Affliction

forms of living

Stefanos Geroulanos and Todd Meyers, *series editors*

Affliction

Health, Disease, Poverty

Veena Das

FORDHAM UNIVERSITY PRESS
NEW YORK 2015

Visit us online at www.fordhampress.com.

Library of Congress Cataloging-in-Publication Data

Das, Veena, author.
    Affliction : health, disease, poverty / Veena Das. — First edition.
        p. ; cm. — (Forms of living)
    Includes bibliographical references and index.
    Summary: "Affliction: Health, Disease, Poverty inaugurates a novel
way of understanding the trajectories of health and disease in the
context of poverty. It traces the unfolding of illness within families, local
communities, neighborhood markets and in occult worlds. Privileging the
experience of people living in these neighborhoods it asks how can global
health be made to take this experience into account rather than escape
from it?" — Provided by publisher.
    ISBN 978-0-8232-6180-2 (cloth) — ISBN 978-0-8232-6181-9 (paper)
    I. Title. II. Series: Forms of living.
    [DNLM: 1. Delivery of Health Care—India. 2. Health Knowledge,
Attitudes, Practice—India. 3. Culture—India. 4. Family—India.
5. Poverty—India. 6. Stress, Psychological—India. W 84 JI4]
    RA418.5.P6
    362.1086'942—dc23

                                                    2014030233

Printed in the United States of America
17 16 15   5 4 3 2 1
First edition

For
Arthur Kleinman and Talal Asad
With whom my agreement runs much deeper
than agreement in opinions.
Thank you for your friendship.

CONTENTS

ACKNOWLEDGMENTS

This book was written over many years in small bits and pieces that came together for me only recently. My main concern has been to understand "what is going on" in the low-income neighborhoods in Delhi where I have worked in different capacities for several years. I thank the following for their generosity in sharing their lives and their thoughts and for letting me benefit from their ungrudging criticisms and support.

To the people in the seven urban neighborhoods described here and to those in the three others that were added later—you have given me reason to believe in anthropology and in my capacity for friendship.

To the ISERDD members—Charu Nanda, Purshottam, Geeta, Rajan Singh, and Simi Chaturvedi—your work and dedication sustains our common endeavor, and your fierce commitment to the possibility of doing something for those whom you meet in the course of your work is life-giving. To Devinder, Bablu, Varun, Anand, and Roopa—and also to Pushpa and Zargham—thank you for cheerfully accomplishing the various tasks that made the work at ISERDD a pleasure.

To my colleagues at Johns Hopkins University and to our graduate students—I thank you for sustaining a serious intellectual life despite all the travails of the past few years.

To Clara Han, Naveeda Khan, and Aaron Goodfellow—thank you for the care with which you have read some of these chapters and for your astute comments.

To Ranendra Das, Jishnu Das, and Jeffrey Hammer—thank you for your openness to anthropology, which has permitted me, in turn, to be open to certain forms of economic reasoning.

To Saumya Das and Christiana Iyasere—thanks for clarifying my queries on medical matters and being ever ready to engage even when we have vigorous disagreements.

To Sanmay Das—I am ever grateful for the gentle way in which you raise questions—they are never bouncers but rather like googlies that are oh-so-beautiful.

To Manoj Mohanan, Brian Chan, Diana Tabak, Nomita Divi, and Grant Miller—my gratitude for your active participation and enthusiasm for training the next generation from different walks of life.

To Yasmeen Arif, Aditya Bharadwaj, Rita Brara, Pratiksha Baxi, Janet Carsten, Roma Chatterji, Christopher Davis, Didier Fassin, Paola Maratti, Deepak Mehta, Michael Moon, Sylvain Perdigon, Shalini Randeria, Bhrigupati Singh, and, Jonathan Spencer—thank you for your engagement with my work. The discussions with each of you over the themes explored here took place in various settings—in a kitchen, a café, a classroom, during a walk, in a seminar room, on the phone—but each discussion left an indelible mark.

To the four anonymous reviewers for the Press—I thank you for the care with which you read the manuscript and your criticisms, which were crucial to my revisions of the text. I hope you recognize your imprint on the final text.

To the Institute of Advanced Study, Paris, thank you for a fellowship in 2009 and the opportunity to present my work in several thought-provoking sessions, and to Claude Imbert and Carlo Severi for helping me fine-tune the philosophical implications of my arguments.

To Anne Lovell, Stefania Pandolfo, Sandra Laugier, Pierre-Henri Castel, and Richard Rechtman—your generosity in sustaining discussions on the theme of madness has been crucial for me to think of the ordinary in new ways.

To the participants in the Critical Global Health Seminar—thank you for the opportunity to look at themes in global health from a fresh perspective.

To the graduate students in my proseminar class in 2013—Ghazal Asif, Swayam Bagaria, Önder Çelik, and Mac Skelton—thank you for the semester-long discussion that is reflected in several chapters of the book.

To Andrew Brandel—thank for your intellectual enthusiasm as well as for your help with the logistics of bringing the book to completion.

To the members of the Governing Board of ISERDD—Ranendra Das, Roma Chatterji, Kuriakose Mamkoottam, Amitabh Mukhopadyay, Deepak Mehta—thank you for your vigilance and your support.

To the staff of Fordham University Press and especially Thomas Lay, Eric Newman, and Teresa Jesionowski—I thank you for your careful editing and attention to detail. It is a treat to work with you.

To the late Helen Tartar—your words echo and echo in more ways than I can say. I miss your delicacy of touch.

To the late Harry Marks, whose presence at Johns Hopkins was like the pure gift—I thank you for the most memorable discussions on whichever subject our fancy took us to.

To Audrey Cantlie, who sadly passed away in the ninety-first year of her life when she was in the middle of writing a book on Wilfred Bion and Jacques Lacan—your intellectual spirit and your love for learning have sustained me since we first met in 1978. I was blessed to have your friendship.

To Nayan, Lucas, Uma, Ayla, Lalita, Kiran, and Uma Jaan—thank you for just being there.

Finally to Stanley Cavell—your words live in my work in whatever way I can receive them—they give it life.

The author wishes to acknowledge the following publishers for generously granting permission to reproduce revised versions of chapters originally published in their respective journals and books and to co-authors for agreeing to let me publish the papers jointly written under my name.

"How the Body Speaks" (chapter 1) is a revised version of the chapter written jointly with Ranendra K. Das titled "How the Body Speaks: Illness and Lifeworld among the Urban Poor." In *Subjectivity: Ethnographic Investigations*, edited by João Biehl, Byron Good, and Arthur Kleinman, 66–97. Berkeley: University of California Press, 2007.

"Mental Illness, Psychiatric Institutions, and the Singularity of Life" (chapter 3) is a revised version of "Mental illness and the Urban Poor: Psychiatric Institutions and the Singularity of Life" (written with the assistance of Rajan Bhandari and Simi Bajaj), published in *Enchantments of Modernity: Empire, Nation, Globalization*, edited by Saurabh Dube, 402–28. New Delhi: Routledge, 2009.

"Dangerous Liaisons: Technology, Kinship, and Wild Spirits" (chapter 4) is a revised version of "The Life of Humans and the Life of Roaming Spirits," published in *Rethinking the Human*, edited by J. Michelle Molina and Donald. K. Swearer, 31–50. Cambridge, Mass.: Center for the Study of World Religions, Harvard Divinity School, 2010.

"The Reluctant Healer and the Darkness of Our Times" (chapter 5) was previously published as "The Dreamed Guru: The Entangled Lives of the Amil and the Anthropologist," in *The Guru in South Asia*, edited by Jacob Copeman and Aya Ikegama, 133–55. Abingdon, UK: Routledge, 2012.

Veena Das
Delhi, 2013

Affliction

Affliction: An Introduction

To arrive at a mode of writing that would allow a world to be disclosed, a world in which life pulsates with the beats of suffering and also with the small pleasures of everyday life, is a daunting challenge. Such suffering as I seek to describe in this book is often absorbed in the everyday and yet scars it with a sense of things being not quite right, even a sense of suffocation and foreboding. Over the years, I have learned how to be attentive to the manner in which ordinary moments might contain within them memories of great violence or suffering. However, suffering that is assimilated within the normal and yet not fully absorbed in it is much more difficult to decipher.

I have titled this book *Affliction*. The title did not come to me as a result of deliberate thought—rather, it became a kind of haunting word, as I was absorbed in my field notes while composing the different chapters of this book. I know that it is hard to hear this word without the sensory experience that Simone Weil's examples draw from us of a suffering that goes beyond physical pain and beyond even ordinary suffering (Weil 1951). Yet Weil is a Christian mystic, and the longing for God as well as the story of the suffering of Christ are integral to the texture of her thought. My attempt is to see if I can use this term while making it mean otherwise. Said differently, I want this term to lend itself to an environment and to sensibilities that might sometimes call on God but are not necessarily looking for a Christ-like figure to lift them out of the abyss that is made up of a kind of corrosion of everyday life that seems to take away from many the capacity to engage life. Not everyone succumbs to this suffering in the same way, even if their souls are marked by what they have had to endure. Many people within the same environment move from one threshold of life marked by bleakness, even abjection, to some other threshold at which they seem to engage with others, laugh, eat, have sex, look after children, greet visitors. I am interested in these subtle movements between these different thresholds of life (see Esposito 2008; Singh 2012). My sense is that although much literature in psychology or behavioral economics tries to ask what makes for the resilience of some people as opposed to others—the more interesting question is, How do the movements between these different thresholds of life carry the marks of suffering endured, of betrayals, as well as small acts of kindness that have made it possible for some to survive while others die? And how has an everyday ethics been honed out of these experiences? Perhaps the idea of *malheur* captures the kind of despair and misery that I encountered, but it still falls short of the way in which people can muster the energy to make life habitable for those they feel intimate with or responsible for.

At first glance it might appear that the difference between *affliction* and *malheur* corresponds to the difference between a subjective experience of suffering and the objective conditions that account for the unequal distribution of suffering, or the difference between a theological move in which suffering poses questions of theodicy and an analysis that privileges the economic and political conditions rooted in political economy. My stake in this book, however, is to overcome these distinctions, for I do not wish to bracket either questions relating to institutions and objective conditions or those that relate to experience and the processes of subjectivization. I contend, however, that none of these terms may be treated as a "given" in anthropological analysis. Experience is not a transparent category, for its essential feature of opacity makes the work of tracking it much more difficult than many authors assume; nor are the character and functioning of institutions such as the state, the market, the neighborhood, and the family apparent right at the beginning;

one cannot simply point to them as one points to a chair or a table. These objects emerge through the process of description.

Weil (1951) presents the image of affliction as a parasite that has established itself within the body. She speaks of how when an apprentice gets hurt or complains of being tired, the workers and peasants express the condition as that of the "trade entering his body." Though Weil repeatedly insists that these forms of secular "affliction" are the same as the feeling that God has absented himself from the world, the most moving descriptions of her own state of affliction are best expressed in Christian terms. "Affliction constrained Christ to implore that he might be spared, to seek consolation from man, to believe he was forsaken by the Father. It forced a just man to cry out against God, a just man as perfect as human nature can be, more so, perhaps, if Job is less a historical character than a figure of Christ" (Weil 1951, 72). She is right that affliction bears a close relation to physical pain, which she sees as an irreducible part of affliction, although the latter cannot be reduced to physical pain. And although one could find a comparison between the affliction expressed in the cry of Christ asking why God, his Father, has abandoned him with emblematic scenes in Sanskrit literature (some of which Weil alludes to), my focus is not on the dramatic potential of the great moments in which heroic figures are caught in the grip of a decision but on the ordinariness of the suffering of many people I came to know that calls out for description and analysis. Didier Fassin and his colleagues, in a book called *Afflictions* (2004), give compelling accounts of life lived with the AIDS epidemic in South Africa, as they describe how words were spoken and heard by women who were trying to gather food, find lodging, or working to extend the life of a child. A famous line in an Urdu poem that would sometimes come unbidden to me during my fieldwork was "*ek bakhiya udheda, ek siya, yun umr basar kab hoti hai*"—unraveling one stitch and putting in place another,[1] how can life be lived in this manner? Yet this is exactly how life was lived.

Can the terms *affliction* and *malheur* together or in a hyphenated relation carry the weight of lives in which even those who had been able to overcome a severe illness or had cared for a sick or dying relative were left with a feeling that such experiences had darkened their world, or that the world had lost

1. I realized later that the lines are from Faiz Ahmad Faiz's poem, *Sheeshon Ka Maseeha Koi Nahin*: "There is no messiah of crushed glass."

some of its benign quality? In the end this is not a book that takes sides on the question as to whether anthropology is slipping into a "suffering slot," as some claim, and whether it should instead turn to the search for the "good" in human life (Robbins 2013) for the simple reason that I do not understand how these two modes of doing anthropology are put into opposition in the first place. Though I return to some of these issues in the Conclusion, the greatest challenge to me is to find a way to make my prose commensurate with the sense of endurance I found among the people struggling to secure everyday life. If I myself get caught in a swirl of emotions created by the tight embrace of forms of living and forms of dying, I have nevertheless tried hard to protect the reader from being overcome with these emotions.

Ackbar Abbas (n.d) and his colleagues have provided us with a manifesto of how to think of those objects that do not lend themselves to existing theoretical templates. They call this "poor theory" to capture its provisional character. Among other characterizations of poor theory, the manifesto says: "Poor theory suggests not a resignation to epistemological futility but an openness to that which outpaces understanding. Objects of analysis present, in their contingency, in their being unsystematic, a degree of intransigence that frustrates mastery. The intractability of the object throws into relief the possibility of error in our methods." I propose that a good place to start is with an open acknowledgment of the difficulty of theorizing the kind of suffering that is ordinary, not dramatic enough to compel attention. We need to problematize the taken-for-granted definitions of the poor that identify them as recipients of charity or welfare, whose life projects are crafted primarily around issues of survival. Instead, I propose to pay close attention to their ethical projects, which include the failures that haunt their relationships.

Different Shades of Suffering and the Burden of Anthropological Description

For almost fourteen years now, since 1999, I have been working with ISERDD (Institute for Socio-Economic Research in Development and Democracy), a small research organization that some of my colleagues from the University of Delhi founded to document and analyze the transformations taking place in the lives of the urban poor in that city. I describe the circumstances under which this organization was born in a recent paper (V. Das 2014b), and the following description is taken from that account.

In 1984, in the face of the devastating violence against the Sikhs in the wake of Mrs. Gandhi's assassination, I was able to find the resources within my community of friends and colleagues in Delhi to insert my own efforts within the collective efforts to contest official renderings of events. We were able to act in those fraught circumstances by lending what expertise we had to the task of documenting the deaths and losses in the violence against the Sikhs, especially in the peripheral areas of Delhi. One part of this reporting was to adopt protocols of data collection and reporting that could stand up to bureaucratic scrutiny in order to assess claims and get some kind of official acknowledgment of the harm done to survivors.

In the case of the terrible industrial disaster of Bhopal too I was able to find some way of being helpful because a community of lawyers, NGOs, and other activists were there to provide the framework within which legal action could take place. But this is when I also learned that justice was not a matter of everything or nothing (see Das and Kleinman 2001). My book *Critical Events* (1995) was born out of this milieu of conversations.

I do not remember the sequence of events, but conversations at home and among my close colleagues at the Delhi School of Economics led me to think more closely about further questions that arose from my prolonged involvement with the Sikh survivors of Sultanpuri, one of the peripheral areas of Delhi where I worked. I remember the small events then—a woman stopping me on the road one day and pointing to a spot where she said that her husband had been killed, not in the riots but in the course of a neighborhood quarrel that escalated and that no one came to help for fear of annoying the local "big men." We were torn by the question of what responsibility devolves on us in such circumstances.[2] Just the simple fact of spending so much time in the slums in 1984 and 1985 made me realize that we could not draw boundaries between the everyday forms of deprivation that I was seeing in urban slums and the events of escalating violence that we were engaged in documenting. I also realized that anthropological evidence of the kind that could be used for serious advocacy on such issues as sanitation, health

---

2. The "we" here refers to the network of teachers and student volunteers working with me in 1984–85, prominent among whom were Mita Bose, Sanjib Datta Chowdhury, Aman Singh, and Roma Chatterji; others lent their labor when and if they could. I should like to reiterate that such activism that contests or tries to modify official policies on various issues is very much part of the political scene in India. A rich literature has begun to emerge that brings the anthropological eye to the understanding of these networks of actors. See, for instance, Fortun (2009) and Riles (2001).

care, or everyday forms of violence was simply not available. Even in the legal case against Union Carbide in the Bhopal disaster, we (a loose configuration of activists) were stumped by the fact that we could not show what the morbidity patterns were among the poor under normal circumstances—so our claim that the increased morbidity among the poor as a result of exposure to methyl isocyanate was not easy to demonstrate in court.

This set of disappointments led to another kind of curiosity—what would it take to systematically document the transformations in health conditions of the urban poor? It was in order to find a systematic way of doing research in such settings that some of us researchers in Delhi founded the Institute of Socioeconomic Research on Development and Democracy (ISERDD). Our aims were modest and evolved through trial and error. We planned to recruit staff for the institute from low-income localites. These would be first-generation college students, and and our plan was to train them to investigate their environment. In time ISERDD developed many projects of an interdisciplinary character with researchers from various institutions, using mixed methods of surveys and ethnographic interviews.[3]

I should add that ISERDD also offers medical and educational assistance to poor families in Delhi and sometimes runs workshops and focus-group discussions to address issues of interest to people living in slums and low-income neighborhoods. In the process of participating in the activities of ISERDD over the years and conducting my own research with the assistance of ISERDD members, I have absorbed so many nuances of everyday life at ISERDD that although I try to indicate clearly the kind of information that I gathered through my own observations, that which was the result of collective efforts with ISERDD, and what became available through participation in focus-group discussions and activities generated by ISERDD's community projects in the chapters ahead, I realize that some kinds of knowing simply happened through our collective efforts in which it was not easy to mark out the boundaries of each other's thoughts. One simply could not draw a line between something marked "research" and something marked "life."

Let me pause now and give a flavor of the way in which you might come upon suffering within a scene of the ordinary in any of the seven neighborhoods from which the accounts that follow emerge. Because of financial and

3. See chapter 7 for the description of some of this work.

other constraints, we at ISERDD started by working on seven neighborhoods at different levels of income in Delhi in 1999 and then gradually expanded to include two more low-income neighborhoods to get a better representation of Muslim neighborhoods. Subsequently, two of the high-income neighborhoods were dropped after the completion of the health surveys. ISERDD staff maintained contacts with sample households in all other neighborhoods and also participated in various events of a public nature, such as political meetings, festivals, marriages, and sporting events. The last phase of expansion was in 2011 when ISERDD launched another study on citizenship for which one neighborhood from the earlier studies and three new neighborhoods were added. I have had very little contact with the high-income neighborhoods, but others have written on the data that ISERDD collected. Although a lot of work that we did was collaborative, the essays here are from the earlier phases when ISERDD members were still learning the craft of research, such as conducting surveys, doing interviews, and mapping basic facilities. As the different studies progressed, the role of ISERDD members changed. They played a crucial role in projects directed by other researchers in partnership with ISERDD (Jishnu Das, Jeffrey Hammer, Manoj Mohanan, Michael Walton, Grant Miller, Roma Chatterji, and Deepak Mehta). A project that held special importance for me was the training of ordinary people who had little education and hardly any work experience who were recruited from the slums to act as standardized patients in a study to assess the quality of care of practitioners in rural and urban areas. Rather than give a schematic account of these processes, I aim to allow the role of ISERDD members and the research methods used to emerge in the following chapters in the process of the substantive descriptions of health, disease, and poverty.

Walking and Greeting

One day as I was strolling through the streets of Kathputli colony in West Delhi—a locality made up of street performers who had settled there through the initiative of an NGO founded by Rajiv Sethi, the famous designer and advocate of street arts—I stopped to talk to a local leader. If you read accounts of this locality on websites and in interviews with Sethi, you get the sense of a magical world in which people live in houses designed as tents in a neighborhood that replicates an imagined life when street arts were nourished by rich patrons and loved by the populace.[4] If, however, you spend time in these streets every day, as ISERDD members and I did, you see the dirt and the squalor—the drains that do not work, the pools of water gathered in the streets that enter the houses, the inebriated men—and you hear the accounts of sickness and death; you meet the women who are indeed great artists and who often narrate accounts of performances in faraway countries—Germany, Sweden, America—but who struggle here in the streets of Kathputli colony with rarely having enough food, with frequent sickness, with tuberculosis, with children going astray. Their narratives bring forth the intermittent presence of storied figures such as Sethi and Madam Stella and their famed rivalry. These great personages are like spectral figures or like the playful gods of Hindu mythology who can give huge bounties but who then disappear for long periods, unable to hear anything about the perils that stalk the everyday life of their devotees. The money some artists earn sporadically during their small trips abroad to represent Indian living arts disappears quickly in commissions and debts they have incurred—the local favorites of these distant gods seem to live in slightly better houses but do not fare much better in terms of health or education.

Scene One

We stood in a street corner of this famed locality, talking to a local leader. A young man came and stood next to us, looking us over with curiosity. Pointing to him, the local leader said, "This is my son, my son from the second. There

---

4. See, for instance, "Jim Goldblum Tells the Story of Kahtputli: The Colony of Wooden Puppets." www.framedmagazine.com.au/Jim-Goldblum.

On the question of how the community was formed as an artists' commune, Goldblum says: "You know, it's interesting because originally it began organically in the 1950s. It's in this area of Delhi called Shadipur Depot; it used to be like a jungle. Basically, all of these itinerant performers from different regions of the country and different artistic tribes would come to Delhi to perform, and then they would go back on their routes. Though, as television and radio became available in the rural villages, the routes got upended so they needed to move into the city. So more and more artists started to permanently move into the city and into these tent camps, then eventually they moved into mud huts and dung huts. Then, in the 1970s, an Indian designer by the name of Rajeev Sethi—who had spent a lot of time in New York and in Paris working for Pierre Cardin and Ray and Charles Eames, you know, he was in Andy Warhol's factory—had this sort of very Western idea of an artists' commune." www.framedmagazine.com.au/Jim-Goldblum.

are three other children." "So you have four children?" "Yes, four children from the second." "So this is your second wife?" "Yes, the first one died. She had two children." "So you have six children?" "No, the woman died, and her children died too."

I was struck by the pronouns—*her* children—not *my* or *our* children.

Scene Two

We are now in Punjabi Basti, a slightly more affluent colony in the middle of efforts to become what is known in official parlance as "regularized," which would give residents certain entitlements to water, sanitation, and electricity and provide security of tenure (for a detailed description of some of these processes see V. Das 2014a and V. Das and Walton forthcoming).

ISERDD members were recruiting households for a survey in 2011 on citizenship directed by Michael Walton and me. They were explaining consent procedures and filling out demographic forms. This is what one of them recorded in a field diary that all surveyors were expected to maintain. The original entries were in Hindi, which I translate here.

Urmila Ji is a forty-year-old woman who readily agreed to participate in the survey. We began to fill the basic demographic form. When we came to the column on number of children, Urmila Ji suddenly began to cry. "What should I tell you? Earlier I had four children but now I have only three." I asked, Should I come back another time, but she insisted I stay—"Bhaiya (brother), how often does anyone come to my door to listen to my story?" Then she told me how her son who was four years old died last year.

"He was playing on the terrace with some children of the neighborhood. The terraces don't have railings or bordering walls [*chajja*] here. His attention must have wavered [*dhyan chuk gaya hoga*]. Suddenly I saw my neighbors carrying him and shouting that he had fallen from the terrace. He was alive and conscious then. My husband was not home, but my neighbors helped me to take him to the nearby government hospital. They admitted him to the ICU and did a brain x-ray. They could not find anything. But he began to vomit that night, and his face was swelling. We begged the doctor, please do something. The doctor asked for another x-ray. We could see the boy was sinking, but he just said we have to wait and watch. Then a technician told us that in cases of head injury you needed a CT scan, not an x-ray. The doctor was so rude when we asked that instead of x-ray, a CT scan should be done—are you the doctor or am I the doctor, he said. So we insisted that the child be immediately discharged from the hospital, and we rushed him to a private hospital where a CT scan was done, and they said, he should have been immediately operated upon as there was bleeding in the brain—but now it was too late. Due to that doctor I had to wash my hands of my child [*bacche se haath dhona pada*] [a metaphoric expression for the loss of the child—author's explanation]."

In a recent paper (J. Das, R. K. Das, and V. Das 2012) we describe the surprising finding that while women who had suffered cumulative adverse reproductive events in their lives (miscarriages, abortions, stillbirth, child death) showed very high levels of depression, their spouses did not. We suggested that men do not register these events through the language of emotion, and that is why mental health questionnaires based on itemized symptom lists do not capture how they feel. In the first scene we heard a man saying that the children who had died were "her" children referring to his dead wife. In other cases we found that men use mythological analogies comparing themselves to warriors who have laid down their weapons or make textual references far more than women do (cf. Desjarlais 2003). The death of a child can surface in a woman's account in the most quotidian manner, and grief can pour out along with accusations and blame for the death. This woman came from Punjabi Basti, a neighboring locality to Kathputli colony where households are a little more affluent, and people enjoy better education and higher incomes. But this factor did not seem to make any difference in how physicians treated them in public hospitals.

Scene Three

We move to another locality in West Patel Nagar, in a neighborhood very similar to Punjabi Basti. I was visiting a family in which a widowed woman, Savita, lived with her adult son and her husband's elder brother, Prakash. I greeted the old man, who was wearing a frayed kurta (tunic) and pajamas with no pullover or warm wrapping. He was shivering in the cold. Reading my worried expression as I looked at him, Savita said, "There is no point in talking to him, Sister. He will not wear any hand-me-downs—see, my son even got a new sweater for him, but he says that he can smell a Muslim in it [*isme musalle ki bu aati hai*]."

In our conversation it emerged that Prakash had been admitted to a psychiatric institution as an in-patient about forty years ago because he suffered from hallucinations and could become violent. His hallucinations have continued over this entire period. They always involved a scene in which Allah, the Muslim God, had abducted him. When in the grip of this psychic drama, Prakash always spoke in a female voice and enacted a fatal attraction toward Islam because of his love for Allah. (I witnessed one enactment, but otherwise it was Savita who related all this to me.) He was saved every time, as he told me in a calmer moment, through the intervention of Shiva, the Hindu God of destruction, famed for his cosmic rage as well as his love for his devotees. Savita related all this with a touch of irony, occasionally bursting into laughter.

I learned that because Savita was widowed at a young age, her larger biradari (collateral kin) insisted that a male guardian was necessary in the house, even if this male was diagnosed with a serious psychiatric impairment. Prakash was discharged from the psychiatric institution on the insistence of the family and against medical advice and moved in the house with Savita and her son as their guardian. He had been on regular medication (Lithium) that a local practitioner had prescribed when he moved into this area, but he had neither seen a psychiatrist for the last thirty or so years nor been evaluated for continued medication. Savita obtained the medicine from a local pharmacist, and if he became too troublesome, she administered sleeping pills to put him to sleep.

Is this a case of abandonment? Savita, as a young widow left with a young son to raise, dependent on what money she could make from sewing and selling garments in the neighborhood and on the charity of kin, was compelled to accept someone with a severe psychiatric disorder as her guardian. Her brother-in-law's symptoms speak of mysterious ways in which fraught relations and impossible desires circulate between Hindus and Muslims. Abduction by Allah perhaps recalls the violent scenes of abduction and rape that he might have witnessed as a young child at the time of the Partition of India, or perhaps he just sensed them (see V. Das 2007). Clearly, the experiences of this man were not accessible to me—I was fenced off, both by his illness and by his family, from any close contact with him. But I learned how his life could be rendered through the life of his family, of which he was a nominal head as well as a dependent relative. We are invited to look—not at the interiority of a person—but at the reverberations that occur in those who are in relations of estranged intimacy with him.

The Ordinary, the Eventful, and the Quasi Event

I take a detour to try to think of the scenes I describe in relation to recent work that that touches on similar issues. I first consider Elizabeth Povinelli's work on the notion of abandonment and the possibilities of what she calls "imminent critique." Povinelli is interested in understanding suffering that she describes repeatedly as "ordinary, chronic and cruddy rather than catastrophic, crisis-laden and sublime" (Povinelli 2011, 132). I share her important insight that there are no overlapping, transcendental categories standing over and above the flux of everyday life through which we might generate meaningful critique, just as I share her concern with the fragility and vulnerability of everyday life (V. Das 2007). But within this similarity I sense a clear difference. I want to spell out what is at stake in this difference. Toward the end of this section I contrast Povinelli's rendering of quasi events with what Clara Han (2013) calls "critical moments" and then turn to the notion of quasi events proposed by Da Col and Humphrey (2012) to capture (as on a camera) the small ways that the everyday can be turned slightly around and to ask how these small turnings can morph into catastrophic and critical events. But first let me return to Povinelli's discussion.

At the conceptual level, I see everyday life in my work as "evented" (V. Das 2007). Povinelli, in contrast, is at pains to distinguish what she calls "quasi events" from full-fledged "events." In her words,

> If events are things that we can say happened such that they have a certain objective being, then quasi-events never take the status of having occurred or taken place. They neither happen nor not happen. I am not interested in these quasi-events in some abstract sense, but in the concrete ways that they are, or are not, aggregated and thus apprehended, evaluated and grasped as ethical and political demands in specific late liberal markets, publics and states, as opposed to crises and catastrophes that seem to necessitate ethical reflection and political and civic engagement. (Povinelli 2011, 13)

Povinelli goes on to note that in the structuring of sentiments under late liberal forms, crises and catastrophe seem to demand an ethical and political response whereas quasi events can be allowed to pass. Thus the latter need publicity and the aid of techniques such as statistical aggregation or amplification through the media to elicit a political or ethical response. Yet, as she says, the deployment of a statistical imaginary to awaken a slumbering critical public faces a central paradox. "By transforming the invisible, dispersed, and uneventful into the visible, compact, and eventful, statistics obliterate the very nature of this kind of death. Rather than understand this kind of lethality within its own term (dailiness, ordinariness, livedness), we demand that it conform to the spectacular event and its ethical dictates of empathic identification" (Povinelli 2011, 153). As an example of how quasi events obscure notions of cause and effect, Povinelli recounts that her indigenous friends do not attribute the lethality of their conditions to the agency of the state since many deaths are not caused by direct violence—say, in the hands of a policeman—but rather by policies that seem distant to them, impersonal and without agency.

True to her theoretical impulse, Povinelli builds her argument in her book by showing how ordinary events in the lives of her indigenous friends become "events" by the manner in which the state picks them out for policy interventions or street-level bureaucrats pronounce judgments on them. Paradoxically, It seems to me that this mode of theorizing itself casts the state as the privileged organ of "seeing," standing above the flux of everyday life—every so often it halts the ethnographic description in the book, turns it from its tracks on the register of the everyday in order to show how a "quasi event" does or does not become an "event" by introducing a person who stands in for some outside agency—a social worker or a schoolteacher. These figures are all proxies for the state or for the media. It seems to me that what Povinelli achieves, despite the programmatic statement cited earlier, is not so much an escape from the abstraction of the idea of quasi event to its concrete unfolding—but rather that the insertion of the state as a transcendental category halts the ethnographic unfolding to propel us into the realm of publicity.

Allow me to elaborate this notion with the help of a case study that I take from Povinelli's text:

A year before the sea voyage I described in the last chapter, a schoolteacher visited a sixty-year-old woman who was dying of oral cancer in an Indigenous community—the birthplace of those on the voyage. Inside the cinder block house where the dying woman lived were a series of rooms, unfurnished, except for old stained mattresses on the floor, where dogs with scabies sometimes slept, a single-framed bed in the front room . . . and a wobbly table on which stood a broken television set. In the kitchen were carcasses of various animals and fish, opened jams, loaves of bread, sugar, tea, bowls, and pans with days-old remainders of cooked food, and running through them all various sizes of cockroaches, The inside toilet had been backed up for weeks. There was no hot water. When we bathed this dying woman we boiled water on the stove in old flour drums. Sewn through all of this were the syringes, empty pill bottles, new and used bandages used to care for this woman, and beer cans, wine coolers, and other addictive substances her relatives were using as they stayed there. Many people on the porch were drunk, stoned, or hung over. . . . When the schoolteacher entered the house, she too entered a heightened condition of static. She found herself unable to enter the doorframe, and then found herself blushing, hot, with what she later described as "embarrassment." The scene she witnessed, the broken nature of the dying woman's home, the ruined infrastructure, the infestations of insects and vermin, the garbage and medical waste strewn about paralyzed her. Who she was before she entered the doorframe was different from who she was afterward. Who or what was to blame? (Povinelli 2011, 135–36)

The house where the old woman is dying is described here through the eyes of a camera that seems to record *for the schoolteacher*, the signs of disrepair— the wobbly table, the broken television set, the blocked toilet. We can almost feel how the teacher shrinks back at the sight of crawling cockroaches and stoned men and dogs with scabies. The description is in the service of a larger argument about the conditions of abandonment under late liberalism, and it seems essential to Povinelli's project that the reader comes to experience what it was for the schoolteacher to see this scene in this way. What is obscured from view in this mode of argumentation is how this form of abandonment unfolds in the lives of kin and neighbors—all of whom Povinelli is intimately engaged with but refuses to yield to her readers. Is this because at this point further ethnographic elaboration would come in the way of better theorization since it is only its conversion to an event that will allow a critique of the state under late liberalism? After all, Povinelli does not spare the reader the horror or disgust at the blocked toilets and the crawling cockroaches—so the point at which the break occurs asks for more reflection on what might be at stake for us in reflecting on this suffering that is ordinary and cruddy.

On another occasion Povinelli takes us to a case of a young man who suffers from multiple ailments and is, by his own admission, an alcoholic. She witnesses an argument that develops between this man and his older aunt. He claims that his body is his—he could do what he wants to do with it. "He knew the risks; they were his to take; how he gambled with his life was his business" (Povinelli 2011, 154–55). As Povinelli explains, these were his words—"risk," "gamble," "my body." His aunt, however, drew on a different imagery and argued that his body was not an individual possession. "No, that is not your body; that is my body. When you die, my body will suffer and die." Yet this second discourse of socially consubstantial bodies in which the fate of one body was linked to another, not through empathy but through a notion of a shared "one body" between kin, according to Povinelli, was already defeated. How so?

Here Povinelli gives a generalized description of the changes in political and economic arrangements in Australia under a decade of conservative leadership under the prime minister, John Howard. These changes have meant that there is a privatization and individualization of wealth—there is a rolling back of welfare, and the sources of public care have shifted from the state to the private realms of family and individual. I have no quarrel with this description at the macro level. However, how these new values fold into the Indigenous communities with whom Povinelli has had such a long and intimate contact is not allowed to surface since larger political and economic changes are simply juxtaposed with a story such as the young man's references to his own body as his possession. But juxtaposition cannot do the work of showing the pathways through which the larger changes are absorbed in individual lives.

In short, the question for me comes down to whether the ethnography is meant to illustrate a theoretical argument or whether theory might be built into the ethnography itself. In my reading of her text, the epistemological techniques that Povinelli describes so well of turning quasi events into catastrophic ones can explain such processes as mediatization, creation of a scandal, and mobilization of a new public by manipulation of affects, but it cannot tell us how and when a young man is abandoned or a mother gives up trying to shore up a deteriorating relation with her son. In replicating the technique of moving rapidly between, say, an argument between a young man and his aunt, or the scene of decomposition in a dying woman's house, to state policy under late liberalism, we lose the opportunity of knowing how these quasi events unfolded within these lives and not others. It might well be argued that theory gains by leaving behind the ethnography at the points at which Povinelli does that—but even at the risk of making the reader lost in the ethnographic details I provide in later chapters, I want my reader to enter that doorway and not turn away after a first impression. By proposing slower movements between the general conditions of life in the neighborhoods I describe and the singularity of lives, I present a different picture of what it is to think of anthropology as a "dwelling science"—grateful to Povinelli for her wonderful formulation of what anthropology could be as "imminent critique" yet not persuaded that one can fully dwell with others, especially with those separated by the distance of living conditions, class, and different ways of enduring the misfortunes that fall on one.

This is perhaps the reason that I get pushed out into other domains in which I engage with those who are my interlocutors in the fields of global health, health economics, or health policy—those who are engaged in thinking about how to improve the conditions of the poor so that they can enjoy better health. I recognize that some of the work in these disciplines is in alignment with the projects of global institutions that are far less interested in diseases that might corrode the everyday life of people living in low-income settings and far more invested in the concern that those diseases can travel and pose a threat to those living in upper-income countries in the West, either directly or indirectly through the resources that have to be spent on keeping the apparatus of biosecurity intact. However, I do not think that these fields of inquiry and intervention are a monolith with no internal differences and conflicts. What I have learned from my engagement with these interlocutors from other disciplines has led me to combine traditional forms of fieldwork in anthropology with surveys and experiments in the field, and to improvise new methods to address problems that arose in the process of fieldwork itself. I contend that the people I worked with in the low-income neighborhoods were not fully enclosed within the local either—they too showed a great interest in engaging with worlds that they comprehended only vaguely or intermittently but about which they learned by putting into use whatever resources they could muster (see V. Das 2014a and Das and Walton forthcoming for examples of this kind of engagement with the nonlocal).

In the chapters that follow I develop an argument that the experience of illness creates incoherence. Even as this experience is absorbed in the everyday, there is also a sense that illness goes beyond the grasp of the categories that are available—that someone else might know more about what you or someone you care for is suffering from. Hence, the contradictory impulses I found in which people sometimes normalized what was happening to their bodies—"this is the body of aging"; "all babies when teething get some fever or some diarrhea"—and at other points searched high and low for a remedy. In siding with these contradictory impulses I have come to realize that ethnography might be simultaneously a mode of dwelling with, but it is also a mode of striving against the social world, as if our forms of belonging also entail the possibility of doubt and disappointment with the worlds we dwell in (see Khan 2012 for a subtle analysis of this impulse in a different context). Perhaps another look at quasi events from other perspectives might be helpful.

In a recent book Clara Han (2013) gives a compelling account of the braiding of care and violence in post-Pinochet, neoliberal Chile in which she uses the idea that there are critical moments that arise in the lives of the families she studied which could sometimes be contained through subtle forms of aid offered by extended kin, friends, or neighbors, but at other times went far beyond what neighbors or friends could offer by way of help and care. The economic model that successive democratic government in Chile employed, despite the rhetoric of the debt owed to the people for the pernicious violence of the Pinochet regime, had perilous effects on the poor. These effects were not a result of direct repression but came about through a reorganization of labor regimes, ready availability of credit, and the stoking of consumer aspirations that encouraged people to live beyond their means. In such an environment a "critical moment" might appear, says Han, when, for example, a family runs out of money and there is no food to be had on credit. Or a catastrophic illness might lead to unexpected expenditures in the family leading to still heavier borrowing. Although there is a strong ethic of "endurance," the signs and symptoms of such distress break out from the tight boundaries of "family affairs" and spill into the neighborhood. Han describes acts of silent kindness through which neighbors provide help—say by inviting a hungry child to share a meal on the pretext that too much extra food had been cooked or by offering to do chores for a harassed mother balancing a job and her domestic duties. Elsewhere I have called this kind of attentiveness "ordinary ethics" (see

V. Das 2012). However, there is also a darker side to neighborhood gossip in Han's account, for a woman may come to be known as a "bad pay"; though courtesies are maintained in face-to-face relations, neighbors might well turn their backs on such a person. In other words, there is fragility to the give and take of everyday life born out of an ethics of proximity.

In a thoughtful response to several comments in a symposium organized by the journal *HAU: Journal of Ethnographic Theory,* on her book, Han (2012) explains why she resisted settling on the notion of abandonment used both by Povinelli and Jãomo Biehl (2005) in their respective works on the poor or in other ways marginalized people. Han explains that both authors treat the family and neighborhood as simply registering the effects of larger neoliberal values, whereas for her, the relations at the local level have some autonomy even if they are not immune from the effects of neoliberal policies. In her own words:

> Despite significant differences in ethnographic description, abandonment in both accounts is elaborated as an effect of "market values" and as the outcome of an ethics in which prevailing definitions of "the good" hinge upon these values, which have encroached on, politicized, or have anchored within the local and the domestic, while also globally producing differential distributions of lethality. In contrast to these values, relational practices or an ethics of consubstantiality manifest accountabilities and obligations to concrete others that, from Biehl's vantage point, are today in decline, or from Povinelli's vantage point, present alternative social projects that must endure their constant being-in-potential. . . . In my ethnography, I engage that "continuous time in which quasi-events unfold in the family or between friends and neighbors" (Das) and "the tactics people deploy to share or absorb, divert or refuse the hardship of others" (Allison)[5] as a way to expand our perceptive range on the subtleties of relationships and material pressures that may not be perceptible under a notion of abandonment. (Han 2013)

Let us now turn to the third notion of quasi event. In their introduction to a special issue on the themes of contingency, morality, and anticipation in everyday life, Giovanni da Col and Caroline Humphrey (2012) meditate on

---

5. The references to Das and Allison in this citation relate to their comments in a book symposium on *Life in Debt* in the journal *HAU: Journal of Ethnographic Theory.* See Allison (2013) and V. Das (2013).

the figure of luck and the small turnings that people might try to engineer that deflect everyday life from its accustomed paths of repetition and routine. Drawing on Charles G. Seligman's foreword to Edward E. Evans-Pritchard's (1939) book on Azande witchcraft as "a normal event of everyday life," Da Col and Humphrey (2012) distinguish such "quasi events" from large historical events that are clearly marked as ruptures. Like witchcraft, illnesses too might be seen as "normal events" or quasi events that make aspects of the everyday that were otherwise hidden come to light or reorient relationships—I have characterized this aspect of uncertainty and contingency as the lining of everyday life with a shadow of skepticism. The circumstances under which such doubts become world-annihilating doubts as in the cases of madness or possession, which some of the following chapters describe, testify to the lethal potential of the everyday not quite captured in Seligman's characterization of the way witchcraft could be absorbed in the everyday. I argue that small suspicions, betrayals, and hurts can escalate into something bigger (without necessarily the intervention of the state or media) that might poison everyday life, as Jeanne Favret-Saada's (1980) stunning work on witchcraft accusations also shows.

In any case, illness discloses the fact that everyday life might be any or all of the following. First of all, it may be regarded as the site on which small misfortunes turn the direction of habit ever so slightly without constituting a full rupture from ordinariness—in such cases we might consider everyday life as the site marked by ordinary realism (Laugier 2013), which guides how people are able to care for each other. Second, it is the site on which the technologies of the state and the market act from the outside distorting close relations of kinship or locality defined by proximity. Finally, we can find ourselves in the grip of skepticism as we lose out footing, thereby revealing everyday life itself to be a scene of trance and illusion. The following chapters might thus be seen as contributions to the further development of the theories of everyday life and the urge to violence against it.

The Context

A recent report in *JAMA*, the *Journal of the American Medical Association*, summarized the state of health care in India under the title "Gaps in India's Health Care" (Friedrich 2013). The report was based on a paper that my colleagues and I had published in the journal *Health Affairs*; some of the findings had been hotly debated in the media (see J. Das, Holla, et al. 2012). Our paper was an account of a study in the poor neighborhoods in Delhi and in three rural districts in Madhya Pradesh, which had used twenty-two simulated standardized patients who went incognito to practitioners of medicine and presented them with three common diseases—chest pain, asthma, and childhood dysentery. In all, these standardized "patients" covered 305 practitioners and made 926 visits in the course of the study. We found that a majority of practitioners in the rural areas did not have medical degrees. Practitioners in urban Delhi, though trained in some system of medicine, did not fare much better than their rural counterparts in terms of ability to diagnose a disease or the treatment they offered. Surprisingly, there was little difference between trained and untrained practitioners, as most failed to adhere to a simple checklist provided by the government. On average, a practitioner spent three minutes with a patient, and the rate of correct diagnosis and treatment was abysmally low.

Although it is not difficult to discern that health care for the poor is seriously deficient by simply walking around the neighborhoods, to have our impressions confirmed in such a striking manner was a surprise. Although I have something to say later on the question of measurement—its uses and misuses in relation to the kind of care that the poor receive (chapter 7)—here I want to provide some background, in the light of which we can read the specificity of the cases I describe later.

The low-income neighborhoods in Delhi are saturated with a large number of practitioners in the adjoining markets. One could find seventy practitioners on an average in a radius of one mile from any residential street in the neighborhoods we studied. These practitioners ranged from those with degrees in alternate medical systems such as BAMS (Bachelor in Ayurvedic Medicine and Surgery) as well as practitioners trained in biomedicine (MBBS). One of the chapters ahead (chapter 6) describes in some detail the proliferation of degrees held by medical practitioners in the Delhi neighborhoods. Here I note only that regardless of the kind of training they had received and the degree they held, there was little difference in the diagnostic categories that different kinds of practitioners used or the treatments they dispensed, including antibiotics and injections. It was very rare to find practitioners with degrees in alternate systems of medicine such as Ayurveda using technical terms such as *panchakriya* (a technical process to cleanse what is regarded as the inner body), although shared folk notions pertaining to classification of food as hot and cold or reference to humors could be detected in advice given to patients on diet, for instance.

Many recent findings on health care behavior confirm that the poor visit medical practitioners more frequently than the rich (Das and Hammer 2004; Banerjee and Duflo 2011). This is partly a consequence of the wide variety of practitioners that are available in the markets that function in the vicinity of neighborhoods in which poor people live. There seems to be an increasing demand for receiving treatment for ailments that might have been treated at home earlier. People use pharmacies and practitioners to get diagnosis and treatment (see chapter 1; also Kamat and Nichter 1998). Although earlier literature suggested that people classified diseases between acute and chronic and that they often resorted to alternate systems of medicine for chronic diseases while opting for allopathic treatments for acute diseases (Bhardwaj 1975), this distinction has collapsed as these systems of medicine have become much more interactive taking on a hybrid character in practice (Langford 1995). Because practitioners working in low-income neighborhoods are not highly competent at arriving at correct diagnosis and tend to treat on the basis of symptoms alone, many chronic diseases present as series of acute episodes. Even tuberculosis can take up to three months to be diagnosed by poorly trained practitioners who are frequently the point of first contact for the patient, despite public health campaigns and checklists of symptoms that are distributed by the government (see Sreeramareddy, Qin, et al. 2014).

Finally, there is a fascination with technology among the poor. In the scenes I presented above, one would have noticed the ease with which people employed terms such as x-ray, CT scan, MRI—and it is a paradox that in the poorest localities one can find advertisements for the most sophisticated technologies. Most households will take out x-rays, or CT scans, or results of blood tests, from shelves or trunks in which they are kept, to show a visitor as proof of the gravity of their illnesses. The combination of density of practitioners in one's neighborhood with the temptations of new technologies gives medical objects a magical aura. It makes medical care commensurate for some purposes with other forms of relief that people seek—such as relief from afflictions caused by spirits or by black magic wielded by an occult figure on behalf of a neighbor or a jealous relative. Instead of binaries of folk medicine versus biomedicine or people's explanatory models versus biomedical models, we find a curious mixture of categories, medications, healers, diagnosis, and divination. It is not easy to discern how the figures of a physician, a healer, an exorcist, or a practitioner in black magic might form a single series—figures of alterity or of mimesis? Are these different types of healing occupying a homogenous place in the lives of people?

A fundamental question that arises throughout this book is that of discerning what kind of being a disease possesses. Can a disease be normal? Is the opposite of normal to be seen as pathological or simply as the critical? Are healers simply technicians or are they conduits for occult forces? Are the expert discourses through which questions of health and disease are materialized in policy decisions, exercises in technical reasoning, or are these signs of "moon talk"? In moving through these questions I am also moving between many different planes in this book. On the one hand, I wish to show how singularity of lives might be seen as the coming together of multiple forces—political, economic, affective, aesthetic—and on the other hand, I also want to reflect on what these lives might tell us about the grand projects of health reform initiated by global health programs or national programs that seem to inhabit parallel worlds, no less full of magic and sorcery as the ones inhabited by my respondents. The swirling affects that these sometimes contradictory perspectives create will become slowly evident, but I confess that I cannot offer a resolution or a grand conclusion—the ending is simply a place where the book comes to rest.

A Brief Overview

The overall structure of the book is as follows. The next chapter ("How the Body Speaks") focuses on one specific neighborhood and looks at the way in which people interact with the practitioners, the duration of illnesses, and the frequency of visits to the practitioners. It asks how people understand their illnesses and finds that there are no firm epistemic understandings of why illness happens. People often put together a narrative of illness that borrows vocabularies from different medical systems (Ayurvedic, allopathic) as well as vocabularies of the occult. I conclude that there are no well-made ontologies that could explain the movement between disease as it inhabits human bodies versus when it exists as an abstraction in textbooks or other discursive forms.

The following three chapters (chapters 2, 3, and 4) take up specific cases concentrating on an illness trajectory within a family—each case shows how an illness is dispersed over people, relationships, and technologies. I treat the local ecologies in these cases as the plot, both in the sense of a narrative plot and a plot (as in a plot of land) on which a story might grow. Chapter 2, "A Child Learns Illness and Learns Death," describes, through the eyes of a child, a woman's struggle with tuberculosis and her subsequent death. The chapter traces the dawning realization of family betrayals, the obligations the child takes on himself, which shows that children are often led to become bearers of knowledge that is not theirs to possess, knitting words and the world in an uncanny manner. In the next chapter, "Mental Illness, Psychiatric Institutions, and the Singularity of Lives," I describe what happens to a young person whose madness unsettles the family to the extent that the neighbors and wider kin become implicated, taking sides and finding temporary respite in what the outside world has to offer. There are no final resolutions, but when there are moments of pause in these relentless family quarrels, we see a different face of medical institutions and the state than were apparent in the first case described in chapter 2. The final case study presented in chapter 4, "Dangerous Liaisons: Technology, Kinship, and Wild Spirits," shows how new medical technologies enter these neighborhoods and expand the sphere of kinship obligations. Instead of finding the ethical in the fulfillment of these obligations, the chapter argues that the problem becomes that of limiting the force of these obligations. Parallel to new technologies are new figures of the occult that emerge, such as roaming spirits through whom the morality of the village and that of the city are put into a subtle clash, reflecting the impossible demands that have to be negotiated in the light of these new technologies.

Chapter 5, "The Reluctant Healer and the Darkness of Our Times," takes us into the life of an *amil*, a Muslim healer, who practices in one of the neighborhoods. We see the knitting together of fantasy, history, and memory in his rendering of the dangers he struggles with as a Muslim healer as he inhabits the thin line between legitimate knowledge and clandestine knowledge—*nuri ilm* (the lighted knowledge) and *kala ilm* (dark knowledge). The ability to heal appears in this narrative as both a blessing and a curse.

In chapter 6, "Medicines, Markets, and Healing," I look at the way that practitioners with different kinds of training, including apprenticeship, see their own practices of healing. Several oppositions—between what is normal and what is critical; between medicine and poison; between the rhythms of the world and those of the disease in one's body; between slowness and speed; between gift and commodity—unfold in these narratives of illness and healing. I explore how money, gifts, and other material embodiments of transactions, in which the body is the temporary habitat for uncanny forces, function as reminders of the fragility of the real.

Chapter 7, "Global Health Discourse and the View from Planet Earth," engages a diverse set of literatures from behavioral economics and global health to see what changes have taken place in foundational agreements about policy regarding the poor. How has the emergence of ideas of global public goods, demands for greater precision in measuring outcomes of health interventions, and the pressures for standardization changed what is regarded as "common sense" about the behavior of the poor? There is a shift of scale in this chapter, but I do not conceptualize the chapter as providing an overarching theory for understanding the relation between health and poverty. Rather I try to ask how theories embedded in the everyday experiences of patients and healers might be made to speak critically to the expert discourses of global health.

Finally, the conclusion returns to various ways in which illness figures in this text and asks how we should understand the suspicion against narrations of illness in both literary studies and anthropology. Can we learn about health and disease in the context of poverty yet also speak to existential concerns about the fragility of everyday life? What is the place of the patient's experience of his or her illness that gives shape to (or not) to medical knowledge in the clinical encounter? Can we speak of the clinical interaction as based on knowledge? And finally, how do our methods form theory and vice versa when the evolving understanding of my field sites was also contiguous with new forms of cooperation that I developed with my fellow researchers from ISERDD (the research and advocacy organization that I had founded with some colleagues in Delhi) as well as with researchers from other disciplines whom I collaborated with. In what way am I able to maintain my deep attachment to ethnography as a way of knowing while maintaining openness to other ways of thinking about health, disease, and poverty?

I see this book then, as an opening of conversation rather than the end of a journey. The analysis and ethnographic descriptions about poverty, prevalence of disease, or state of health that I offer retain a certain tentativeness. What I have succeeded in showing is the differential distribution of life chances and the surge of aspirations on the part of the poor for improvement in their material and social conditions. Beyond this, though, we see a complex range of normalities through which the poor strive to bring about a different everyday. Yet their experiences of illness, care, and search for remedies do not set them apart as wholly others but rather as those with whom we share certain existential moments. I have seen my task, above all, as that of rendering knowable the lives I encountered. I do realize that more than in any other work that I have done, the experience of working on the project to look at affliction in terms of not only a theology of suffering but also a political economy of everyday life has brought out all the intellectual and emotional frictions with which I live. I hope, nevertheless, that if someone from one of these neighborhoods were to read this book some day in the future, she or he would not be disappointed.

ONE

How the Body Speaks

In this chapter I describe the ways in which illness is made knowable in the course of clinical and social transactions in one of the neighborhoods, Bhagwanpur Kheda in East Delhi. As discussed in the introduction, illnesses might be seen as examples of quasi events that get inserted within the routines of everyday life but that can also morph into critical or catastrophic events that can rupture ongoing relations. This interplay between the ordinary and the catastrophic, the normal and the critical, vital norms and social norms is what concerns me in this chapter.

As is well known, the "illness narrative" has emerged as a classic genre in medical anthropology that focuses on the contrasting perspectives of patients and physicians on illness. In the eighties when the idea of the illness narrative gained currency in medical education, the focus was on the patient's construction of her or his experience, and the goal was to confront the power that physicians, as the holders of expert knowledge, exercised in clinical settings. Thus, eliciting illness narratives and patients' "explanatory models" within the clinical encounter served an important therapeutic and pedagogic purpose:

Arthur Kleinman (1989), for instance, used this notion with stunning effect in his critique of psychiatric practice. The critical force of the concept of illness narratives came then from the potential to interrogate the dominant modes of biopower (Foucault 1991). In the Conclusion I discuss the hermeneutic suspicion that came to be attached to illness narratives as a genre in literature and in medical pedagogy in some detail. I introduce some of those issues here, but the main burden of this chapter is to capture the importance of illnesses that were seen not as dramatic instances of rupture in everyday life but as part of the scene of the everyday in my field sites. I have juxtaposed the different types of findings—results of the weekly morbidity surveys that we conducted and accounts given by households of what any illness entailed in terms of expenditure, therapeutic choices, effects on household income and children's schooling, along with the sources from which medications were obtained. I have also considered the accounts of specific illnesses collected as illness narratives offered by patients and by other members of their families. I am interested in catching the resonances and the tensions that lie between these different modalities through which illness experiences in these neighborhoods were disclosed to us.

Since its formulation, the concept of illness narratives has developed within medical anthropology in two different directions. The first is a greater refinement of the narratological qualities of the telling of illness experience, and the second is greater attention to the economic and political conditions within which illness experiences are formed. The shifts between these analytical positions are not uniform across the discipline, but they provide a lens through which we can see that for many analysts the world is becoming more violent and more disorderly, which affects the way we look at even quotidian experiences of illness. One of the most important anthropologists who has consistently worked on these issues, Byron Good, emphasized the linguistic and narratological qualities of the illness narrative in his earlier work—not only pointing to genre and emplotment but also showing how the context of the telling may influence the way that the story is organized (see Good 1994). Whereas this move opened the way for a subtle analysis of the complex relation between experience and representation in illness narratives, it also shifted the weight of analysis from the context of health seeking to that of storytelling, bracketing the important tension between the indexical and symbolic aspects of medical complaints. Other scholars also analyzed illness narratives as part of the postmodern experience of illness, suggesting that modern and postmodern denoted two different (even successive) styles of living with ill-ness—"a modern style that accepts the authorized medico-scientific narrative and a post modern style in which patients reclaim power as creators and nar-rators of their own distinctive stories" (Morris 1998, 25; see also Frank 1995). These formulations underscored the manner in which the patient as the speaking subject could wrest the self from the dominant expert discourses on illness—yet it gave little importance to the materiality of the conditions within which people fall sick and seek therapeutic interventions. The emphasis on meaning completely eclipsed the specificity of the conditions within which people experienced health and illness; it was not even clear whether the voice of the patient was an embodied voice or whether it functioned as a grammat-ical or literary voice alone. Interestingly, other work in medical anthropology has shifted the focus to illness as indexing the disorder of political and eco-nomic conditions in the postcolonial scenarios of civil wars, economic col-lapse, and high rates of AIDS-related mortality (Farmer 1999; Good et al. 2008; Fassin 2007).

In his later work Good explicitly distanced himself from the unitary coher-ent subject of medical or psychoanalytical discourse that he felt characterized his earlier work, arguing that a dispersed subjectivity better captures the expe-rience of precariousness in the contemporary world (see also Butler 2004 on vulnerability as a condition of the contemporary). As Good puts it now:

> For much of the literature on subjectivity the term "subject" references the *sujet* of the French psychoanalytic, poststructuralist, and feminist writing, locating discussion on theoretical territories that evoke strong reactions among anthro-pologists. And for good reason—the poststructuralist suspicion of the "human subject" and the focus on "subject position" over lived experience leads too often to thick theory over thin ethnography. (Good 2012)

This is an important call for reinstating the thickness of ethnography, but it perhaps overstates the distinction between lived experience and the concepts through which we apprehend the world—much of the burden of my argu-ment in this and other chapters is that concepts are crafted out of this lived experience but that these concepts need not have the character of a well-organized narrative with clear plot lines and well-recognized social actors. The disordering of narrative is part of the sense of bewilderment about what it means to have *this* illness in *this* body. At least in the low-income neighborhoods I studied, patients were not able to accept the idea that practitioners could provide authoritative definitions of what they were suffering from.[1] The critique of illness narrative as a genre performs the important function of shifting attention from the literary to the material conditions under which disease and disorder arise, but this critique also signifies a fatigue with having to deal with the fact that there is suffering in the world (see Han 2013). I return to these conceptual issues in several of the following chapters and especially in the Conclusion.

Making Illness Knowable

Although every culture has recognizable lexical terms that point to the presence of an illness, these terms do not constitute a closed system within which the experience of bodily discomfort or a sense of ill-being can be irrevocably placed. Rather, as Christopher Davis (2000) points out, diagnostic categories are the starting points or building blocks for constructing therapies. Thus, though common understandings may exist of the terms that make up a diagnosis within a shared culture, significant variations can exist in ideas about which of these categories fit together as individuals struggle to match therapies with illnesses. Further, there are no hermetically sealed cultures, which can provide fully constituted and coherent cosmologies within which illness is experienced, diagnosis made, and therapies are sought. For one thing, cultural understanding of illness has become deeply entangled with biomedical categories, for although biomedical categories and therapies have reached different parts of the world in very different ways, the condition of medical diversity, medical pluralism, and hybridity is now universal. This fact raises significant questions about how concepts of health and illness travel. How are these concepts translated, and how do people deal with different expert cultures in making intimate bodily experiences available for therapeutic intervention?

1. Throughout the book I use the term *practitioner* to register the fact that medical markets consist of many kinds of practitioners with a bewildering array of degrees. Rather than use terms such as *quacks*, I have opted for a neutral term— people themselves used the term *doctor* or the Hindi *daktar*, though qualifications are added in the form of adjectives—MBBS wala, Bangali, jhola chaap—that is, one with an MBBS degree, one from Bengal (usually a euphemism for untrained practitioners), or one who caries medicines in a cloth bag. See especially chapters 6 and 7 for further discussion.

In order to address these issues I begin at the simplest level with notions of complaint, symptom, and diagnosis as they arose in response to simple questions. "Were you sick this week?" "If yes, what was the complaint?" "Who diagnosed this problem?" "Do you know what disease you had?"

These questions were posed to sample households as part of a weekly morbidity survey conducted in seven neighborhoods in Delhi over a two-year period (2001–3) preceded by one year of preparatory work and piloting of research instruments in 2000.[2] The survey was carried out by field researchers at the Institute of Socio-Economic Research in Development and Democracy (ISERDD), under the joint direction of an interdisciplinary team (Ranendra Das, Jishnu Das, Carolina Sanchez, and myself). Approximately three hundred households (1,620 individuals) participated in the survey; the refusal rate in the recruitment phase was less than 1 percent.[3] Six households moved out of the localities in the first two years, complicating efforts to survey them on a regular basis. Morbidity surveys were conducted in two yearly cycles—a weekly survey lasting seventeen to eighteen weeks, followed by monthly surveys during the rest of the year (sample characteristics are described in the appendix to this chapter.) Although several other surveys were conducted periodically, here I take the results of only the first round of the surveys.[4]

2. In an earlier paper jointly authored with Ranandra Das, I mistakenly put the first year of the survey as 2000, which was actually the pilot phase of the survey (see V. Das and R. K. Das 2007).

3. The number of households fluctuated slightly during the survey period as some households moved out or were temporarily unavailable due to visits to the village. However, at no time, did the number of households fall below 285.

4. J. Das, Hammer, and Sánchez-Paramo (2012) conducted an interesting experiment to compare the impact of recall periods on reporting of illness and on the expenditure incurred. Using a sample of 205 households that could still be located from the original sample, a second round of morbidity survey was conducted in 2008 by the ISERDD team. Households were divided into a control and experimental group. After four weeks of following the original survey design, the experimental group was surveyed once a month whereas the control group was surveyed weekly. The authors show a significant impact of the time element on illness recall—however, the effects were much more pronounced for the poor than for the rich. The poor are shown to use practitioner visits more than the rich in the weekly recall surveys as compared to the monthly recall surveys. The authors theorize that while the period of recall has no impact on catastrophic illnesses—the poor forget ordinary illnesses of short duration more rapidly—thus these become normalized as part of life. Perhaps the puzzle as to why the rich report themselves to be sick more often than the poor that surfaces in the literature periodically might have something to do with survey designs rather than the state of their respective health status.

The survey design used three methods to elicit accounts of illness experiences, each of which captured different aspects of illness. (All the interviews took place in the homes of the respondents. Although the ISERDD team also collected data on the interactions between the practitioners and patients through observations in the clinics of 291 practitioners, spending one day in each practitioner's clinic, these data enter this discussion only as background for patient accounts in this chapter.)[5] The first method of soliciting names for various illnesses was to ask questions posed in the questionnaires developed for the weekly morbidity surveys. This method helped identify the categories people used to express deviation from a state of health. Although we constructed our questionnaire to elicit a sequence of events as a story—the sequence resulted from the order in which the questions were asked, whereas in interviews conducted later with patients with particular diseases (e.g., TB), people constructed their own sequencing of how the story was to be told. For the survey, the illness account moved from reporting an experience of illness that occurred in the household that week to naming the practitioners consulted, the medications received, and the expenses incurred. Instead of adopting the usual survey method of eliciting information in a single interview (or in some cases in a follow-up interview some months later), fieldworkers from ISERDD contacted households every week for the first four months and then once every month for the rest of the yearly cycle. Thus, they were able to record the course of illness as it developed, as well as the therapeutic regimes that patients undertook over the course of the illness. This frequent contact between field researchers and households was very important for tracking the intersection between household decision making and the course of the illness, but it cut up the telling of illness-related events into weekly episodes.

The second method we used followed directly from our initial observations that in the course of describing their illness experiences, people offered many other insights that called on different realms of sociality and different ways of reckoning time. For example, the story of the illness in many cases was also the story of kinship relations, of who helped and who betrayed; in the course of the interaction over survey questions respondents often went into other stories of how the episode of the moment related to earlier episodes of their own or others' illnesses, or they reflected on the social and economic conditions in which they lived. Not all illnesses invited such reflection, indicating that significant variations existed in the way different illnesses were

5. For an analysis of the data collected on practitioners see J. Das and Hammer (2004).

experienced: Some illnesses were passed over in a casual manner; others led to more stories about engagement with different social and therapeutic contexts. Illness in the latter sense revealed itself to be profoundly social. To capture this aspect of illness experiences and to understand the relation of failures of the body to failures of one's social world (including the specific conditions that constitute poverty), the ISERDD team of fieldworkers recorded such observations even when the accounts did not seem to have an apparent relation to illness and therapy, as defined in biomedicine. Fieldworkers who conducted weekly surveys kept diaries in which they recorded the conversations that occurred in the course of the interviews, although these conversations did not seem strictly pertinent to the questions they had asked. Over time, I found that stringing together these scattered observations gave me several clues to unfinished stories, evolving tensions, and linguistic patterns, such as use of euphemisms or irony to express a range of affects through which illness was wedged between the self and others.

Finally, fieldworkers at ISERDD were trained to use the typical illness narrative genre to conduct detailed interviews with at least one member of each household in the first year. Senior members of the ISERDD research team (Rajan Singh, Purshottam, Simi Chaturvedi, Geeta, and Charu Nanda) conducted these interviews and recorded them when households permitted them to do so. The ISERDD team made every attempt to see that different persons in each household had an opportunity to speak with the field researcher at some point during the year. The weekly surveys permitted the survey population to speak about the ordinariness of many illnesses such as colds and coughs and mild, short-duration fevers. In contrast, the ethnographic open-ended interviews allowed respondents to address the dramatic nature of illness and to discuss what was at stake. Together, these interviews revealed the diversity of contexts in which survey participants experienced illness. At one end of the spectrum, illness was seen as a deviation from life that was easily absorbed into the normal; in these cases, it was part of the normal flow of life. At the other end of the spectrum, the story of an illness could be haunted by the sense of a failure of the body and of social relations. How did people move between these registers of the normal and the pathological, or better still, the normal and the critical? In the eloquent formulation of Davis (2000), medical systems may be understood not only in terms of what they do as therapeutic interventions but also in terms of what they allow people to say.

The Lexical Terms

The lexical terms employed to refer to illness or to abnormal bodily sensations are the linguistic means through which illness acquires a social existence. To respondents who answered in the affirmative to the question "Were you sick this week?" surveyors first asked, "What was the problem/discomfort?" (*kya taklif thi?*). The answers revealed important overlaps between the notion of the symptom, the medical complaint, and the idea of discomfort because the term *taklif* could cover all three. Many of the answers to this question used terms that Davis (2000) calls "primary terms"—those offered without elaboration. These terms rendered illness unproblematic and absorbed it within the normal ups and downs of life. The second kind of response consisted of an elaboration on antecedent events, the physiological location of the discomfort, and attribution of illness to the specific economic conditions in respondents' lives; or a sense that the body itself was failing. In the third category were responses that viewed illnesses either as failures of social relations, especially of kinship and neighborhood, as the result of magical manipulations, attempts at divination, or other ways of accessing the sacred. Though explanations of illness could, indeed, be characterized in this way, none of the respondents' stories fitted neatly into one or the other category. Rather, their experiences of illness were ones of movement, swirls of emotions, with explanations, narratives, and therapies navigating among all these categories at one time or another. Though illness is often talked about in the language of otherness—as the work of the other on the body—I agree with Davis (2000) that experiences of illness move between the registers of the ordinary and the extraordinary, centered in one's social and material worlds yet carrying the power to propel one outside these worlds.

In the rest of this chapter, I build my argument on the basis of discussions that took place in the ordinary give-and-take around illness that fieldworkers recorded in their diaries in the course of their weekly visits to the households. I also draw on the long interviews that two of us (Veena Das and Rajan Singh) conducted with members of the households. Yet I think that the quantitative data we collected helped us think of the dimensionality of the problems faced by the households—how frequently people were ill, how often they accessed practitioners, and the sources of their medicine.

In the following discussion, I make a distinction between "sick weeks" and "full episode" (both are constructs for purposes of analysis), since the former

Table 1. Example of a data segment

Week	Were you sick this week?	What was the problem (taklif)?	Is this the same sickness as last week?[a]
1	No	—	—
2	No	—	—
3	Yes	Fever	—
4	Yes	Fever	Yes
5	Yes	Fever	Yes
6	No	—	—
7	Yes	Boils	—
8	No	—	—

[a] Fieldworkers asked this question only if a respondent reported an illness both in the previous week and in the survey week. They recorded chronic conditions, such as diabetes, separately.

tells us how often people were sick and the latter tells us how long the illnesses lasted. Because fieldworkers recorded the data they collected through the morbidity questionnaire on a weekly basis, initial information was coded in terms of the story of sickness that week.[6] Obviously, many illnesses lasted more than one week. To capture this distinction, the data were coded both in terms of sickness weeks and illness episodes. For example, table 1 shows the entries for Ajay in one eight-week segment.

The fieldworker coded Ajay's information in different ways. First, the table records two episodes, based on the fact that Ajay reported he was ill with fever in weeks 3, 4, and 5; because he said that the fever was a continuing one, it counts as one episode of illness. After reporting no illness in week 6, Ajay reported boils on his body in week 7, which counts as the second episode. However, we also record that in the total of the eight weeks, he reported illness for four weeks and hence had four sick weeks. Clearly, two measures of temporality operate here, and though these measures get entangled in the narratives, the distinction is useful for interpreting data on practitioner visits and on the extent of self-medication (V. Das and R. K. Das 2006; J. Das and Sánchez 2002). Table 2 gives the distribution of acute episodes in the sample

6. The survey instruments were developed during a one-year pilot phase in 2000 with a sample of forty households in four localities and were finalized by Addlaka, Das, et al. (2000).

population in the first year for one round of weekly surveys, and table 3 gives the duration of the episodes.

These tables illustrate two important points that will be of use when considering the narratives. First, about 52 percent of the sample population experienced one to three episodes of illness in a four-month period, and second, a large proportion of illness episodes (nearly 70 percent) lasted less than one week. Only 24 percent of the population reported no illness. Of course, the illness burden was not equally distributed across localities, but no straightforward relation was evident between income and illness burden. For instance, though the shanty cluster in NOIDA (New Okhla Industrial Development Authority) and the households in Bhagwanpur Kheda were next to each other in their average reported income, NOIDA had the lowest reported morbidity and Bhagwanpur Kheda reported the highest. Although a nuanced analysis of the differences by locality and income is not possible here (but see J. Das, R. K. Das, and V. Das 2012 for the absence of a direct relation between income and mental health), we can safely state that the poor and the rich tended to have different types of diseases. For instance, TB was found in all low income

Table 2. Numbers of persons with numbers of episodes (Period: 17–18 weeks)

Number of episodes	Frequency	Percent	Cumulative percent
0[a]	384	23.69	23.69
1	352	21.71	45.4
2	282	17.4	62.8
3	209	12.89	75.69
4	136	8.39	84.08
5	105	6.48	90.56
6	62	3.82	94.39
7	51	3.15	97.53
8	24	1.48	99.01
9	7	0.43	99.44
10	7	0.43	99.88
11	1	0.06	99.94
12	1	0.06	100
Total	1,621	100	100

[a] Recording the number of episodes as 0 and the frequency as 384 means that 384 individuals reported no episodes of illness in the data set, and this number constitutes 23.69 percent of the total number of individuals.

Table 3. Duration of episodes

Week	Frequency	Percent	Cumulative percent
1[a]	2,566	69.65	69.65
2	669	16.16	87.81
3	196	5.32	93.13
4	85	2.31	95.44
5	53	1.44	96.88
6	38	1.03	97.91
7	19	0.52	98.43
8	8	0.22	98.64
9	10	0.27	98.91
10	4	0.11	99.02
11	8	0.22	99.24
12	5	0.14	99.38
13	3	0.08	99.46
14	4	0.11	99.57
15	2	0.05	99.62
16	3	0.08	99.7
17	3	0.08	99.78
18	8	0.22	100
Total	3,684		100

[a] This table records the number of weeks that each episode lasted. Recording the episode duration as 1 and the frequency as 2,566 means that 2,566 episodes (69.65 percent) lasted one week.

localities, but not a single case was reported among the upper income groups. Finally, the burden of chronic disease (as defined in biomedicine) was significantly higher among the upper-income groups, partly because the number of older people in that population was higher and partly because their access to better quality practitioners led to easier recognition of chronic diseases such as diabetes and hypertension. This finding does not mean that feelings of chronic and debilitating conditions were absent among the poor—simply that the symptoms they reported as chronic conditions were often a result of illnesses that were not diagnosed and hence kept recurring.[7]

7. See chapters 6 and 7 for a further discussion of the medical environment and comparison of private versus public health facilities in terms of quality of care using different measures of quality.

With this background on the overall disease burden, I move on to consider how respondents employed notions of complaints, symptoms, and diagnosis in the narratives and see what light these notions throw on the construction of illness, local ecology, and the subject.

Primary Terms: Illness and Normal Deviation

When the respondents in the survey described their illnesses using various lexical terms with little or no elaboration, we found that they attributed such disorders to the routine ups and downs of life—changes of season or changes in the body due to normal transitions in the life cycle. For example, they described various kinds of colds and coughs—*sardi, zukam, nazla, cheenk, khansi, gala kharab*—cold, runny nose, sneezing, coughing, and sore throat as "seasonal." To refer to a fever, they sometimes used the Hindi word *bukhar* and at other times they used the English word "viral" (*viral ho gaya*—viral has happened). Apart from attributing some ailments to seasonal variations and hence assimilating them to normal rhythms of the environment, respondents also attributed certain ailments to normal changes in the life course. Thus a baby could be having "diarrhea due to teething," a young girl's stomach pain could be due to menstrual cramps needing only dietary interventions, and various aches and pains were considered normal for old people due to *budhape ka sharir*, "the body of aging." Certainly, contests still emerged over these definitions, but these contests centered on whether a condition was normal for the current season or phase of life or whether the evocation of normality was being used to mask a lack of care for the ill person. I give two examples below.

Minakshi was washing clothes when Rajan went to interview her. She said that she had slight fever. "Viral fever," she said, "change of season, everyone is getting it." They then went on to talk about other things.

In contrast, Ballo, an old (perhaps in her late sixties) widowed woman in Bhagwanpur Kheda, who lived with her son, his wife, and unmarried children, constantly complained of stomachache, feelings of weakness, and lack of appetite; she insisted that she had a "heart condition" or perhaps "TB"—*dil ki bimari, ya shayad TB*. Ballo's husband had died a year before our survey began, and no one in the family was clear about the cause of his death. His son said he had been admitted to a referral hospital for TB, so the father could well have died of tuberculosis. However, the man's widow, Ballo, said that her husband had had a heart condition and had been admitted for disease of the heart (*dil ki bimari*). Such confusion of categories was not uncommon. Ballo was reported as "head of the household" when we collected demographic information at the initiation of the project: I noticed tensions over her status in the family that had a bearing on her illness. In the eighteen weeks' duration of the survey, Ballo reported as sick for eleven weeks. Precise information on her illness was missing for the remaining seven weeks—one week because the households could not be surveyed and for six weeks intermittently because she went twice to visit her married daughter in a village on the outskirts of Delhi to "get treatment." Her daughter took her to a local practitioner trained in biomedicine with an MBBS (Bachelor of Medicine and Bachelor of Surgery) degree for consultation. She showed the fieldworkers a couple of prescriptions that the practitioner had given her: the diagnosis given was "old Koch."[8] That such antiquated terms circulate among practitioners, even trained ones, is indicative of the different kinds of lives diag-nostic categories live in this environment. Throughout the survey period, Ballo's son bought medicines from the local pharmacist by presenting him with an old prescription. These medicines included capsules for acute or chronic viral hepa-titis for three days; Liv 52 for improved liver function, intermittently during the whole period; and Pyrazinamide, a first-line anti-TB drug, for two weeks inter-mittently. Underlying the history of intermittent drug treatment, ranging from powerful anti-TB drugs to medicines for improving liver function, was Ballo's demand that she receive more attention from her son and daughter-in-law. However, whenever the daughter-in-law was interviewed, she would say, "*Bud-hape ka shrir hai aisa to hota hi hai par, amman mein sahan shakti kam hai*" ("This is the body of old age; such things happen, but amma has no capacity to tolerate"). Ballo's visit to her daughter's village was to show her displeasure with her son— she stayed there for four weeks, pronouncing herself to be much better after she returned. Her daughter sent her some medicines intermittently from the practi-tioner in the village via a Delhi Transport Corporation bus driver who lived in that village and happened to be related. The entry in the last week against Ballo's

8. Robert Koch is the German physician and scientist who discovered the *Mycobacte-rium tuberculosis*, the bacterium that causes tuberculosis (TB). He presented his findings in March 1882. Earlier tuberculosis was known as Koch's disease—so it is interesting to find this usage among the practitioners in these low-income neighborhoods in Delhi.

name recorded that she cited "mild TB" as diagnosed by the village practitioner. In this period, this family had spent 350 rupees, more than 1 percent of its annual income, on medicines, which, from a biomedical perspective, were useless for treating Ballo's medical conditions.

Ballo's case shows another way in which the "normal" was positioned in the lives of the poor. Her representation of her illness was made up of complaints that she had picked up from previous encounters with the medical system, especially during her husband's illness. Thus, while she represented her illness as "heart trouble" sometimes and "*thodi bahut* TB"—mild TB—at other times, her daughter-in-law represented her complaints as normal for the aging process and thus not as signs of illness at all. Did the availability of categories such as "heart trouble" and "mild TB" allow Ballo to reconfigure somatic changes that might have been considered "normal" for an aging person into categories of disease? In an influential paper on the cultural inflation of morbidity during decline in mortality, Ryan Johansson (1991) seems to suggest that such a process might indeed be taking place: "In general social scientists cannot or should not attempt to relate morbidity and mortality during the health transition because morbidity is made up of phenomena of several different kinds, each of which relates differently to sickness and death." He further states that "the more diseases there are, the more likely are individuals to think of themselves as sick or to be diagnosed by a professional as sick. In this way the incidence rate is a function of the culturally recognized stock of diseases, along with the propensity of ordinary people to classify biologically suboptimal states as sickness according to culturally standardized breakpoint on the health continuum" (Johansson 1991, 44).

I agree with Johansson that the availability of categories may expand the possibilities of how to think of bodily discomfort, but I question the categories of "ordinary people" and of "culturally standardized breakpoint" on the health-sickness continuum. Instead, I suggest that the concrete experience of illness in the family and local community, along with the actual nature of the clinical encounter, makes up the stock of knowledge through which people represent illness categories and seek therapies. A tremendous struggle takes place as people try to determine how to authorize the "real": Are these symptoms indicative of "mild TB" or of old age? The notions of normality or pathology take shape in this struggle within a set of family dynamics, as Ballo's case shows.

Another Idea of the Normal

A second way in which the notion of the normal emerged in the interviews was in the experience of the illness within the materiality of the lives of the poor: What was normal, they asked, for someone who was living in these conditions and doing this kind of work? The following entries in the diary maintained by Shoyab Ahmad, a field assistant who conducted the survey in NOIDA, illustrate this point. (All entries were in Hindi—my translation.)

> September 3, 2001—household no. 9086. When I reached R's house, I found her sitting outside washing vessels. On seeing me, she put out a charpai [jute string cot] for me to sit on and asked me to be seated. I asked her about her husband's work, and she said that he goes out in search of work every day, but until now, he has not been able to get anything. I asked, how are you managing? She said that they are managing by borrowing money from neighbors. The baby had loose bowel movements but there was no money to take him to the doctor; but he was probably teething—so he would get better—but if they had the money, she would have taken the child to Khan (the practitioner visited most often in this locality, who has a degree in "integrated medicine").[9] She said, "We are poor; our children have to get by with what we can give them."
>
> September 4, 2001—household 9092. As I was going to S's house, I met his son, who was sitting outside. I asked him how everyone was in the house. He said everyone was okay but that his papa was not well. As I was talking to him, S came back from taking a bath at the public pump and said his *nazla* [cold] was worse, and he had pain in the lower part of his abdomen. He said that he was getting it

9. The degree in Integrated Medicine which used to be offered in some medical institutions at least till the late fifties was replaced by degrees in specific alternate streams of medicine such as Ayurveda (Bachelor of Medicine and Surgery in Ayurveda); Unani (Bachelor of Medicine and Surgery in Unani Medicine), etc. Though I have not been able to find definitive evidence of the way this degree was administered, the sprinkling of older practitioners who claimed that they had a degree in Integrated Medicine in Delhi seems to indicate that this option was available earlier.

treated privately. "I don't mind spending four hundred or five hundred rupees—but when things become expensive—one has to consider the government hospital. I know that things won't go well in hospital [*durgati hoti hai*], but it is our helplessness [*mazburi*]. Now I have to go to hospital to get admitted." On the next visit, S had not gone to a hospital—he had obtained medicine from the local practitioner: "As long as my hands and feet are moving, I have to work. The pain has subsided."

The second example is from an encounter I had with Z, a young man who was sitting outside his house and greeted me. I was not sure whether he was inebriated, but I asked him why he had not gone to work. He said, "My mind is not okay today—I get such disturbing thoughts, I am feeling so angry, I have pain in my head—I have to go and get some medicine." At this point, he held his head between the two palms of his hands and bent his head as if in despair. I joked, "Maybe you had too much to drink!" "No madam ji, people do not understand. Everyday, I have to lift such heavy weights. I feel my body collapsing. If I do not take some drink, I will collapse. Now I get these tensions, these terrible headaches. I have to do something. This doctor will give me some medicine that will make it a bit better, and then again it will happen—but what can I do? I have to find some way of getting relief. Just as I have to drink some to make my body fit for work."

In such cases, the question of what is normal is mediated by the questions, what is illness and what is treatment under conditions of poverty? I heard the expression "as long as my hands and feet are moving" as the trope through which Z represented the laboring body. Among the poor families in the ISERDD sample only 20 percent had jobs in the public or private sector (one third of the total sample that includes upper- or middle-income families); 10 percent worked informally as hawkers, rickshaw pullers, housemaids, or unskilled labor in factories and shops; and 44 percent were outside the labor force but sometimes engaged in domestic production, doing piecemeal jobs for minor industries in the area (see the chapter appendix on the sample characteristics). Most people had only intermittent employment and thus had a persistent feeling that they were on a threshold, in danger of not finding work, or one step away from a serious illness that would throw them into debt. They also lived in fear that the nexus of relations through which they maintained their jobs, obtained loans, or found a doctor in a public hospital would somehow collapse. Households had some cash flow, but it was irregular. Though even the poorest households managed to have some disposable income, any large expenditure propelled them into debt.[10]

The practitioner market and the therapeutic practices that practitioners offered in these localities show how attuned they were to the material conditions of the households in the neighborhood. Low- and middle- income neighborhoods are full of practitioners from alternative streams of healing (Ayurvedic and Unani) who have received some training in biomedicine as part of their curricula (Langford 2002); but regardless of the type of training and degree they had, their typical therapeutic strategy was to dispense medications for two or three days at a cost of twenty to thirty rupees and to ask patients to come back if they did not feel better. If a practitioner felt that a patient required more expensive medication, he or she sometimes wrote a prescription for purchase at the local pharmacy. Households often saved such prescriptions and took them to the local pharmacist with the complaint that the symptoms had recurred.[11] In more than 13,000 data points in the ISERDD survey, respondents reported visiting more than 300 different doctors in a total of 1,200 practitioner visits. Less than 30 percent of all practitioner visits were to public hospitals or government dispensaries. The use of government facilities was higher among the poor than among the rich, except in one area of upper income households where many residents were employed in government service. Subsequent research has shown the generality of such patterns and is discussed in chapter 7 in greater detail. Tables 4 and 5 show the distribution of various types of actions that respondents in Bhagwanpur Kheda and NOIDA (the two localities with the lowest-income profile in the sample) took

10. Catastrophic health expenditure is traditionally measured as out-of-pocket health expenditure that exceeds some fixed proportion of household income or a household's capacity to pay. This particular measure leads to the result that catastrophic health expenditure goes up with increases in income. Rama Pal (2012) proposes a different measure—expenditure on health is catastrophic if it reduces nonhealth expenditures to a level that the household cannot maintain consumption of necessities any more. Using the new measure, Pal shows that the incidence of such health expenditures goes down as income increases. Bruno Van Damme et al.'s (2012) letter to the journal *Lancet* recapitulates their experiences in Cambodia—viz., that such expenditures lead the poor to cut back on consumption, take children out of school, sell productive assets, or take loans at high interest rates, further eroding their capacity to maintain necessary consumption. This finding strongly resonates with my own experience of talking to people about these matters.

11. On the failure of regulation of pharmacies and of medical practice, see V. Das (1999), Jesani, Singhi, and Prakash (1997), and Kamat and Nichter (1998).

in response to reported acute illnesses during a typical week in the first year of the survey period. Respondents in Bhagwanpur Kheda took no action in 21.75 percent of cases. The figure is considerably higher for NOIDA, where respondents took no action in nearly 43 percent of cases. However, people typically consulted a practitioner rather than the pharmacist for treatment. Further, even in cases coded here as self-medication, patients often used earlier prescriptions or obtained refills.

On the basis of the data presented here we can now fill in the larger picture of what health seeking looks like in this environment. We can see that 70 percent of illness episodes lasted less than a week (see table 3), and people made high use of practitioners. Even though households often reported such deviations (short-duration morbidities) from health as "normal," whether these conditions could be treated even at this low level of medical competence, depended on the cash in hand. In most cases, the patient's need for relief combined with the practitioner's (mis)understanding of the pharmacopoeia carved out the therapeutic strategy. There is an interesting assemblage here of biomedicine as embodied in the local strategies of care and the household as located in the materiality of the informal economy, which is characterized by

Table 4. Actions taken on reported illness in Bhagwanpur Kheda

Action	Frequency	Percent	Cumulative percent
No action	319	21.75	21.75
Only practitioner	508	34.63	56.37
Only pharmacist as doctor	48	3.27	59.65
Only self-medication	389	26.52	86.16
Two or more actions	203	13.84	100
Total	1,467	100	100

Table 5. Actions taken on reported illness in NOIDA

Action	Frequency	Percent	Cumulative percent
No action	319	42.25	42.25
Only practitioner	248	32.85	75.1
Only pharmacist as doctor	8	1.06	76.16
Only self-medication	123	16.29	92.45
Two or more actions	57	7.55	100
Total	755	100	100

precarious employment and small flows of cash. Through this assemblage, both biomedicine and households mutate to create a unique neighborhood ecology of care. What kind of illness narrative do patients produce in this exchange and translation of illness categories in their lives? I offer low-blood-pressure (low-BP) syndrome as an example of this process.

THE LOW-BP SYNDROME

In one of the first interviews I conducted even before the pilot phase of this project, Priti, a young woman with two daughters, told me that she suffered from low blood pressure. She complained that she suffered from persistent body ache, blinding headaches, weakness, and sadness. "I have no life in my hands and feet. The world appears to bite me. I feel like leaving everything and running away." When I asked her if she knew what she suffered from, she said without hesitation that she had low BP. She stated that she consulted a local practitioner, using the term "family doctor" in English for him. The doctor did not measure her blood pressure, but whenever she felt that her symptoms were becoming difficult to bear, she went to the pharmacy and got a mixture of capsules and pills that she consumed for a couple of days. I found that there were others in these areas who referred to their complaints as "low BP" and that there was little difference in the way that practitioners and patients used the term. Weakness, giddiness, headaches, and sadness were often attributed to low BP, which, in turn, was often attributed to the "tensions" inherent in the conditions in which people lived. However, this category does not appear to belong to either the "folk" or the "expert" category; rather, it carried the trace of the clinical encounters typical of low-income neighborhoods and their particular ecology of care. Practitioners in low-income neighborhoods did not seem to distinguish between diagnostic categories and symptoms (on which more in chapters 6 and 7). Thus, households in these neighborhoods tended to use what would be diagnostic categories as descriptive of symptoms.

Members of higher-income households used the same terms in very different ways. Thus, when such households reported that someone had a "BP problem," the meaning was much closer to the biomedical meaning, at least to the extent that they understood that BP reflects a particular measure, although this fact does not mean that they would fit the profile of compliant patients. It is thus difficult to endorse Johansson's (1991) very general claims about "the culturally recognized stock of diseases" or the "propensity of ordinary people to classify biologically suboptimal states as sickness according to culturally standardized breakpoint on the health continuum." Neither of these categories—"ordinary people," "culturally recognized stock of diseases,"—is transparent; instead, we must treat them as emergent categories.

Instead of thinking of symptoms and diagnostic categories as arising from culturally standardized practices of classification, perhaps we might shift the weight of explanation to the regimes of labor through which both body and temporality were produced and consumed in these local settings. As is well known, analyses of the working day in the factory (Marx 1887) or work in the disciplined regime of the prison (Foucault 1977) objectified the experience of time into homogenous and equivalent units. The worker's or the prisoner's body is put to labor, and the question for the capitalist in the first case and the state in the second case is how to ensure the reproduction of the laborer's or prisoner's body. Questions of a living wage or the minimum nutrition necessary for the prisoner arise out of this consideration.

In contrast, temporality in my field sites was intimately tied to the experience of the precariousness of work and the irregular flows of cash in the household. The intersecting temporalities of work, cash flows, and the therapeutic practices of local practitioners created certain ways of dealing with illness that emphasized immediacy and the short term rather than investment in proper diagnosis and cure as the case studies in the next three chapters will show. This situation in turn stems from the failure of the state to regulate practitioners and pharmacies so that categories such as "a little bit of TB" or "low BP" and the related modes of treatment with intermittent and (from the biomedical perspective) inappropriate drug use have come to dominate the health-seeking practices and health delivery in these localities. The state does not act here to regulate the proliferation of practitioners with spurious degrees or little training in medicine. But then, there is not much difference between the way that practitioners in low-income neighborhoods, whether with training in biomedicine or training in other streams of medical education, treat patients or dispense medicines (see also J. Das, Holla, et al. 2012). As a result, practitioners who cluster on the fringes of the city and give the local moral worlds their particular character become conduits for the distribution of pharmaceutical products in these neighborhoods.

OUT OF THE LOCAL: OTHER THERAPEUTIC SPACES

Though 70 percent of the illness episodes reported in our survey lasted less than one week, more than 6 percent of episodes lasted three or more weeks. In such cases, families in low-income neighborhoods, despairing of the therapeutic choices available locally, began to seek alternatives outside the regime of the local. One cannot describe this journey via a straightforward model of vertical or horizontal resort. The households were not consistent in their decisions about which illnesses were best treated through specific therapeutic systems (for example, they did not consistently seek allopathic solutions to acute diseases or homeopathic ones to chronic diseases); instead, they thought about which networks of information and influence they could activate. The practitioners in these localities generally reported that when they could not manage a disease using the resources they had, they provided a service to patients by referring them to private, but more expensive, medical facilities.

All of us at ISERDD were intrigued by the fact that the billboards outside the office of some (but not all) practitioners displayed rates for various kinds of diagnostic tests, yet we could find no sign of such facilities in the offices of these practitioners. "How do you do these tests?" I asked one practitioner. The practitioner, an active member of the National Association of Practitioners of Integrated Medicine, told me that he knew a good diagnostic laboratory in the area, and he received a small commission for referring patients there. Others did not display billboards but nonetheless acted as brokers between patients and providers of more sophisticated facilities or specialists. If the disease was seen to worsen and a practitioner began to fear that death might result, he advised the household to take the patient there.

In chapter 6, I describe the sense of foreboding some practitioners felt that they were not competent enough to handle difficult cases. In such a scenario, some households were able to borrow enough money to deal with emergencies; others accessed such facilities for a few days, decided they could not sustain the expense, and tried to find someone who could get the patient treated in a government hospital. The other route for patients was to access a public hospital—recall that 30 percent of all visits to practitioners were to public hospitals.[12] In such cases, the capital required to sustain treatment was

12. See chapter 7 for a further discussion of the medical environment and comparison of private versus public health facilities in terms of quality of care using different measures of quality.

often a "contact"—often a relative working in a hospital as an orderly or a janitor who could push the file ahead so that the patient could access the doctor without a long delay. We found several variations in patients' accounts of their treatment in the public hospitals. In the lower-middle-class area of Jahangirpuri, many households had effectively learned how to access the Jagjivan Ram Hospital in the area, but except in cases of TB, they could rarely sustain long-term treatment because of the demands on time. In other areas, such as NOIDA, the distance from a public hospital made access very difficult, whereas in Bhagwanpur Kheda, many patients claimed that they were told that the private medicines would work better even for TB, for which they received some but not all medications. Nevertheless, use of public health facilities was higher in Bhagwanpur Kheda than in NOIDA. To illustrate how patients came to use diverse pathways of care, I offer some ethnographic vignettes of therapeutic failures in the next section

MEENA: A CASE OF TUBERCULOSIS

I present Meena's case, which has haunted me for a long time. I describe her case to show how difficult it is to decipher what kind of clinical trajectories were available to her. The confusion that we find in her narrative at least partly reflects the confusions that arose from a very confusing medical landscape for diseases that do not get cured easily or speedily. In the next chapter I describe her illness through the eyes of her young son, Mukesh. There is some overlap between these two renderings of the same illness, but one might also see these as different experiences even as each is touched by the other. I found the way mother and son tried to ward off danger and protect each other resonant with the way Didier Fassin (2010) thinks of survival, following Derrida, as the capacity to think of life with and beyond physical death. If one thinks that I can never live the death of another, then the account offered in this and the next chapter might move one to imagine how we do make the death of another something that is also ours.

Meena lived with her husband, their two sons, and her husband's father in one of the mud huts in the shanty settlement of NOIDA. Her husband held a job as a janitor in the U.P. Waterways Department. The family had a regular but small income. At the initiation of our study (August 2000), Meena reported that she suffered from tuberculosis. She said that her first episode of TB had occurred three to four years earlier and that she took medications for a long time—perhaps seven months, perhaps one year.

However, on another occasion she told one of the fieldworkers that she had suffered from TB for the past eight years and that she had "never been cured." She described a complicated story about having a breast abscess after her child's birth, followed by a minor surgery as well as fever, cough, and weakness. This illness, she said, referring to her TB, happened when she lived in the village with her conjugal relatives while her husband came to the city in search of work. Following is an extract from an interview by Rajan Singh.

> RAJAN: So, in your conjugal family, did you know that you had TB?
>
> MEENA: In the beginning, I did not, and the doctor also did not say that.
>
> RAJAN: Then you were having cough and fever and weakness.
>
> MEENA: Yes, they gave me lots to eat, but still the weakness did not go. Then I became okay when they took me to Vrindavan [a pilgrimage town in North India associated with Lord Krishna as a child].
>
> RAJAN: Government hospital or private?
>
> MEENA: Government hospital—there the checkup and everything was free, but you had to buy medicines from outside.
>
> RAJAN: How long ago was this?
>
> MEENA: Eight years ago. I took medicines for three months. Then I became healthy.
>
> RAJAN: So did the doctor ask you to stop the medicine?
>
> MEENA: No, but there was no money (to continue). For three months, my husband's father [*sasur ji*] bought medicines, but then the money ran out, and no one helped. (Original text in Hindi, translated by Bhrigupati Singh)

From the village, Meena moved to NOIDA to join her husband. She said that she was healthy for some time after moving to the city, but then her symptoms recurred after her one-year-old daughter died. When we began our survey, she reported that she had completed a course of TB medication recently but was still feeling very sick and weak. In the initial weekly survey period of four months in 2001, Meena reported that she was ill with various symptoms ranging from cough to fever during eight of the sixteen weeks. Because she had already completed a six-month course of TB medications recently from a government dispensary and had been reported cured after a sputum test, she did not return to this dispensary for treatment of her symptoms in these eight weeks. Instead, she intermittently sought treatment for relief of symptoms from a private practitioner in the area, who had a bachelor's degree in Ayurvedic medicine and surgery, He gave her a range of medicines, from analgesics to antibiotics. Her mode of accessing medical care was typical of many people in the area—that is, a mode in which practitioners treated symptoms by dispensing medications for a day or two for a consolidated fee of twenty to thirty rupees. This period was difficult for her in another way because she suspected that her husband was having an affair with a married woman in the neighborhood. During conversations, Meena said she feared that her husband would send her off to the village where his mother lived, on the pretext that he could not care for her adequately, and she worried that he might even marry the other woman. Meena wanted desperately to recover her strength so that she could attend to household chores effectively and keep her place within the conjugal family.

Toward the end of the first year of our survey in 2001, Meena's condition seemed to have worsened to the point of an emergency. She was beginning to cough bloodstained mucus and was constantly coughing. The neighbors remarked that her husband had tried first to get her admitted to a private hospital in the neighborhood but did not have the money to make the advance payment demanded by the hospital. Eventually, a relative who was employed as a ward boy in a government hospital in South Delhi managed to get Meena admitted under another name on the pretext that she was his dependant relative. Meena stayed in the hospital for six months. By the time she was discharged from the hospital after the six-month stay, and returned home, the Pradhan (headman) of this cluster of jhuggis (shanties) had acted decisively against the woman with whom her husband was presumed to be having an affair as a result of complaints from the neighborhood.[13] Consequently, the woman's husband was persuaded to send her to back to the village to live with the husband's extended conjugal family. Meena had now taken another course

13. The perspective of various neighbors was always present. The jhuggis were so tiny that most women did their work in the street—thus any visit by us occasioned general commentaries on the neighborhood, including comments on births, visits to the village, children, husbands, thefts, politics, and everything else under the sun. This was the public life of the neighborhood, and one participated in it purely by being there.

of TB medication, and the hospital discharged her with instructions to complete the course of medications. She was required to go to the hospital outpatient department to receive medication, but her husband managed to get her name transferred to a DOTS (Directly Observed Therapy, Short Term) center nearer their home. Meena completed the remaining course of medications from the DOTS center. For the next three months, she was free of symptoms and put on some weight. One could detect the altered effect even in the small entries in the diary of Purshottam, who was then covering her household for the survey.

EXTRACTS FROM PURSHOTTAM'S DIARY

Today looking at Meena ji's face [ji is an honorific in Hindi used for all elders], one felt that she was a little better. I asked Meena ji, "How are you?" She smiled and said, "Now I am better. I went to get medicine for Rahul [her younger son]." She showed me the medicines.

A few days later, Purshottam recorded in the diary that while he was visiting the household, Meena's husband came from the market with a bag of pomegranates and handed them to Meena to eat. (Pomegranates and grapes are among the most expensive fruits and often denote the extra care and affection showered on a sick person.) Meena's symptoms reappeared in the third year of the ISERDD study when the first phase of the survey had been completed, but regular visits were made to the study areas by ISERDD staff and myself for ethnographic work. Purshottam's diary entries record that she lay in bed coughing. At one point, she said to Purshottam, "Brother, I feel broken from inside." On her husband's request, two members of ISERDD took her for a consultation to a referral hospital in Kingsway Camp, where the attending physician was prepared to admit her as an inpatient, though no one was willing to explore why her symptoms kept recurring.

Off the record, one physician told one of us (Veena) that conducting diagnostic tests for multidrug-resistant TB would be futile because the hospital did not have the resources to provide treatment. Meena's husband did not want her admitted to a hospital so far from home, so they went to another DOTS center and provided a false address to avoid regulations regarding zonal treatment centers. Here again, she received the anti-TB regimen under the DOTS protocol but reported serious side effects such as continuous nausea. Her condition continued to worsen, so she stopped taking medications. She died in a private nursing home in December 2003 after being rushed there two days earlier. At the end of her life, the family was several thousand rupees in debt.

Given the weight of the literature on TB and stigma, one might have expected that stigma would play a major role in this illness trajectory. However, the theme that seems to emerge from Meena's story is consistent institutional neglect and incoherence. This neglect on the part of institutions existed in conjunction with the different ways in which Meena's husband moved between care and neglect over the three years. In each episode of the disease, Meena completed the course of medications given by the DOTS center and was declared to be sputum negative and thus "cured." In addition to taking the prescribed first-order drugs in the TB regime, she consulted a private practitioner between treatments and received medicines to address specific symptoms such as fever, pain, and cough. She did not conceal her illness from anyone. The private practitioner she consulted in the locality was well aware that she had consulted various DOTS centers about her disease and that she had been on medication for TB. Though she had the treatment cards that she had collected from the DOTS centers as well as those from the hospital, she did not carry her medical records from one government institution to another. Nor did any practitioner try to get a detailed medical history from her. This lack of interest in patients' medical histories is consistent with the common practice in the area among practitioners trained in all streams (biomedicine, Ayurveda, homeopathy, Unani) who often diagnose recurring symptoms as the "residual" effects of TB that include weakened respiratory functions, coughs, and fevers. They treat these symptoms with analgesics and inappropriate antibiotics, even after the patient has been declared cured by the DOTS center.

Meena's death cannot be attributed to a simple notion of stigma that prevented her from going to a DOTS center for treatment. Her family made no effort to conceal her disease. Paradoxically, the notion of stigma of another kind was pervasive within DOTS centers—the stigma of a noncompliant patient. Meena's family members had to move her from one DOTS center to another because they feared that she would be held responsible for her failure to be cured. As a result of these treatment strategies by patients and their families, we have no way of knowing whether Meena was repeatedly reinfected because of compromised immunity, environmental factors, or concomitant HIV infection or whether she was infected by an acquired or transmitted drug-resistant strain. Meanwhile, the records of each DOTS center classified her as a cured case. We might note that if HIV were to become endemic in such areas, classifying cases of repeat infections would be even more difficult.[14] The literature on TB now distinguishes between patient delays referring to the time taken by patients to access medical care after the onset of symptoms and diagnosis delay as the time taken by practitioners to diagnose TB after the patient has presented with symptoms (Sreeramareddy, Qin, et al. 2014), and it is clear from the review of this literature that failure to diagnose TB is a very important risk factor for delay in treatment. However, this literature pays little attention to what happens when patients manage to reach DOTS centers but find that their symptoms keep recurring despite treatment.

Meena, as we saw, was completely bewildered by the fact that her symptoms kept recurring though she was pronounced cured at the end of each treatment cycle. Throughout her treatment, she ricocheted between despair and hope. If her symptoms improved, she became active in making little improvements in the house, such as paving a little space in front of her jhuggi with cement so that she could wash it and keep the entrance clean. When the symptoms recurred, she lay inside the jhuggi and said, "Now I must prepare for going to Jamna ji [the river near the cremation ground]." Yet she hoped to survive, and even in the last month of her life, her husband tried to take her back to the DOTS center from which she had received the last course of treatment. The nurse in attendance there was not willing to register her case again; she told her that they had done all they could and that their records showed that she had been cured of TB. In the last week of Meena's life, when she was coughing incessantly, her husband took her again to a private nursing home, which admitted her, albeit at enormous cost, and she finally died there.

In telling this story, I do not seek to pit heroic patients against heartless doctors; I am trying to understand how the "letting die" happens even as international agencies and the government participate in the much publicized global Stop TB program. In Foucault's rendering, this "letting die" is itself an aspect of biopower in which a cut is made between those whose lives are enhanced and those whose lives are not worth preserving. In his famous formulation, "Sovereignty took life and let live. And we have the emergence of a

14. According to some estimates, already 21 percent to 40 percent of cases among smear-positive patients in Maharashtra and Gujarat are retreatment cases (see Lambregts-van Weezenbeek 2004).

power of regularization, and it, in contrast, consists in making live and letting die" (Foucault 2003, 247). In his acute reading of Foucault, Fassin (2009) makes the important point that a politics of life is much broader than biopolitics—in that sense, he says, biopower is conceived not so much as power over life but is to be seen in opposition to sovereign power over death. This formulation, however, requires us to attend closely to the way in which different institutions such as family and state are knitted into each other, since the power to deal death is now no more in the hands of a sovereign power but is dispersed over different institutions. We cannot assume that the family simply functions as an agent of the state. I hope to have shown that the way in which the family lets a relation die has a different dynamic and texture of feeling than the way in which the state does so. Thus, terms such as abandonment or triage cannot be employed in a seamless manner as we traverse the milieu of the family and the state, even as we track how the state's signature might be read in the lives of families and local communities.

The micropolitics of families and communities have qualitative differences and variations that are internal to the family (see also Han 2012). I do not seek to paint a stark contrast between the "care" provided by families and the "neglect" of the state. In Meena's life, she faced periods of neglect, when her husband probably just wanted to get rid of the burden of caring for her. She also experienced periods of care, when he would make the long journey to the hospital whenever he could get leave from his work or come home in the afternoon during his lunch break and cook food for her and the children. Kleinman (2009, 2014) has shown us in his extraordinary writing that care has a lighted side and a dark side to it. Even in affluent societies the burden of grief in caring for a loved one whom one cannot save can become unbearable, coloring love with the opposite emotions of anger, aggression, and sorrow.

There were other cases of therapeutic failure as a consequence of TB or other conditions, but the trajectories of family relations and the pathways followed by patients were never identical. Thus an elderly Muslim man who died had not followed the DOTS protocol with any regularity because he felt that he was not treated with respect at the DOTS center, and although his wife and son tried their best to get him to go there regularly, they could not exercise any authority over him. Another woman was cured, but her infant who was born during the time that she was being treated died without any medical worker having given her any advice about whether she should withhold breast milk from the infant or not. There were other cases of accidental deaths of children who fell from a roof while playing or a factory worker who got electrocuted—in all these cases the combination of institutional apathy or incompetence or even humiliation heaped on patients was combined with complex ways in which families could not sustain care.

In the literature on the economic consequences of diseases such as TB and AIDS, one sometimes finds calculations of the impact of deaths on particular populations (the young versus the old, heads of households versus dependents, and so on). The consequences of the death of a young mother for the life of the family, however, cannot be computed in strictly economic terms. During her illness, Meena ceased being an earning member of the family, and paying for her treatments deepened her husband's debt. In this sense, she was an economic liability while she was alive; thus, deaths of unproductive members of the family might be seen as less grievous for the family from a strictly economic point of view. Yet, however much Meena's illness drained the family's resources, her husband and children wanted her to live, mourned for her when she died. Like Simone Weil's (1951) understanding of affliction, the grief caused by Meena's death might live in the body of her children like a parasite, eating one from within as the local rhetoric on grief puts it. The impact of the mother's death on the children, and thus the social and emotional costs of institutional incoherence in the treatment of TB, cannot be computed in strictly economic terms. But more important, we should ask what the loss of a mother might mean to the children: How do they learn to read their social environment or to trust institutions that seem to have failed them so dismally? Such questions will resurface in the next chapter as I describe how Meena's son learned what it was to live with her death.

Deadly Intimacy

While walking through the streets of the low-income neighborhoods in Delhi, one sometimes came across billboards that assure a cure for *uppari chakkar* (misfortunes caused by occult forces) at the same times as they carried advertisements for various diagnostic tests and treatments for varied conditions. Thus a billboard proclaimed: "ct scans, blood test, sugar test, pregnancy test also available. Here you can be treated for uppari chakkar." The original with its combination of Hindi and English words typical of the language of the bazaar in poor neighborhoods read as follows: "*Yahan CT Scan, Khoon Ka*

Test, Sugar Ka Test, Pregnancy Test Ki Bhi Suvidha Uplabdh Hai. Yahan Uppari Chakkar Ka Bhi Ilaj Kiya Jata Hai." Uppari chakkar has a complex semantic range: Muslims might use it to refer to a jinn (a being of smokeless fire) who passing above the human world might sometimes becomes enamored of a beautiful child or a woman and thus might come to possess him or her. Though jinns might be divided between the pious ones and the malicious ones. People want to expel the ones who are responsible for uppari chakkar from the sphere of sociality that they have forcefully occupied. Among the Hindus, this term simply refers to mechanisms through which the ill will of a neighbor or a jealous relative subjects a family to repeated illnesses and misfortunes. The following story of K illustrates this notion.

K traced the beginning of his misfortunes to his daughter's paralysis, which occurred after she received a vaccine from a practitioner in the area who was also a good friend of the family. The girl developed paralysis of the limb probably because the injection was wrongly administered. After some years, K had an accident, and though he was not badly hurt, his vehicle was damaged and he lost his job as a taxi driver. A series of other illnesses followed. Business ventures failed. Though the family had regularly accessed both private practitioners in the area and the public hospital, they attributed the series of misfortunes to the magic done by a jealous neighbor. At the time of the pilot survey in 2000, they told Komila (a fieldworker) that the Hindu diviner (*jhad phook wala baba*) they consulted had not been successful in warding off their misfortunes because he had not been able to do any real harm to the neighbor. They had therefore shifted to a Muslim diviner (*maulavi*) who could use the verses of the Qur'an in a clandestine way, trapping anger in its verses and directing the verses toward harming their neighbor. In a discussion with them, I asked why they thought a Muslim diviner would be better able to deal with their misfortunes. Because a Hindu, they replied, was unable to muster enough anger against another Hindu. A Muslim, K thought, would have a reservoir of hate against Hindus, so he could direct that hate into a powerful spell against the neighbor. The social practices of blaming here do not take the usual fault lines of sectarian conflict, in that the neighbor whom K's family blamed for its misfortune was not a Muslim. Yet K created a collective subject and sought to harness the diffused hate and anger that Muslims supposedly harbor against Hindus to use it against his Hindu neighbor. This situation gives us an insight into how particular Hindus and Muslims were able to inhabit the same local world in ordinary circumstances but could also call on anger and hate residing in imagined collectivities to harm each other.[15] A crisis can draw on these common reservoirs of hate, which are a potential, waiting, as it were, on the door of reality. Yet this kind of crisis can also be given a new direction as the extraordinary story of the Muslim healer I describe in chapter 5 shows. This healer was reluctant to take on the burden of healing but found in the end that in order to move on the side of light, he had to experience what is darkness.

In other instances, people in the neighborhoods placated goddesses with offerings of liquor or performed pig sacrifices to channel the energies of angry gods and goddesses against someone they wanted to punish. There was a widespread notion that illness persists because the social world is fraught with danger: "Someone has done something." Thus, the experience of the neighborhood and of kinship was a profoundly ambiguous one. Support could be found in the local moral world, but the same local world could overwhelm people and force them to act in conflicted and confused ways. This phenomenon explains why people were sometimes able to make successful therapeutic choices in defiance of the voices in their local world, but at other times, as people came to believe that their illnesses went beyond the capabilities of the practitioners and the medicines, they would resort to the clandestine sacred world of gods who required bloody sacrifices and goddesses who asked for offerings of liquor and meat. But rituals do not provide any guarantee either (see chapters 4 and 5). Depending on the experience of the social world, one person might dismiss a symptom as a harmless part of the change of seasons, and another might read the same symptom as evidence of the power of those who seek to inflict harm. Though the narrative flow in any telling might render these events in linear terms, I found that revisiting the story several times made it more complicated with new explanations of symptoms and complaints thrown in, especially if the disease became more recalcitrant in the course of a person's life. Explanations were more in the realm of possibilities, people could move from one to the other as new information or new insights came in or as older explanations simply did not work. Narratives of illness did not have a teleological orientation—perhaps demonstrating that it is life that weaves stories that are themselves points at which a person may rest or move on. As the amil who figures in chapter 5 taught me, the subjunctive mood is the most important mood when one reflects on one's life.

15. For an analysis of how such diffused notions come to the surface during ethnic or sectarian riots, see V. Das (2007), Mehta (2000), and Mehta and Chatterji (2001)

Appendix: Note on the Sample

This note describes the characteristics of the households in the seven neighborhoods of Delhi, India, with which ISERDD studies on urban health and poverty started. Later more neighborhoods were added for another problematic related to an understanding of citizenship.

Of the seven neighborhoods we first chose, three of the neighborhoods were poor, with average monthly household expenditures (in 2002 Indian rupees with a nominal conversion rate of $1 = Rs. 49.09) of Rs. 4165, Rs. 4313, and Rs. 4898, respectively; two were middle income (Rs. 5309 and Rs. 7849), and two relatively wealthy (Rs. 14892 and Rs. 16117). These localities were chosen on the basis of initial contacts; once a contact had been established, the sample of households was drawn randomly by asking every alternate household to participate. In all, 300 households were thus selected with less than a 4 percent rejection rate among those approached. After the pilot phase of testing of questionnaires and establishing contacts and mapping basic facilities in 1999 and 2000, these households were observed over a period of two years, using a mix of weekly and monthly recall surveys with detailed information on individual health and health care–seeking behavior. In addition, demographic, income, and consumption modules were administered three times in the two years, and special modules on mental health and reproductive outcomes were administered between the twelfth and twenty-fourth month of the study. Over the two-year period of this phase of the study, attrition was less than 5 percent in the sample.

On average, the individuals in the sample are young (with a median age of twenty-two), poorly educated (50 percent of all individuals are illiterate or have less than a primary education), and live in nuclear households with an average of 5.4 members per household. Joint families, as defined in terms of coresidence of married sons (or, more infrequently, daughters) and parents in the same household are less frequent: 73 percent of households are—fully nuclear in the sense that they consist of a head-of-household, his spouse, and their children (in 4 percent of these households either the father or the mother of the head is coresident), and another 24 percent report a married son and daughter-in-law living together with the head. In these cases the median age of the son or daughter-in-law is twenty-eight. Less than 2 percent of households report more than one married son living with them.

Among all individuals in the sample, 43 percent are married and among those older than eighteen, this increases to 76 percent. A small minority (4 percent) is either widowed or separated. About 50 percent of those fifteen and older are employed, resulting in 1.5 income earners per household, although only a third of them are in the formal sector (public and private). Finally, 47 percent of the adults (eighteen and older) are migrants into the city, relative to 33 percent for the sample as a whole.

Average age and education are higher for the rich, although employment rates are not substantially different across income groups.

A comparison of the ISERDD sample to representative samples of Delhi from the National Family Health Survey (1998) and the National Sample Survey (2000) showed that the ISERDD sample looks very similar to both these representative samples, although households in the ISERDD sample are slightly richer than in the National Sample Survey (this could be attributed to the later date of the ISERDD sample).

TWO

A Child Learns Illness and Learns Death

In the section on therapeutic failure in the previous chapter we briefly met Meena, who suffered from tuberculosis and died despite multiple rounds of first-line therapy. This chapter looks at Meena's illness and her subsequent death through the eyes of her son Mukesh. Georges Canguilhem's (1991) characterization of disease as an experiment with life provides a powerful framework not only for understanding the life of the individual organism in relation to its environment, but also the relationships within which the organism is embedded and which shape the course of illness as much as they are shaped by it. In my attempt to understand the reverberations of Meena's illness, I ask: How do children learn to set individual norms for themselves in relation to the adult world by learning to place themselves within relationships as illness and misfortune erodes their taken-for-granted categories of understanding? I argue further that although adults try to bring children within the world as they know it best, they sometimes acknowledge that there are experiences to which children might give expression that are beyond the reach of adults. It is as if adults have some dim knowledge or suspicion that the world that children have come into is marked by a strangeness for them; that the children are in possession of languages, which are of adjacent worlds that are not fully known or even knowable to the adults (see especially Cavell 1979; Khan 2006). I claim that such a view of both adulthood and childhood casts these categories as unstable, since the contour of each comes to be formed in relation to the other.

As we shall see in the course of this chapter, children can become ventrilo-quists voicing the desires of adults; and they can invest themselves in role performances that cast them as as-if adults (see Ferenczi 1949 for such pro-cesses in the specific context of sexual abuse of children). I came to know Mukesh, Meena's older son, from the age of eight till he was twelve. He lived in a shanty settlement in Sector V in NOIDA within the National Capital Region at the periphery of Delhi. This neighborhood was at the lowest level of income and assets among the seven localities in the original sample. I hope to show that demonstrating how children learn to make a world within the contingencies of family politics, state institutions, and the unpredictability of adults has great potential for rethinking the indeterminacy of the social as it absorbs the biological.

The idea that the child is not a tabula rasa on whom society simply imposes its own projects has been vigorously interrogated in research on children (Prout and James 1997; Pufall and Unsworth 2004). But even earlier, the impor-tance of understanding childhood as a period of creativity and self-formation and its implications for our theories of social action was underscored in George Herbert Mead's distinction between children's play and games and in the decisive importance of the concept of "I" in his thinking (Mead 1934). As the German sociologist Hans Joas (1997, 118–19) has argued, the "I" in Mead is regarded as a source of unanticipated spontaneities that surprise the actor no less than her or his interactional partners. The observations on childhood and the transition from concrete others to the generalized other were import-ant for Mead as providing the basis for understanding how a system of ethics could take societal regulations into account without reducing individual development to mere adaptation to the social. To that extent, understanding children opens a door to answering questions about the regime of the social itself. In recent times, others have drawn attention to the importance of regarding children as philosophers or theologians in the light of not only experiences of, say, illness or death but also because of the philosophical per-plexity to which children often give expression (Matthews 1980, 1992).

I am much in sympathy with these ideas that break from an earlier powerful tradition of regarding children as simply unformed potential adults. However, I am interested in another dimension of experience—namely, that of the ordinary as strange or uncanny, which is particularly relevant in the context of illness or death with which children were frequently confronted in my field sites. I do not derive my sense of the uncanniness of the ordinary from a general philosophy of life but from the particular way in which a complex layering of family relations with the institutions of the state came to define the quotidian in the overall context of poverty and deprivation and created the sense of reality as precarious. For me the idea of the child as hovering around the social, stealing rather than formally learning language and then slowly putting the world together as his or her own, provides a haunting picture of what I shall call scenes of instruction. Such scenes of instruction contest our usual ideas of socialization as adaptation to pregiven norms without making the opposite blunder of presuming that the self can be created ex nihilo. I am interested in exploring how the illness of a caregiver, a much-loved mother, deforms one's world and how such a world is put together, however precariously, again.

In the last chapter, we saw the trajectories of illness and consequent actions in Bhagwanpura—one of the localities in the larger study. Now we move to the shanty settlement in Sector V of NOIDA, where forty of the sample households were located. I refer to this settlement as a jhuggi cluster—the popular term for shanties, huts, and other temporary structures put up by the poor on various stretches of land in the city, though in official parlance this is an unauthorized slum or squatter settlement.[1] Elsewhere I have described the precarious position of these neighborhoods and the ambiguous legal position

1. According to the 2021 Master Plan of Delhi adopted by the Delhi Development Authority (DDA), the unplanned settlements in Delhi are divided into the following types: resettlement sites, designated slums, urban villages, regularized unauthorized settlements, unauthorized settlements, squatter settlements. There are different degrees of security of tenure for these settlements. So, for instance, designated slums have rights against eviction under the Delhi Slum Act of 1956; many of the resettlement sites came up under the government's own initiative in various periods but most notoriously during the beautification-cum-sterilization drive during the national emergency in 1976 (Tarlo 2003) and thus enjoy permanent lease over the land allotted to them; urban villages are those claimed under different government notifications in which land was converted from agricultural land to that used for building; and regularized unauthorized colonies are those which received official recognition from time to time. According to different estimates, about 50 to 70 percent of the population of Delhi lives in these "unplanned settlements."

they occupy, since, on the one hand, the jhuggis have been made on occupied land, and, on the other hand, the courts have given a stay order so that residents cannot be evicted till the government can supply them with alternate housing (see V. Das 2011).

In this chapter, I am particularly interested in the way in which children register the biological rhythms—births, illnesses, deaths—in their lives. There were fifty-four children between the ages of five and fifteen among the forty households in this neighborhood, and although, as I have said, we collected systematic data on morbidity and mortality in these households through survey methods, it is the usual anthropological practice of hanging out in the neighborhood that generated much of the data on children that provides the broader context within which I present the story of one child in this chapter.

One of the members of the ISERDD team, Purshottam, whom we met in the last chapter, was particularly engrossed in getting to know this neighborhood well since 1999. I often accompanied Purshottam and chatted with men and women whom I met in the course of their normal routines. Since the jhuggis were very small, it was a normal practice for people to carry on many of their activities in the street. Women engaged in cooking, washing clothes, or simply sitting on their haunches in small groups and chatting. Men would often lay out string cots at the entrance of a street and play cards or just snooze as if the streets were their homes.

As Purshottam and I went around from one house to another from 1999 to 2003 getting acquainted with people in the area, we were followed by children curious about what we were doing.[2] Slowly we began to engage the children in conversation while they went about their daily life—as they carried water or carried a younger sibling or walked between school and home. Thus, instead of any formal interviews we simply took notes in our field diaries on conversations, or we recorded events of interest such as quarrels that broke out or complaints that we heard children make among their peers. In the

---

2. What I call a neighborhood here is defined by cluster of jhuggis, some made with mud and straw and others with different stages of being converted into pucca dwellings made with bricks, plaster, cement, and asbestos or tin roofs. Rooms rarely have any windows. In the daytime it is very rare to find a child within the house, as life is mostly lived in the street where people cook, eat, bathe, play cards, or sit on string cots and gossip. Since most residents work in the informal sector, there are no fixed hours of work. In the other low-income localities such as Jahangirpuri or Bhagwanpur Kheda where there are built houses it is more common to find children within the house.

beginning of the school year we sometimes accompanied children to school in NOIDA, mediated with their teachers over report cards, school fees, and sundry other matters. I did not define myself as engaged in an ethnography of children. Instead I thought of them as part and parcel of the ethnography of the neighborhood.

The stories of illness we found in the course of our ongoing interactions with people in these neighborhoods were not clear-cut in terms of plot, narrative coherence, or delineation of characters. As I stated in the last chapter, stories could change shape, be picked up or discarded much as therapies could be picked up or discarded. In part, the very strangeness of the world for the poor and the sheer force of contingency produced constant shifts in delineation of character and plot. Particularly for children, the kind of knowledge to which they became accomplices was often hard to bear. Whereas in the case of fiction, plot often refers to the series of events consisting of an outline of the action of a narrative, there are other meanings of a plot, such as "ground," that might be more appropriate here. In the sense of ground, plot may be taken to refer to the soil on which the story grows.

Mukesh: A Dwelling and a Building

Mukesh was about eight years old when we first met him in the jhuggis in NOIDA. He lived with his mother, father, younger brother, and grandfather. Mukesh's mother, Meena, suffered from tuberculosis for many years and despite completing at least three courses of anti-TB medication, she was not cured.[3] She died in December 2003. Meena's two sisters were married to the two brothers of her husband: They lived in the same neighborhood, but relations between the families were fraught with conflict. Meena's husband and his father were both employed by a contractor of the state-run water board (UP Jal Board) as cleaners. They reported a stable but meager income. Throughout the period when the ISERDD conducted regular surveys, small amounts

---

3. There is some evidence that an informal triage is practiced in the DOTS centers so that patients who are not likely to comply in the judgment of the attending nurse or physician are simply not registered, thus excluding the poorest and the most marginal populations from the program (see Singh, Jaiswal, Porter, et al. 2002). So the failure to attend to Meena when she presened with symptoms that might have been indicative of MDR-TB was probably not exceptional.

of cash were available to the family, but demands ranging from food, school supplies for the children, medicines, and money spent on Mukesh's father's drinking severely constrained their capacity to engage in any projects that required commitment of money for any length of time.

In the first year of the pilot phase of our study (2000), Mukesh remained one of the small crowds of children who hung around Purshottam and me as we trudged from one jhuggi to another, filling forms and gathering basic information about the residents. To recapitulate the main events in Meena's case as described in the last chapter: She had completed one course of the first-line treatment against TB when we first came to know her, but she was extremely weak. After a brief period of being free from symptoms she had begun to complain of intermittent cough and fever. Our first set of impressions about Mukesh was from snippets of conversations with his mother. In one such conversation in 2001 Meena confided to a member of the general survey team that she feared her husband was having an affair with a neighbor whom Meena described as a loose women (*gandi aurat*, lit., dirty woman—a term that could cover a range of meanings from a prostitute to a woman with loose morals). Here is how Lathika, the field assistant, noted it in her diary.

> Meena cried today. She said that Mukesh was very angry with his father because he had seen him walking hand in hand with this other woman in Hadola [a nearby market]. [Meena said,] "She is a dirty woman. She makes alliances with men—her husband seems helpless—he says nothing to her."

Over this year, Meena began to fear that something ominous was going to happen. Her husband began to say that he might leave Meena in the village with his mother so that she could get rest and clean air. Such a strategy of coping with illness is not uncommon among many households, but it can signify a range of affects from genuine concern for the sick person to the first step in abandoning a sick wife. In fact, since NOIDA had a large number of migrants, trips between the city and the village were quite common, but leaving a sick person back in the village was a gendered strategy that is generally resorted to by men rather than women. In my interactions with Meena and her neighbors I began to viscerally feel her fear of being abandoned. The children of the household, however, remained somewhat vague in my imagination though they figured often in the mother's narrative.

Mukesh and his brother, Rahul, were both shy and awkward in my presence. Both boys would simply run away if directly addressed. In the course of the first four months of my fieldwork, I found one occasion when neither Meena nor her husband was at home. Finding Mukesh sitting outside the dwelling, I asked him if he would help me fill the forms about illnesses in the family that week. He was probably flattered to be recognized as a trusted informant. He told me that Rahul had suffered from an attack of asthma (*dame ka attack*). Then he went into the room and brought out a whole sheaf of papers—one of these was an old prescription for a broncho-dilator for Rahul. As I was leafing through the papers I found results of diagnostic tests for Meena and a DOTS (Direct Observation Therapy) treatment history record. I was muttering to myself that I could not understand why Meena was not getting better if she was taking the medicines regularly when Mukesh suddenly interrupted me and said, "Madam ji,[4] when she gets angry with my father, she does not take medicines for many days." I said, well, you are going to school; you should explain to her that she must take her medicines regularly. He threw up his hands and said, "We are but *children*. Who will listen to us?" After that, he collected the papers, shoved them somewhere inside the room, and ran away.

It appeared to me that Mukesh was on the edges of conversation in the house; he was aware of his father's transgressions and fearful of what this might mean for his mother and himself, but all he could do was to inform his mother about what he saw and try to protect her from the dangers of the illness and the dangers of a world he barely understood. In taking the role of her protector, he worked with bits and pieces of information that came his way— guessing at what are the consequences of adult desires, such as that of his father for another woman

Boundaries and Bridges

Though I had been visiting the locality regularly since 1999 (even before the formal study of the neighborhood began) , it was not until much later that I

---

4. The use of honorific *ji* along with the English term Madam seemed to place me as someone akin to a schoolteacher—at some stage I made a transition from being Madam ji to Auntie ji.

got to know Mukesh well, though I could never get Rahul's attention except
for fleeting moments. It happened that in late July of 2001, I was walking
around the neighborhood. The heat was intense, and a lot of children were
just hanging around, half naked, whiling away the time. The school year had
begun, and so I said teasingly to a couple of children, "Bunking off school, are
you?" In the previous year many parents had told me that they would get the
children admitted to the neighborhood government school. The government
had announced the policy that no child would be deprived admission to the
primary schools for lack of documentation or on grounds of performance.
Schooling at the primary level is free in government-run schools. In addition, children of scheduled castes,[5] to which most households of this shanty
settlement belonged, were entitled to free schooling, uniforms, and school
texts. I had carefully and repeatedly explained this to the parents in the previous year. I also knew that at least for part of the year Mukesh had attended
a private school. When I asked him if he was going to continue in the same
school, he said, "Papa says there is no money." Mukesh had decided that he
now wanted to join the government school where schooling was free,
although he was very skeptical if there was much learning to be had there
(*vahan khas padhai nahin hoti*).

From my inquiries of Mukesh and the other children, I learned that when
parents had gone to the school to secure admission for their children, the
teacher in charge of admissions had demanded that they produce either a
birth certificate if they were joining the first grade or a school-leaving certificate if they were joining a higher grade. In the absence of either certificate,
they were to produce an affidavit duly signed by the Patwari (the lowest-level
government official of an administrative block); and if they had none of these
papers, then they had to pay Rs. 180 (approximately US$4.00 in 2001) osten-
sibly so that the school could get the necessary affidavit. Most children,
of-course, did not possess birth certificates since they were born at home or in
the village, and parents did not even know that they required birth certificates.[6] In Mukesh's case, he did not possess a school-leaving certificate because

5. Scheduled castes refers to a number of previously untouchable castes which have
been recognized for affirmative action. In many parts of the country such castes refer to
themselves as Dalits (lit. oppressed castes), but in this locality the preferred term they used
was SC (abbreviation for "scheduled castes").

6. The situation has changed considerably as people have become aware of the need to
collect various kinds of certificates to access government entitlements.

he still owed a month's fee to the private school he had attended. No adult had the time to run around to get an affidavit signed from the Patwari because most were daily wage laborers, and even the ones who were without work went around searching for work during the day so that going in search of the Patwari would have meant loss in wages.

Incensed by this story of what I saw as extortion from the school, I gave a brief lecture to whoever would listen that they must go and meet the principal and demand their right to be admitted. Mukesh's father had come home for lunch, and since he is literate (having studied until fifth grade), I again told him of the announcements made in several government handouts that no child would be denied admission to primary school because of lack of documentation. He promised to go the next morning to see the principal.

As I was at the point of crossing the water pump that used to separate the neighborhood from the main street,[7] Mukesh came running to me and burst out, "Papa will never go—he never has the time and the principal will not listen to him." He pointed to two other children whose fathers had paid up the money and who had been allowed to join the school. He had brought his exercise books from last year, and he held those out toward me, saying, "See, how well I did." (I do not know whether he had come running to me out of his own sense of urgency or because his mother had told him to do so, but it would have still required some courage on his part to thus approach me.) I first tried to evade his entreaties and then finally relented and said I would come in the morning and take Rahul and him and any other children who wanted to come with me to the school. I said I would not promise anything but would try to argue their case before the principal.

What happened next is best described as a comedy of errors but with some happy consequences. In the light of our earlier discussion (in the introduction) of De Col and Humphrey's (2012) notion of quasi events we might even think of it as a bit of luck that could change the direction of the routines of everyday life without constituting a rupture. I went to the school with the children and demanded to see the principal. As might be anticipated, my

7. The pump does not function now, but most people have running water drawn from the municipal pipes from the main road that have been connected to household taps through various arrangements with local entrepreneurs. Thus an illegal market in water has emerged along with other small but significant changes, such as the addition of septic tanks that obviated the need for people to use the streets or parks as toilets or for daily ablutions as they had in the past.

presence there created a stir. Most parents standing in groups around the teacher in charge and pleading for their children to be admitted were poor, and many were illiterate. In that crowd, my clothes and my appearance stood out. The principal assumed that I was a government official who had come to do a spot-check of the school, though I did not introduce myself as one. Despite my explanations that I was doing research among the slum dwellers, the principal could not quite fathom why I was there with these children. Here is an extract from our conversation (in Hindi), constructed from memory (my translation).

> V. Principal Sahib, I am part of an organization. We are working with families in the jhuggis on the problems of the slum dwellers. All these children had come to get admission, but your school is demanding money from them. Where are these people to get Rs.180? These are scheduled caste children, and the government is supposed to be doing everything to get them into school, not keep them out of it. (There were many appreciative nods from the motley crowd of parents standing outside. The principal asked them to not crowd the entrance to his office and to go to another room where their cases would be heard.)

> P. No, no, Madam Ji, there is surely some misunderstanding [*galatfahmi*].

Turning to Mukesh, he asked, did you go to any school earlier? Mukesh nodded but was clearly quite apprehensive.

> P. So did they not give you school-leaving certificate? See, Madam Ji, the rule is that a certificate must be shown so that we can put him in the right grade. If he does not have this then we need an affidavit.

I pressed my case for admission, arguing that they could see his schoolwork or give him a test to determine in which grade he should be admitted. In the course of the conversation the principal offered the following explanation.

> P. Madam Ji, you have not understood our plight. Please look around. In this school we do not have even mats for the children to sit on the floor. There is no almirah for the principal to keep his papers safely. I admit we take money from the children, but it is to get these essential things.

This gave me an opening. The principal's complaints about the lack of any facilities for the children were quite valid. I said I would not be able to give any money but would be delighted to give some things for the school. I urged him to admit the children from the jhuggi cluster without the hassle of papers and certificates though I did not tie up the gifts with the promise of admission. (This does not mean that the principal did not understand this as some kind of a bribe, although he too maintained the fiction that these were two separate events.) I bought the school some jute matting for one of the classrooms and a small steel almirah for the principal. These were duly entered in the school stock register, and the children were admitted without birth certificates; each child was assigned August 15 (Independence Day) as his or her date of birth. For many years after, I would occasionally visit the children in school and would be roped into reading stories to them. The teachers and the principal were never clear as to my identity. I said truthfully that I was not a government official. I also did not behave like one, but they often suspected that I had the power to report them to some higher authority.

The Physiognomy of Mukesh's Words: The Prepolitical?

In some of the famous passages relating to the child in *Philosophical Investigations* (Wittgenstein 1953), the picture of the child and her learning of language and hence of coming into a form of life, evokes the idea of her coming into a strange country. Similarly, it seems to me that the entire episode of Mukesh's reentry into school was like coming into an adjacent world whose languages were obscure but not without the possibility of divination. I say "divination" rather than "interpretation" of "deciphering" in order to signal that the coming into this world for the child was rather like interpreting omens, signs, and portents.[8] As Mukesh tried to gauge how the opportunity of

---

8. I think here of Pedersen's (2012) lovely essay on a day in a Cadillac where he describes how the young men in urban Mongolia would sustain hope by reading the omens and signs of the day in a hopeful way, despite consistent failures, such as the failure to recover money owed to them or to find a job or make a business investment work. Pedersen says that hope is the poor man's good fortune, for it allows him to see the present moment as if it contained the possibility of a different future, however unrealistic.

my presence in his neighborhood could be made into something that could work for him and as he watched the transactions with the principal, he was not learning about a stable world but rather about the essential incoherence of institutions in his world. Learning about the world of certificates, documents, and bribes and also guessing whether parents would (or could) come up with the resources for a child to continue in school (in NOIDA at least) had the character of divining the gestures and signs that attached to adults rather than, say, applying incremental knowledge to learn how to read. The only way that residents in the neighborhood could interpret the actions of the school principal in his demand for certificates and affidavits was to see it as a bribe: It fit with their experience as well as with the rumors about the state that circulate in the city (cf. Gupta 1995, 2012). Yet for the children the full implications of such entities as bribes and certificates were not fully in place so that often the questions of securing admission translated into the question of how invested their parents were in putting in the efforts to get them into school.

What is interesting for me, then, is the way that Mukesh read the politics of the family—his father's ambivalence toward the whole affair and his mother's passionate investment in his education must have given completely contradictory impressions of what was expected of him. I feel that this accounted for the combination of despondency and hope with which he had run to me to get me to intervene. One might ask if the father's ambivalence toward Mukesh's schooling arose from the poverty of the family that made even the small amounts of money required for school supplies difficult to sustain or whether it stemmed from a desire to escape the obligations of looking after a sick wife and children. There is no sure way of answering such a question, for as the famous saying in Zande goes, one cannot look into another's heart as if it were an open basket. What is relevant is Mukesh's own sense that he needed to please his father to keep his father's anger against the mother in abeyance. I can give several examples of quotidian events when I would find Mukesh not in school but fetching water for a nearby tea shop or taking leave to run errands for a wedding in the hope of getting some small money as tips. Yet he was also responsive to his mother's desire to see him as an educated youth, and when he did well in school, his father too expressed some pride in him.

After he completed the primary school the issue of work versus school began to intrude in his life with greater force, as small opportunities for earning money arose in the neighborhood. In his discussion on children as philosophers, Gareth Matthews (1980) discusses a story he crafted for fifth graders in which they were asked to reflect on the question of whether a single person could be divisible into different parts. He shows how in thinking about this question either in terms of bodies (I am sitting still but my eyes are moving, so do I have two parts—one sitting still and one moving) or with regard to the conflict between desire and reason within oneself (one part of me wants another cookie, but another warns that more would make me sick)—children dealt with questions of divisible selves and what that entailed for establishing responsibility. In the case of Mukesh similar issues about conflicting parts of the same self were not framed in response to hypothetical questions; rather, the question of whether to pursue his studies or drop out of school was premised on Mukesh's ability to read his mother's hope and his father's bursts of anger against him; or he needed to interpret talk that was not even directly addressed to him, as the following account noted in my diary reveals.

> Mukesh said that Papa and Mummy had a fight—Papa was going out in the morning on Sunday, and Mummy said where are you going because she thought he was going to buy a *thaili* [locally brewed liquor sold in pouches]. He got very angry and said wherever I am going is not your business—I give you and your children enough to eat—after that what I do, whether I spend money on drink or on gambling is my affair. Who are you to interfere?

Childhood, Hierarchy, and Styles of Dependency

Let us put this discussion in the context of the literature on hierarchy and styles of dependency in South Asia. Several scholars have emphasized that the aim of socialization in India is not to make children into autonomous adults but to teach them to act as relational beings within a realm of hierarchical relations (Kurtz 1992; Trawick 1990a). In his exquisite descriptions of the various genres of trouble telling in Bangladesh, James Wilce (1998) describes the way in which everyday interactions teach children to take a stance of assertive dependence toward adults. He argues that even young children learn the meaning of complaints from the way in which their tears are responded to, but in the process they also learn that the caregiver herself is not an autonomous decision-making person, for she might herself be a dependant with little power within the structure of familial relations. In the Punjabi families that I have described earlier, younger women or women who are living as dependent relatives in a joint family are not expected to respond to a child's crying—they must let an older women take care of the child so as to affirm faith in the elders of the family and in the cardinal principle of kinship that children belong to all (V. Das 1976; see also Kurtz 1992; Trawick 1990a). The manifestations of hierarchy are complex, and managing them in everyday life as opposed to simply affirming them as structural principles is a delicate task for both inferiors and superiors.

The literature on South Asia then alerts us to the play of power within the family and especially how children learn the meanings of tears, admonishments, silences, and restraints as not only emanating from the caregiver but from her *position* in the larger (often joint) family. Unfortunately, there are not many descriptions of how wider forces such as sectarian or caste conflict or violence of policemen or local officials fold into the politics of the family and affect children .

In the episode of the school admission I described, one might be tempted to think that Mukesh was performing an assertive dependence that Wilce (1998) sees as typical of socialization of children in Bangladesh. However, it seems to me equally important that Mukesh had learned to decipher what was irresolvable within the family structure and thus needed the mediation of an outsider in order to resolve the impasse created by the demands of the school. Children in the neighborhood learned in various ways that there is a powerful world that they located outside their neighborhood, in relation to which their position was vulnerable not only as children but as poor and thus suspect in the eyes of the outside world of policemen, government officials, schoolteachers, and government hospitals.

It was a taken-for-granted assumption in the neighborhood on the part of both adults and children that this powerful, yet unpredictable world could be accessed only through intermediaries or through brokers. The normal linguistic practice was to describe these intermediaries as paths through which a way could be paved into the wilderness of government bureaucracies. People often referred to the strategies for accessing these worlds as *"jan pahchaan nikali"*—to have extracted an acquaintanceship, or *"rasta nikala,"* to have extracted a path. For instance, at one stage when Meena's medical condition required emergency attention, her husband found a way of getting her admitted to a public referral hospital for TB by finding a relative who worked as ward boy there and who helped secure a hospital bed for Meena by pretending that she was his wife. Meena's husband explained to me that because

Meena came under the jurisdiction of a DOTS center near their house and had a card that recorded her as cured, he was certain that the hospital would have simply sent her back for treatment there. Although I concede that such fears are not always justified, we collected enough evidence in these neighbor-hoods to be able to state that they are not completely unfounded (as described in the preceding chapter). These arbitrary practices created the conditions of possibility for what I have elsewhere called a brokered self (V. Das 2004) and are typical for the lives of the poor in urban settings. It is this context that explains how Mukesh came to imagine that he could overcome the obstacles presented by his family situation by aligning himself with Purshottam and me in a similar relation of brokerage. Before he got to know us well we must have fitted into the picture of the intermediaries on whom children pick up infor-mation from fragments of gossip in the neighborhood.

There were also cases in which Purshottam and I were assimilated to the category of outsiders from whom information had to be protected. One morning we were shocked to learn that a young woman who was pregnant and already the mother of a seven-year-old girl had died of severe burns a few nights earlier. Her hut was locked. Inquiries from the Pradhan (headman) revealed that the woman had been making tea when the kerosene stove burst, and now her husband had taken their daughter to leave her with her grand-parents in the village. Another neighbor said, though, that the woman had poured kerosene and set herself alight in the course of a bitter quarrel with her husband. The neighbor said that the woman might not have wanted to kill herself, but by the time anyone could do anything to save her it was too late. The neighbor also said that when the police came, the child had given a "cor-rect statement" (*sahi bayan*). When I asked what that meant, she explained that the child had said it was an accident; otherwise, the man would have got into much more trouble with the police. The "correctness" of the account from the local perspective was for the child to reiterate the father's version of the event. Obviously, we could not determine whether it was a case of suicide or a homi-cide, but everyone was agreed that it was not an accidental death. Yet the child had told the policemen that it was an accident-the neighborhood supported her in this because it was in no one's interest, as the residents maintained, to have the police probe into neighborhood affairs. Although this is an extreme case, there were other examples that show how children learn or decipher for themselves that the correct response to any inquiries about fights, injuries sustained during quarrels, or a man's aggression against his wife was to feign complete ignorance. Were they learning to enact a certain kind of citizenship in these gestures of ignorance?

A basic presupposition of liberal theory about children is that they are pre-political beings (cf. Boli-Bennett and Meyer 1978). As astute readers of Imman-uel Kant, such as Isabel Hull (1996) has argued, Kant equivocates between a universalizing view of humanity and a definition of the human as citizen. The exclusionary force of citizenship, Hull argues, puts various barriers to recog-nizing children, the mentally impaired, the poor or economically dependent, and women as political beings. The view of children as prepolitical has been contested in some stunning ethnographies of the role of children in political movements, including war (Cairns 1995; V. Das 1991; Scheper-Hughes and Sargent 1998; Stephens 1995; Reynolds 1996, 2012), but there is still a ten-dency to assume a distinction between children who are embedded within fam-ilies and other categories of children such as street children, child warriors, or child prostitutes. It is the latter categories of children who are seen to be most directly engaged in the field of politics. The everyday life of children in these neighborhoods suggests that that the soft knife of everyday deprivations, fear of death and disintegration, and the sense of vulnerability with which such children live makes them extremely sensitive to the processes of politics and especially to the politics through which the boundaries between legality and illegality are negotiated in everyday life. Thus it seems to me that it is not so much that children are excluded from politics in liberal political regimes as that the kinds of politics that children such as Mukesh engage in, are not rec-ognized as politics through which the margins of the liberal state are defined.

Will You Live, Mother?

The children's understanding of the outside world was astute, but they were also vulnerable, small, and scared, in need of adult protection. I asked Mukesh once if he recalled any occasion when he had been truly scared, and he said when his newborn sister had died. And then, he said he was also scared when Rahul (his younger brother) was born in the village because he became blue and was rushed to a nearby dispensary. "I followed them, and I saw the nurse there pick him up by his legs and thump him on the back—then they gave him an injection, and then he revived." This might have been a story he had heard in the course of family conversations and recast as something he had witnessed.

But Mukesh attributed his sense of dread to his having witnessed Rahul so close to death. Scholars who have explored children's relation to death reveal that children with incurable disease not only know that they are dying but have questions and thoughts that are often blocked for discussion because of parental anxiety and the adult view that children do not possess such knowledge (Bluebond-Langner 1978; Silverman 2000). Yet because these studies are based in Western milieus and do not deal with overlapping issues of poverty and deprivation, we do not get to understand how death is experienced within the kinds of worlds in which every child has some experience of the death of a sibling or a neighbor.[9] My own rendering of this aspect is closely tied to whether Mukesh was the one who brought up the topic for discussion.

I sensed that the biggest source of fear and sadness in Mukesh's life in the four years that I interacted frequently with him was the illness of his mother and the prospect that his father might abandon his mother. It was not easy to get a child alone for a conversation in NOIDA because children always hung around in groups, so the voice of one child was always complemented or contradicted by another. I realized the full extent of Mukesh's fear when his mother was hospitalized under a false name (as I have described earlier). Mukesh was sitting on a cot outside his house when I asked how his mother was doing. He said, "I am very scared, I think she is dead, or maybe she has been killed, and they are making up the story that she is in hospital." So great was his dejection that I completely internalized his fear and went to the hospital to find her. That is when his father told me that she was admitted under another name—after that I asked the father to take the children to visit her. It was on this occasion that Mukesh told me another story. I try to retell this in his own words as best as I can recall them:

> One year back when we went to visit the village on some wedding. My mother had been ill, and my father said that we will visit my *bua*'s village [father's sister's conjugal village]. So Rahul, my father, and my grandfather went to take a bus. When everyone got into it, and the bus started, I suddenly jumped down, and I stood alone at the bus stop. The bus had gone a little farther when my father and grandfather realized that I was not on the bus. They said, where is he, where is

9. Nancy Scheper-Hughes's (1992) powerful ethnography of child death in Brazil is a deservedly admired critique of the idea of the universality of mother love, but she does not tell us anything about how children experienced the death of their siblings.

he? So they stopped the bus and then walked back and found me standing at the bus stop. I said I am not going anywhere unless you take mummy with us. They tried to tell me that my mother was too weak to go for a social visit, but I said, no I will not budge from here. Then we all went back and then came to Delhi with my mother. I was scared that perhaps my father was going to take us all and return to Delhi and leave my mother behind in the village. He was probably making some excuse to leave my mother behind. I took a lot of beating for this, but I said no, I am not going to go without my mother.

Why did Mukesh bring up this story when he was telling me about his fear that his mother had died? It seems that the memory of a past event when he was younger reminded him of a time when he had been able to control his father's action by becoming an "unreasonable" child, and the father for all his ambivalence toward his sick wife had responded to the fears of his child though he had also given him a thrashing for his disobedience.

I asked Mukesh if it upset him that his father had beaten him. He laughed and said that elders had to sometimes beat children because otherwise children will go astray. "Anyway my father beats me only when my misdeeds have gone beyond counting. He says, why are you accumulating your bank account [meaning bank account of misdeeds]? See today is Thursday—by this Saturday, something will happen which will just tip the scales."

Mukesh's justification of the obligation of adults to correct children by sometimes beating them was given in the context of an episode when he had not committed a mistake but was willing to pay the price for getting his mother home. Yet in articulating this as a judgment on his father he repeated the community wisdom. This often happened if we ventured to ask children their *opinions*. but if they offered reflection through examples then we could see how the norms and justifications acquired a different dynamic in relation to the specific needs of the moment such as protecting a mother from the father's wrath. In these examples we can see how words such as "bank account" acquire a particular salience within a form of life.

Mukesh became aware in the third year of our research that Meena's symptoms were recurring and that she was despairing of ever getting well again. He would ask me, "Will she get well?" Purshottam and I tried to reassure him, but privately we suspected that Meena was probably suffering from MDR TB (multidrug-resistant tuberculosis) but was only receiving first-line drugs at the DOTS centers. As I said earlier, the protocols at the DOTS centers led to an undercounting of patients who get reinfected: The policy of treating only easily identifiable and easily treatable patients led to an abandoning of such cases as that of Meena's (see also Singh, Jaiswal, Porter et al. 2002).[10]

When I returned in July 2004 for a visit to Delhi, I learned that Meena had died. I went to offer my condolences. Mukesh sat quietly hardly looking at me. However, when I was at the point of crossing the road, which leads to the cluster of jhuggis, he ran toward me. I saw he had a card in his hand. It turned out to be his report card. He had successfully passed the fifth grade and now needed to move to middle school. As he showed me his report card, he said, "Mummy said you must stand first in your class—see, I did get a first division."

I will not go into a full account of this aspect of the story except to say that Mukesh had found out that the only good government school was at a small distance from his neighborhood. He did not want to go to the school that was closer because, according to him studies in that school "were dismal." His father was not very keen for him to go to the school he liked because though schooling was free, there were requirements of textbooks and a uniform that would eat up a lot of money. At that time in late July the national polio campaign was being implemented. Mukesh was given a job on a daily-wage basis in the campaign. His work consisted in going from house to house to tell parents about the day on which polio drops would be dispensed. He was receiving Rs.50 per day, and my impression was that this had his father's approval. Was it the economic condition of the family or the hassle of arranging the admission in a school where he feared he would meet new obstacles that deterred the father from actively pursuing Mukesh's desire to be admitted to this particular school? It seemed like a combination of all these circumstances, but I decided to help out. As on other occasions, Mukesh was more confiding when away from his father's eyes. He described the last day of his mother's life.

10. A program for MDR TB patients started under the DOTS Plus strategy was initiated only in January 2002 in the domiciliary treatment area of the Lala Ram Sarup (LRS) Institute of Tuberculosis and Respiratory Diseases, a tertiary referral institute in Delhi. The first cohort of 126 patients was treated at the institute but only patients with laboratory-confirmed MDR TB status and those who resided in the area could be included. It was out experience that in DOTS centers generally, the patient who had already received treatment but had recurring symptoms was simply marked as "cured" (see Singla, Sarin, et al. 2009).

She was admitted to a private (nursing home). I sat with her till two o'clock at night. I pleaded—eat something, do you want something? But she was very weak. She would open her eyes and say just sit here by me. I said, you will live (lit. dwell), won't you, mother? Then I came home, and then she died. Rahul does not even believe she is dead—he says she has gone to the village. Now he plays all the time, does not listen to anyone. When you had gone away to America, she kept saying, show me that you can come first. I showed you I got high numbers—didn't I? But I could not show her how well I had done.

Mukesh passed the entrance exam for the school and was admitted. He was very apprehensive that his father would scold him that he had secured admission in this school where expenses were much higher than the other one. I bought him the school texts and two uniforms. I urged him to continue to help in the house and not to provoke his father's anger. When I visited him later that year, he had passed sixth grade but was finding the studies much harder. Though his father and grandfather both said that he had become careless and was not studying properly, I was not certain what kinds of messages he was receiving from them. Once when Meena was alive, she had told me that Mukesh had witnessed a fight between her husband and her, over the affair with the other woman. Mukesh had been furious and had even tried to hit his father. Meena had confided. "I thought I am making preparations to go to Jamuna Ji—if his relations with his father get so weighed down with conflict, who knows whether his father will look after him when I am gone." The reference to Jamuna Ji is the honorific reference to the Yamuna river in the city on the banks of which Hindus are cremated. Meena was then already shaping the present in relation to a future when she would be absent from the father-son relationship. Now that future had arrived.

In my understanding, Mukesh's desire to study merged with his mother's desire to make him a future that would be different from that of his neighborhood. Another observation Mukesh made was that "Papa was a *bekar* kind of person before he got married to Mummy." The term *bekar* is one of those words that can do a handyman job, referring to a wide range of meanings. It can connote a benign affect of being useless to the more disparaging one of being uncouth, and in this context it could even touch on criminality. So I asked him to explain what he meant. He said, "Papa used to just hang around with other young men, and they would get into fights and do all kinds of *bekar* things. It is Mummy who made him into a decent person—the only thing left from those days is that he drinks, but Mummy made him promise not to get into fights and to do physical violence [lit., *hathapai*—fighting with hands and feet]." I think it might take some while before these complex family relations unfold and have an impact on Mukesh's desires to make a different kind of future for himself.

It might help to put these issues in perspective by considering that out of the fifty-four children ages five to sixteen among the forty households in NOIDA who are included in our study, only twenty at the time of the first survey were in school. In the neighborhood of Bhagwanpur Kheda that is next to NOIDA in terms of economic criteria such as per capita income and assets, and basic facilities such as *pucca* housing, there are only five children in this age group, out of a total of sixty-nine, who are dropouts from school. The local environment of NOIDA jhuggis posed formidable challenges for children to continue their schooling: Given that Mukesh had constructed himself as the person who keeps family relations in order, it was difficult for me to gauge how long his will to pursue his studies would be sustained in the face of the possibility that his father might return to becoming a *bekar* kind of person, now that his mother was gone.

Thoughts Toward a Conclusion

In summarizing the challenges posed by the "new paradigm of childhood" Prout and James (1997), like many others writing in this genre, emphasize that children actively shape their social world. Although the exhortation to see the world from the standpoint of children is well taken, I have tried to show that the categories of child and adult are not stable categories; for instance, consider the manner in which Mukesh moved between the role of the caretaker, the one who tried to ensure that the interest of his mother was preserved, as well as the child who was frightened to even ask his father whether his mother was alive when he suspected that no one was telling him that she was dead. Thus the boundaries of childhood and adulthood are not given in advance; they are created in the context of actual interactions between adults and children.

James Spilsbury and Jill Korbin (2004) suggest the metaphor of dance to capture how adults and children negotiate contexts in which children might need the help of an unknown adult within a known neighborhood. In making a case that children should be seen as important stakeholders in devising neighborhood security, they state, "Less often are these adult-child interactions viewed as negotiations, in which both adults and children weigh risks and benefits and in which both parties believe that they influence the ultimate outcome" (203). This is a reasonable picture of adult-child interactions when the adults are unknown and children have been taught which kinds of adults to trust in an emergency and which to avoid. If dance is to be seen as an iconic image of social life as Susanne Langer (1957) suggested in her early work, then gestures as symptoms or signals of our desires would call for analysis and not a weighing of risks and benefits. The force that we exercise on each other in the formation of a dance is in the nature of virtual force. Although the metaphor of dance is illuminating for conceptualizing embodied action and of steps that move in relation to cues as these are received in the process of the dance itself, it does not quite reflect the processes through which children place themselves in the adult world within the context of poverty, fear of state institutions, and scenes of illness and death or the way in which they invent themselves between threat and possibility.

In foregrounding the complex layering of familial politics, the politics of state institutions and the attempts made by one individual child in the face of his mother's illness and death, I have tried to show how culture might be rendered not only as a set of dispositions but also as a context that enables or disables an individual to acquire certain capabilities. In this sense to participate in a child's lifework or his inspiration toward life has been for me to recollect the dream of life. I offer Mukesh's world not as an example of some general conditions of poverty and dispossession (although we also learn about these) but as an example of how the child might teach us that the social is never simply reproduced. With Mukesh we learned what it is to suffer not only death but also birth, as he tried in his quest for schooling, in his work of keeping the father from becoming a *bekar* man, in keeping his mother alive to the father, to give some form to the event of becoming his mother's son.

I met Mukesh accidentally a couple of years back in 2011. His father had remarried soon after his mother's death and named his new wife after his first wife—a common gesture in the case of a second marriage to communicate the social role the new wife steps into. Mukesh never did finish school: "You paid for my books and my school uniform," he said, "but 'mummy ji' (referring to his stepmother) was never supportive. I had to fetch water and to cook before I left for school. In the end it was because I was sent to school hungry that I think I could not cope." He told me that there had been a scandal about a girl he wanted to marry because she was of a different caste. His father had beaten him with a leather belt when he came to know of the affair. Because Mukesh could speak a smattering of English now and is smart, he had got a job as a delivery boy in a fast-food restaurant. When I saw him, he was smartly dressed and had a wristwatch and a cell phone. He told me he now attends church in a middle-class neighborhood where he said he feels a sense of peace because unlike Hindu temples, there is no noise or crowds, or people jostling with each other to get a *darshan* (viewing) of the deity. "I cannot fully convert." he said, "because then I would not be able to perform the *shraddha* [rituals for ancestors] for my mother. . . . I still love Papa a lot," he mused, "because though he beat me so mercilessly I remembered that when my mother was often very weak, he would cook something for her, however late he had come back from work." Mukesh said he had been looking for me. He wanted to meet me because though he did not remember *everything* that happened when he was eight years old and first met me, he remembered that his mother used to look forward to my visits.

THREE

Mental Illness, Psychiatric Institutions, and the Singularity of Lives

The relation between madness and modernity is a classic space for exploring an ensemble of questions relating to the place of madness in popular culture and the biopolitical state. As astute observers of modernity have noted, there are two poles on which attitudes to madness seem to configure: On the one side there is the stigma attached to madness, while on the other side there is a fascination with madness for its potential to provide a critique of normality and as the site of creativity par excellence. The stigmatization and the ill treatment meted out to those who are defined as mad and consigned to psychiatric asylums was forcefully brought out in the United States and in western Europe at the end of the second world war when conscientious objectors were allocated the task of working in mental asylums. Shocked by the conditions in these asylums, these conscientious objectors acted as witnesses and provided

This chapter was published originally with Rajan Singh and Simi Chaturvedi, two senior field researchers from ISERDD. I am grateful to both for permission to publish it in my book. Their contributions will be evident in the chapter.

the documentation that led to the revelations of the terrible conditions of patients in these institutions (Erb 2006). Paradoxically the postwar period also saw artistic experimentation in cinematic arts in which, above all, it was the dislocation of space and time that resonated most strongly; the experience of dislocation of these two dimensions is also typical of schizophrenia. René Laurman in his critique of this epoch forged the term "schizophile" for gathering the characteristic experiences of madness and the artistic avant-garde movements in art under a generic term (cited in Stastny 1998, 90). In the same vein, Louis Sass (1992) saw a profound intimacy between modernism and madness; he argued that the characteristics of schizophrenia reflected each aspect of the sensibility and style proper to modernity.

One could also explore the relation between madness and modernity in the context of the emergence of the biopolitical state. In his *Histoire de la folie à lâge classique.* Michel Foucault (1972; translated as *History of Madness*, 2006) provided an intellectual paradigm for examining the changing episteme under which madness lost its organic relation to society. Various legal and administrative measures came to mobilize a whole arsenal of techniques of exclusion by which the mad were excluded from society and came to be placed in specialized spaces, separated from the space of the normal. As is well known, Foucault later declared his dissatisfaction with the earlier approach for its emphasis on the repressive powers of the state rather than on the creation of a new disciplinary object. Nevertheless, the relation between "law" as an expression of sovereign power and "discipline" as an expression of biopower have both played a crucial role in the emergence of the biopolitical state as Foucault saw it. Whereas some scholars contend that modernity as a historical regime is marked by the replacement of sovereign power by disciplinary power, the publication of Foucault's lectures at the Collège de France (Foucault 1999), especially on the theme of the abnormal and the dangerous individual, should correct this erroneous impression.[1]

In this chapter, I engage some of these issues, but the center of gravity in my discussion is neither a critique of repression nor the exclusion of the mad

1. For example, Michel Foucault (1999) shows how psychiatry intervenes when the judicial logic is blocked by bringing disciplinary power to attest to the future possibility of a crime being committed by someone due to criminal tendencies that are not yet manifest. This precursor of the dangerous individual from whom society must be protected is a psychological or moral double of the criminal who has not yet committed a crime.

to a specialized realm. Rather, my aim is to track the fragility of relations and of experience that is revealed when madness cannot be absorbed in the everyday—yet it is the case that it is only within this everyday, corroded and shattered by madness though it becomes, that care can be offered. The problem of the other as revealed by madness is not primarily an epistemological problem but one in which a concrete other demands the attention of those who make up his or her social world. I want to explore ethnographically how we can think of modernity as a certain kind of enchantment in the context of the lives of the urban poor to whom it seems that the promises of modernity are both within reach and beyond reach. The assemblage of certain conditions—the failure of medical institutions, the politics of family, and the devaluation of its nonproductive members, along with the lure of the modern in such forms as the ability to speak in English, create a "singularity" through which these conditions come to define the biography of an illness as part of the trajectory of relations that madness puts into question. What I call singularity here relates to certain conditions of possibility, but I do not think that these conditions mechanically produce any one kind of outcome (e.g., abandonment). If the ultimate failure of care in this case may be read as the "letting die" aspect of biopower, then my description will show that the subject of madness is an ensemble of relations rather that an individual—so who or what is allowed to die is something that lies within the knotted relations in which madness itself resides. However, in no case does this conception authorize us to put aside the separateness of the individual or the fact of his or her suffering on the grounds that the subject is not simply the individual. Such is the complexity of the situation that madness brings into existence.

Fractured Narratives

In 2003, the psychiatrist Lloyd A. Wells published an article in the journal *Philosophy, Psychiatry and Psychology* on the theme of madness in which he presented clinical cases to illustrate what he called the phenomenon of discontinuity of personal narrative (Wells 2003). The cases included bipolar disorder, incipient schizophrenia, dissociative disorder, severe depression, and anxiety. Providing us with the perspectives of patients on their own disorders, Wells cited a patient with dissociative disorder who maintained that discontinuities in personal narratives such as Wells observed in her case, were ubiquitous, even in people without a psychiatric diagnosis. I should like to note immediately that the patient's view was not offered as a matter of "opinion" as one might find, for instance, in a conference paper. Rather, it surfaced at the very start of a session after she had been struggling with the sense that she was completely different from other people—hoping that she was not a "zombie." Here is how Wells described it:

> The putative discovery by Mary lay dormant for several months and then resurfaced at the very start of a session, when she began by saying "Damn you, damn you, damn you to hell!"
>
> Startled, I asked, "Why?"
>
> "For not telling me. Why didn't you tell me? Damn you!"
>
> "I don't know what you mean," I replied.
>
> "Yes, you do. You must. About others. About how they really are."
>
> "Can you talk about it?" I asked, rather lamely.
>
> "That I've had it all wrong, thinking, *I'm* all alone with this weird organization of my mind, being in different places in it, in different compartments; being different aspects of me so unpredictably. And thinking—almost my whole life—that that's what sets me apart."
>
> "And now—you think, what?" I asked.
>
> "The truth, damn you, and you know it, too. You must."
>
> "I don't think, I do, though," I replied. "I'm not sure what you are talking about."
>
> "That they're just dishonest. That I'm not different at all—just honest about it."

Wells then posed the question: Can we maintain a theory of narrative continuity of the self in view of the psychopathology he presented and especially in view of the patient's claim to normality. For the moment, I leave aside the question of how to interpret these words as part of *this* form of life—of the patient in the psychiatrist's clinic. Instead, I first look at one example of the responses of some philosophers that appeared in the same special issue of the journal, as they rethink the narrative theory of the self and then ask what this might have to do with the way in which we understand the relation between modernity and madness located in contemporary Indian society.

Let us first listen to the words of J. Melvin Woody (2003), who says, "Lloyd Wells' four examples of loss of self challenge both philosophers and clinicians to ponder just what it is that has been lost in such cases. If a self has been lost, who lost it? And how can personal identity be so insecure that it can be lost in so many different ways?" He then goes on to state that narrative unity or continuity is no guarantee against the experience of loss of self. "The monological character of narrative masks the sociality of the self, the way that each individual self is constituted and threatened by interactions with other selves." For the moment I am bracketing other responses to the paper, for instance, those who maintain that even when the patients point to discontinuities in their respective narratives, they are, in fact, positing the existence of a narrator who can recognize these discontinuities.

Let us ponder the question: Just what is it that has been lost? Or, if a self is lost, who lost it? For me, it is instructive to compare this picture of what has been lost and who lost it to the parable of the boiling pot in Wittgenstein (1953). The relevant paragraph (#297) in *Philosophical Investigations* goes as follows.

> Of-course if water boils in a pot, steam comes out of the pot and also pictured steam comes out of the pictured pot. But what if one insisted on saying that there must also be something boiling in the pictured pot?

In applying this parable to the questions of pain, as if to something inner, Wittgenstein, alluded to the distinction between image and picture—*Vorstellung* and *Bild*. Paragraph #300 sets out this distinction in the following way.

> It is—we should like to say—not merely the picture of the behavior that plays a part in the language-game with the words "he is in pain," but also the picture of the pain. Or, not merely, the paradigm of the behavior, but also that of the pain.— It is a misunderstanding to say, "The picture of pain enters into the language game with the word 'pain.'" The image [*Vorstellung*] of pain is not a picture [*Bild*] and *this* image is not replaceable in the language-game by anything that we should call a picture—the image of pain certainly enters into the language game in a sense; only not as a picture.

Stanley Cavell, in his profound reflections on this formulation—namely, that the image of pain enters the language game but not as a picture that we could "see," asks:

> But wouldn't all these problems about the content of the pot be solved by making the picture of the pot in such a way that you can see inside it—either by giving us a perspective over the rim of its top, or by picturing a glass pot? Wittgenstein's parable does not say that the picture is not like this. Of course these alternate pictures will not seem grippingly pertinent in applying the parable to the question of knowing the pain of others, which is presumably the point. But why not? Perhaps because we would not know what the analogy is to "looking over the rim of its top"; we have no perspective of this kind, or ought not to claim one, on our fellow creatures. And if I try imagining a glass man or woman (not merely a man with glass skin and muscles, but, as it were, glass through and through), I do not know where to *place* the pain. (Cavell 1979, 333)

Taking our education from Cavell reading Wittgenstein, we might then propose that when Wells's patients say that in the course of their illness and recovery, they have lost someone, or they have lost a self that they miss, or that they have lost all that time, we are not likely to be able to understand this by somehow looking inside the person or next to the person to see what has been lost. What has been lost, I suggest, is some way of being in the world. Thus a description of this madness would require a description of how to tell the story as if the person were located, not inside the body but in the network of relations, affects, encounters, in which the body comes to be expressive of something we might call a soul. In effect, to understand the words of Mary, the patient with dissociative disorder, we would have to ask from what forms of life the kinds of words she spoke could emerge and how these words tell us not only about the forms within which experience takes shape but also how we may read the tracks of other sorts of "life" to which the body comes to give expression.

Much research on psychiatric conditions focuses on the moment of the diagnosis treating diagnostic labels as providing the "niches" in the social world, which impose systems of value and normality on the flux of experiences in the heterogeneity of everyday life (Hacking 2002). However, as Sarah Pinto (2012) notes, diagnosis is seldom the focus of the clinical encounter in Indian psychiatric practice; patients are much more interested in receiving treatment in the form of medications rather than finding out the label attached to the disorder.[2] Renu Addlakha's work has also alerted us to the fact that even in hospital settings, the psychiatrists take into account a whole range of social issues, such as whether the diagnosis will stigmatize a young woman making it impossible for her to be married off to a suitable man (Addlakha 2008; V. Das and Addlakha 2007). At best, then, we should think of diagnosis as a dialogical moment, as Byron Good (2012) suggests, but we must also remember that expert knowledge on madness is not confined to psychiatrists alone (see Good and Good 1986). People seek multiple explanations for what has occurred and consult a wide range of experts, including diviners. Madness brings to the fore different, entangled, incommensurable vocabularies of the self, as shown in Pandolofo's (2008; 2014) work on the lines between tradition and modernity in the person of the psychiatrist, the Imam, and the patient in Morocco. In this sense, madness makes evident the precariousness of kinship as well as the unstable character of the institutions that the patients and their caregivers have to navigate (see also Pinto 2011, 2014).

Vocabularies, Networks, Affects

As in the other cases described in the last two chapters, the story of illness here too starts in a low-income neighborhood, Baba Faridpuri in West Delhi. Recall the case of Prakash on whom I provided a small ethnographic vignette in the introduction. He had spent a lifetime wrestling with the psychic drama of being abducted by Allah and being rescued by Lord Shiva. The members of his household managed his illness, using an old prescription for lithium without ever having taken him to a psychiatrist once he was discharged from a psychiatric institution. I reported in the earlier discussion that I was fenced off from any close contact with Prakash by his family and therefore could not get a better understanding of what his illness implied. This was not the case with Swapan's family, whom I describe in this chapter, for they actively solicited the

2. I want to note the publication of two recent books that bring extraordinary insight into the understanding of mental illness within the texture of everyday life (see Chua 2014 and Pinto 2014). I could not engage with these books here because this book was already in press when the other two books were published, but reading them gave me great hope that the suffering of women these authors encountered in their respective field sites will not be simply drowned in grand concepts but will be patiently and attentively heard.

help of ISERDD members to manage Swapan's illness when certain episodes became too intractable for them. The dynamics of care and neglect in the family lead me to engage further with the issue of abandonment. In the last chapter I argued that the processes of abandonment by the family and the institutions of the state cannot be seen as if the former were a mere reflection of the latter, just as we cannot posit the family as merely the agent of the state. I hope that the ethnography presented in this chapter will make for a deeper understanding of the web of connections between familial neglect and institutional neglect without reducing one to the other.

Epidemiological studies of mental illness suggest a correlation between poverty, gender, and what are known as "common mental disorders," though the relation is more complex than a simple correlation between income and these common disorders (see Patel and Kleinman 2003; J. Das et al 2007; J. Das, R. K. Das, and V. Das 2012). When it comes to severe psychiatric disorders, however, there is a serious dearth of anthropological studies (but see Addlakha 2008).

To return to the case in hand—let us think of it as a description of a form of life in which illness trajectories reveal the many vocabularies, the network of relations, the circulations of affect, and the openness of the human to the modes of the nonhuman. Simultaneously, the trajectory of illness tells us about the specific conditions of urban poverty within which the abandonment and the "letting die," of which we saw a grievous example in the last chapter, happens. Let us begin by treating the world that is disclosed through this episodes of mental illness, as somehow made strange since none of the concepts we are familiar with can be taken as given. Thus a psychiatric diagnosis is not an expression of certainty and surety of expert knowledge, nor is a kinship term such as mother, father, son, one that we can assume to be known at the beginning of the story. More than in the case of Meena, where we saw how the categories of child and adult became unstable and porous, in this case kinship relations are constantly shifting so that we do not know when Swapan, the protagonist of this story, is to be seen as his mother's son privileging filiation and when he is to be seen as among the agnates who are wife-receivers, privileging affinity.[3] The illness trajectory is full of footprints through which

---

3. An older ethnography of kinship was much more attuned to these distinctions, as, for example, in Edmund Leach's ([1961] 2004) discussion of the different ways in which a woman might be seen as belonging to her husband's family and the mother of her children or as lent

we can track the failure of institutions, the desire for modernity and how this desire is thwarted, the threats to the givenness of something like kinship and ultimately, of how time does its work. The same illness trajectory reveals another scene of near helplessness—one in which the team of researchers (me included) are caught in an impasse—stumbling from one solution to another, basically as a way of warding off the worst, rather than being able to find the best or even that which is good enough.

In her perceptive work on voice and witnessing on the margins of psychiatric encounter, Stefania Pandolfo (2007, 2008, 2015) reflects on the impossibility of establishing "facts" as she produces a compelling account of madness that places the subject within the proliferation of institutions and codes. Pandolfo talks of the impossibility of constituting the history of the subject and of the collectivity in any other mode except that of the phantasmal. Indeed, one could speak of a phantasmal modernity in the context of the urban poor in Delhi, but I wish to not settle on that point right now. And, indeed, Pandolfo herself shows that despair and hope reside in the same network of relations, institutions, and languages; even in a story in which the outcome invites despair we should not assume that this was inevitable.

The protagonist of this story I will name Swapan (lit., dream).[4] When we met him he was about twenty years old and lived with his mother, father, elder brother and younger sister in Baba Faridpuri in West Delhi.[5] Let me reiterate here some of the characteristics of this neighborhood that nestles at the back of the affluent houses and upscale shops of West Patel Nagar. The neighborhood started as a cluster of jhuggis—temporary shanty houses—that refugees who came from Pakistan erected as temporary shelters. There were also clus-

---

to the husband's family and hence as somewhat like an incubator whose body is assimilated to that of a machine. In the latter case Leach argued that the mother was seen more as the father's wife. Leach thought of these distinctions as possibilities that different systems realized variably. We might think of them as different aspects of the same relationship.

4. Names of respondents in this chapter as in all others are pseudonyms, but here I gave myself the liberty of finding names that somehow matched my sense of the truth of their lives without assuming that I could decipher this truth from some authoritative position. At one level, after all, the naming is just play but at another level these names, my inventions, are evocative of who I was then, in that place.

5. I use the composite term "we," since Rajan Singh, Simi Chaturvedi, and I often met the family together and often divided up the responsibility of talking to different family members or visiting Swapan when he was admitted to the hospital for a short period.

ters of jhuggis of migrants from nearby villages—primarily members of "untouchable" castes who migrated in search of work. Other waves of migrants came from different regions, so that today one can locate different clusters from Rajasthan and Garhwal as well as the original refugees from Pakistan. As the refugees and migrants became more affluent, they converted the *kacca* (mud and brick) houses into *pucca* (cement and brick) houses—adding rooms, terraces, and shops. In NOIDA, the setting for the last chapter, threats of demolition have led to several court cases filed by residents to obtain stay orders against eviction. But in Baba Faridpuri no government agency has attempted to bring in bulldozers because the neighborhood is too densely populated and the network of spidery lanes are very hard to access. The neighborhood, however, does not enjoy the legal status of an authorized colony; so public services such as sanitation and clean drinking water are in a dismal state. Swapan's family has lived in this neighborhood in different houses since his early childhood. His father's father and mother's father were both refugees from Multan, now in Pakistan. His father owned a small cloth retail shop that is losing its economic viability for complicated reasons—some of these will become clear in the course of this story.

I came to be in Swapan's house in January 2001 when ISERDD members had conducted a pilot survey of school children in various neighborhoods in Delhi to assess patterns of self-reported morbidity, but the data collected turned out to have many problems, so that project was dropped from the larger study. Swapan's sister, who was studying in the West Patel Government High School, had insisted that I go with her to the house to meet her mother. On the very first visit to their house, Swapan's mother told me about how her father had migrated from Multan at the time of the Partition. I learned that she was the eldest daughter, that her brother had died in an accident when she was finishing school, and that her father became desperate with worry that he would not be able to find a good husband for her and thus married her off to a boy from another refugee family who lived in the neighborhood. Right on the first day I was made to understand that Rajkarni[6] (Swapan's mother) had regrets that her husband was not educated—not even literate—and that this was a source of major tensions between her sons and her. ("I tell them, he may not be able to read but he has nourished you, raised you, so that today you are

---

6. The Punjabi word *Rajkarni* means a woman who presides over a kingdom—very often the name is bestowed on a girl as an expression of a wish.

able to complain—hasn't he?") Yet she had complaints of her own; most of these were about her husband's younger brother and his wife, who, she claimed, had cheated her family of their property rights. She also complained that the younger brother's shop did much better because they had switched to ready-made garments, but her husband, unfortunately, did not have the confidence to change his ways because he was illiterate. I also learned that her only sister, who is much younger than she is, was married off to an educated man who also ran a successful business. I was witness to the extent of her hostility to the husband's brother when I asked her if I could meet others in the street to recruit them in our sample, and she said categorically, "Yes, but avoid the house next to ours because that is where 'our enemies' live," and then she and her daughter stood outside the door to see that we did not enter the enemy/brother's house.

Our research team first began to sense that there was something wrong when toward the end of the first year of our weekly morbidity surveys in the community study, we noticed that Gudiya, Swapan's sister, seemed to have frequent small injuries—a swollen eye, bruises on her arms—injuries that could happen if she were getting in regular fights or playing active sports. In discussions about illness in the course of our weekly surveys, her mother denied that any of these findings were of any consequence; instead, she seemed obsessed with Gudiya's acne and worried that the acne might make it difficult to find a suitable boy for her in the attempts at an arranged marriage. My colleague, Simi, was the one who first began to comment in her ethnographic diary that Swapan seemed irritable and got into frequent fights. Both Rajan and Simi also noted that the mother was constantly undermining Swapan and nagging him for various faults. The tensions seemed to have escalated after Gudiya passed her tenth grade Delhi board exam. Also, the shop was reporting losses, and in 2002 the family sold their house and moved to a rented place in the same locality.

Swapan was reporting bouts of anger, and we slowly learned that he would beat up Gudiya occasionally. Finally, the dreadful family secret came out that he was showing great aggression toward his mother, occasionally beating her up. The mother pointed to this as a dangerous development. One frequent source of disagreements and heated arguments in the house was the mother's taunting jibes against Swapan about the fact that he had failed in tenth grade but that his sister was now in eleventh grade and might soon become an earning member of the family. Swapan used to sometimes assist in his father's shop, but his father now forbade him to work in the shop because he claimed that Swapan's angry outbursts drove away the customers. My colleague Rajan sometimes tried to engage Swapan, but he clearly did not want to discuss any of these matters; he was sometimes affable and other times simply unavailable.

In August 2002, a psychiatrist[7] volunteered at ISERDD to help patients with suspected psychiatric problems who could not afford a consultation. Members of ISERDD hoped that with his help we could refer Swapan and some others like him to the available medical facilities in the city. The mother was anxious for a consultation with the psychiatrist, but the father was sullen and said to Simi and me, "This is our family affair—why should his [Swapan's] mother have embroiled any strangers in this affair?"[8] On further probing, it appeared that Swapan had stopped bathing, he was rude and uncooperative, and his father was nervous that they would lose face before this physician who was a stranger. However, on the day that Dr. Agrawal visited the house, Swapan came to the room bathed and dressed. Dr. Agrawal spent about an hour with him, and at the end of the consultation, he urged the family to take him to a psychiatrist for a full clinical evaluation. Dr. Agrawal suspected a case of bipolar disorder but thought that with appropriate medication Swapan's symptoms could be brought under control. However, he emphasized that it was important for the family to get a full consultation with a local psychiatrist and work out a therapeutic plan.

For the next few months there was no follow-up. It was clear that Swapan was becoming worse. The family was meanwhile consulting an exorcist, for they felt that perhaps "someone" has done "something." The linguistic strategy of referring to a nameless fear or a hostile neighbor by use of an indefinite noun is common in these areas, as I discussed in chapter 1. In this case, the

7. I am very grateful to Dr. Saumya Das and Dr. Hans Agrawal for twice volunteering their time for periods of up to two weeks and for meeting with families in these neighborhoods that requested consultation and advice. Though Swapan's case was not easily resolved, there were other cases in which the provisional diagnosis itself helped a recalcitrant husband or a parent to seek medical help from government facilities in the area.

8. The dilemma when different members of the family want very different things from the anthropologist is hardly new. Its implications for the discourse of institutional review boards on ethics, which assume that there can be sharp distinctions between life and research and that informants always speak with one voice on what constitutes consent and what constitutes harm, are compelling but difficult to confront—given the power of the therapeutic model in mediating questions of ethics of research.

ongoing conflict between Swapan's mother and her husband's brother's family added to the suspicion that perhaps these relatives were responsible for Swapan's bouts of anger. Because Swapan was particularly hostile to his mother and his sister, his mother took this to be evidence that her affinal relatives were trying to poison his mind against her. His mother told us that Swapan increasingly suspected that his mother was putting something in his food, and so he refused to touch food cooked by her. Initially, we made no comments on their therapeutic choice. Because such strategies are shrouded in secrecy, we had to stay this course very delicately. ISERDD has records of some cases in which families report a temporary suspension of hostilities after they have taken measures to consult with a diviner and performed rituals of exorcism.[9] In this case, though, we could see that Swapan was losing weight, that his anger was frequently out of control, and that his mother was becoming increasingly hostile to him.

I visited the family again to urge that Swapan might benefit from a medical consultation. His mother told me that they had been taking Swapan to various local practitioners, but their medicines did not work. The local practitioners were clearly not able to diagnose his condition—Swapan's mother showed me the empty blister packs of medicine that he was given—it turned out to be Valium, a sleep medication, but Swapan's problem was not insomnia—so it was hardly surprising that the medications did not work.

I was visiting Swapan's family about two months after Dr. Agrawal's visit. I asked his mother if they had thought of taking him to a psychiatrist. Through a friend I had located a psychiatrist who volunteered once a week in a polyclinic where poor patients could consult physicians at a relatively low cost. This clinic, though, was far from their house. In retrospect, I was unsympathetic to the mother's concern that it would take more than two hours to commute by bus one way. I pointed out to her that many people with far lesser means traveled to get treatment and that this was a very good "doctor." I could not talk directly to Swapan because he was not often found at home, and in any case, I thought that his mother would have to help arrange for his visit to the psychiatrist. "He wanders around," said his mother, increasingly angry with him for not trying to get some kind of work. "What can I do?", she said. "He just does not agree. He saw what that doctor from Amrika (Amerca) had

---

9. See Davis (2000) for a superb description of the temporalities of conflict within a lineage group in her study in the Congo and the place of the diviner within this milieu.

written on that paper, and he got very angry. He said, do they think I am mad? He wanted to tear it and throw it away. I took it forcibly and put it in this almirah where he cannot get to it." She told me that Swapan's condition had worsened—that he refused to bathe—that he was not eating. "He says, he will not eat anything touched by my hands. I am his own mother, and he won't eat things touched by my hands. Now you tell me . . ."

Excerpts from my diary in early 2002:

A stroke of luck for me. Swapan came from outside and sat on the bed facing me. Noticing that his eyes were not averted—in fact, he was looking directly at me—I asked him why he doesn't want to go to the doctor. "Who will take me?" he says in a challenging rather than despondent tone.

I say, "I will."

SWAPAN: "My problem is not that I am mad. My problem is that no one takes interest in me." [He uses the English word "interest"—*mere mein koi interest nahin leta*]

VEENA: "What do you mean, no one takes interest in you?"

SWAPAN: "See, I failed in my tenth exam. I was always a good student. Math is my only weakness. I could not pass the math exam. Now what my mother wants is that I should work in a factory—(with emphasis) work in a factory for 1500 rupees a month. Earn money. But I will not work in anyone's factory. I want to pass my exam."

MOTHER (directly addressing me): "You know our financial condition. How much money have I spent on him? We say, be ashamed—a big man—sitting and eating at home—look at your sister—are you not ashamed?"

VEENA: "But what he has is an illness." (Turning to Swapan) "What you have is an illness. Like you have blood pressure or something—you take medicine and you will feel better."

SWAPAN: "Will I be okay (be cured)?" [The Hindi expression *theek ho jaunga* encompasses both nuances of normal and cure.]

Meanwhile Gudiya began to hum a song, her chin defiantly turned upwards—I felt that our conversation, Swapan's and mine, was being devalued. Swapan looked hurt but said nothing. Perhaps Gudiya was trying to show defiance in my presence because she knew that I was aware that Swapan often beat her. I was not able to interpret the condensed conversation of gestures any further.

In any case, Swapan promised that day to let me take him to the psychiatrist, but when I arrived on the promised date he was nowhere to be found.

Over many conversations I continued to try to get the mother interested in the possibility of a consultation, though I was careful to define this as a way of getting along, in the way one gets along with high blood pressure with which she was familiar.[10] She rightly raised the question of finances—where were they to find the money? But then at other times, she would say things like, "I spent so much on him, whereas my daughter needs injections to cure her acne." Slowly it also emerged that the mother, while agreeing that Swapan had a disease as the "doctor from Amrica" had suggested, also thought that there was something else happening. Offering evidence haltingly as if trying out something on me that she knew I would reject,[11] she said, Swapan has been losing weight and is so thin now—but when he is in a rage, he can harness such strength as to beat up his mother and his sister though they try to fight back."[12] How is it," she said, "that he gets so much strength?"—her voice ascending to a much higher pitch. The argument did not need to be spelled out for me—it was only because some demonic being had taken hold of him

10. One's own motives are never fully transparent to oneself, but I think I invested hope here in the psychiatrist, despite knowing how difficult it would be for the family to maintain a regular routine of attendance at the clinic and compliance with the prescribed treatment, both because I thought there was a disease to be dealt with and because I had not seen any other path by way of kinship support or community support in this case. In this sense I was dealing with a very different situation than that reported by Gananath Obeyesekere (1985) in which persons reporting states of mind that could be read as signs of depression were nevertheless able to carry on everyday activities in their social worlds. Yet the discomfort and the sure knowledge that one would not measure up to the expectations of the family, for this was no straightforward contract, created enormous anxiety in me, especially in periods when I was away from Delhi.

11. The informants after all, also read the anthropologist and clearly my demeanor suggests an educated person who might not believe in such occult practices. I should add, though, that I have also had an opposite experience in which one of the practitioners of the occult simply assumed that I wanted some rituals performed but that I was embarrassed to directly ask for them because I was "educated".

12. Referring to herself in the third person here highlights the relationship rather than her individual personhood.

that he could beat her with such force. This "not naming" was a common strategy, and in the course of the three years that Rajan, Simi, and I interacted with this family, we also learned that he had earlier been taken to the famous Balaji temple where demons are compelled to reveal themselves, but that even the temple deities were not strong enough to do this.[13]

Then Swapan agreed one day to go to the psychiatrist. I was not in Delhi, but Rajan and Simi took him to the polyclinic where the psychiatrist saw patients at a reduced fee. ISERDD was able to provide some financial help that met the costs of transport and the doctor's fee, but we all hoped that the family would provide some contribution toward the medicine as a sign of their commitment to treat Swapan. However, he stopped taking the medicine after two visits. The psychiatrist's view was that if Swapan had to depend on the family for medicine, he would not take them. We offered to raise money for the medicine through a charitable organization. Swapan said with great insight, "But what is the point of getting better if I have to live in this environment?" Clearly, we decided, there was nothing we could do but wait.

9. January 2004. Swapan's condition had deteriorated. Two events happened to propel us back into the case. Swapan's mother had complained that he sat and looked at the mirror or the TV screen for hours. I knew that his mother was referring to the fact that demons do not cast a reflection in mirrors, but neither she nor I could voice this explicitly lest the evil forces become unleashed and get out of control. (Obviously, these facts carried a very different significance for the psychiatrist). Further, Swapan now avoided bathing for weeks; he had grown a beard; and his mother claimed that a strange odor came from his body, and his hair was unkempt. More alarming, his mother called us on the phone and told us that he had stopped taking food from the plate—instead when everyone was asleep he snatched food from the cupboard and his arms grew long like that of a monkey. In other words, there were all these other lives now that had taken over his life—his body was now an expression of these other forms of life. Earlier the complaints were that he was not a good son—his membership in the family was at stake—now his membership in the human form of life was at stake.

13. There is an extensive literature on possession and dispossession masterfully reviewed in Smith (2006). On the practices in the Balaji temple, see Kakar (1982), Dwyer (2003), and Pakaslahti (1998).

The Crisis

We were now in the middle of January 2004.[14] The first event that signaled a crisis, as told by the mother, was this: "Last night Swapan beat me up so badly that I lost consciousness. Gudiya here, she was crying out loudly that he is killing my mother. Swapan locked himself in the downstairs room fearing the neighbors would come out and perhaps beat him, but the neighbors did not want to get involved. His father was not at home, nor was my elder son at home. Gudiya and I sneaked out in the street and went to a telephone booth from where we called the police. Now, what could we do? There was danger to life."

The upshot was that two constables from the neighboring precinct came to the house. As Gudiya and the mother told me, the constables heard their account and at first they shouted at Swapan—what kind of son are you? Aren't you ashamed—your sister is studying for her twelfth grade exam. She needs peace—don't you know how much pressure is put on the brain when one studies for a board exam? And look at you—sitting and eating on your parents' charity. A policeman even slapped Swapan. Some neighbors summoned his father from the shop. His father said something to the constable, who now began to admonish the mother. "Why don't you love him? Why don't you give him food? Is he not the child of your womb? Is your daughter more your child?" The neighbors, however, intervened and said that the fights in the family were disturbing everyone. The constables took Swapan to the police station. In a panic, Swapan's father begged a local leader to do something for his son. They went together to the police station, and Swapan wrote a letter of apology and promised to behave in the future. I have elsewhere described such mediations by local leaders, who resemble the Big Men (Godelier and Strathern 1991) as helping create what I called "brokered selves" (V. Das 2004).[15] The mother was crying as she told me, "At that moment in the police

14. The first round of systematic morbidity surveys were completed in 2002, although as explained earlier, other projects have been conducted in the areas under study. Among other things, ISERDD continues to provide educational help and emergency assistance for medical conditions in the neighborhoods where its research projects have been implemented, so the contact with the neighborhoods is maintained independent of any particular projects.

15. The phrase "Big Men" refers to those whose authority does not derive from traditional norms but is the direct result of local transformations brought about by the interven-

station, he [her husband] became his [Swapan's]. He [her husband] gave me *dhoka*—betrayed me. He told me that Gudiya and you can go to your sister's house or wherever you wish—my son is going to stay here." "Now I have become the enemy," she said. "I fear for my life."

The second event that happened was as follows. After the incident with the police, Swapan's mother went away to her sister's house, but she returned after three days. As she said, "How long can one say in another house even if she is my sister?" The neighborhood had intervened, and the door connecting the stairs leading from the ground floor to the first floor of the house had been locked on their insistence. The local leader who had negotiated Swapan's release from the police station commanded that Swapan was never to go to the first floor or to have anything to do with his mother and sister. Swapan was deteriorating. One night his mother discovered that he had begun to defecate in the room. She stood outside in the street and loudly lamented for all to hear: "Let the neighborhood now come and see. Does he belong in a house? Is it my fault?" The powerful combination of symbols of pollution and the woman's voice as lament, forced open a public space in which her plight had to be received. The situation is comparable to the way that the woman's voice forces the secret of her violation into the political, launches her desire for a revenge on the world, as I have described elsewhere for the survivors of the 1984 riots in Delhi (V. Das 1991, 2007); or the power of the mother's curses and tears that Malathi de Alwis (1998) has described in the case of southern Sri Lanka. Ironically, in this case it was not the mother crying out for revenge because the enemy had harmed her child but because the child *is* the enemy. Once earlier relating her story to me, Swapan's mother had said to me, "I pray to god—oh god, lift him up to yourself—can anyone imagine such words, wrenched out of a mother, words asking for the death of the same son to whom she had given shelter in her womb, borne him in pain? He has made his own mother into a *dayan* [female monster]." When I heard her, I thought of the famous discussion in Freud and Lacan of the voice of the dead child awakening his father with the words, "Father don't you see, I am burning?" (see

---

tion of the state or emergence of new markets. Thus the idea of "brokered selves" was to capture the sense that many people have in these neighborhoods that in order to get access to public institutions it is not enough to have entitlements; these need to be backed by those who can mediate between local communities and bureaucrats who hold positions within these institutions.

Caruth 1996). In Swapan's case, the consciousness that had gone to sleep resided in the entire network of neighborhood, kinship, and even a shadowy world beyond, which consists of remotely imagined doctors and researchers like myself, to whom the voice of the mother was addressed.

It seemed to me that the mother's voice had reached an unbearable pitch. Though the neighbors had put a lock on the connecting doors, Swapan still managed to shout curses and threats at his mother, and I suspect that his mother responded with more verbal aggression. Gudiya did not have the confidence that if she called the police again they would respond, because, as she said "*Police station mein to Papa ne hamko jhuta bana diya na* [in the Police station Papa made us into liars, didn't he?]" We hardly saw Swapan because he would disappear from the house for long periods. I began receiving phone calls from the mother every day—do something while you are here—you will go away to America—then what we will I do? I tried to persuade Swapan to seek medical help whenever I unexpectedly found him in the house. I could sense that he was feeling trapped. I was also increasingly frightened that he might violently injure his mother or even kill her, for I could see that she constantly feared deadly assault, and I had no way of knowing how real her fears were. I told Swapan once, "You have been to the police station, once—next time it may be the prison. Why do you want to ruin your life?" He once again agreed we should go back to the psychiatrist. We fixed a date. Rajan, Simi, and I came to accompany him. Once again he disappeared.

Rajan, Simi, and I could not do anything else, but we urged his mother that she had to find support both for herself and her son by involving their extended family. Whatever your quarrels with them, I said to her, this is also their responsibility. "Call his uncles. Call his aunts. Get whatever help you can." One evening, soon after this, Swapan beat his mother badly by stealthily gaining entry to her side of the house. In desperation, she made a phone call to her sister and said, "My life is in danger." Her sister called Rajan and asked that we all should come to their house urgently. I told her that I did not want a stalemate between the maternal kin and the paternal kin. I said, "When you can assemble together someone who can represent the paternal side and someone the maternal side, then we can meet to find a way out." She promised to do so.

When we reached their house, the mother's sister and the father's sister were there. It seemed the father had been there but had just left for the shop. Seeing me, Swapan's maternal aunt began to tell me how much her sister, Swapan's mother, had suffered. I noticed a very important division of voices along the wife-givers and wife-takers. The mother's sister as the accuser took on the role of those who had given a daughter to the house, the father's sister as representing the "wife takers."[16]

"How long will *our sister* keep getting beaten up by *a son* of your side?" Notice that Swapan was now assimilated into the wife-receivers. He was not the son of the mother any more but a member of the agnatic lineage to which his father's sister also belonged. The father's sister appeared ashamed and said that she agreed that something needed to be done. But how can we call the police against our own "son," she asked. I again put it to them that it would be better to treat Swapan like a patient rather than a criminal. We wondered if the various prescriptions he had from the previous visits to the psychiatrist would serve as some kind of certification that Swapan should be in a hospital. I offered to take them to the psychiatrist so they could discuss the difficulties with him.

Swapan's mother, his maternal aunt, Rajan, Simi, and I went to the polyclinic. The mother said, "I have not been out for so long—everything seems so green here." In the psychiatrist's office the mother started to cry, so it was the aunt who asked the psychiatrist what they should do under the circumstances. They wanted Swapan to be admitted to a private hospital, but they had no money. The psychiatrist explained that it would be very expensive to admit him to a private facility and suggested admission in the Institute of Human Behavior and Allied Sciences at Shahadra, which is a public hospital. "Oh, that is the *pagalkhana*—the mad house!" exclaimed the aunt "But we have heard that they tie up patients and beat them there."[17] I was nervous that it might be difficult to get admission there, because they have a long waiting list. The psychiatrist said, "I don't know if my reference will count at all, but it may help." He wrote a referral saying that Swapan had been under his care

16. Although the anthropological literature clearly recognizes that marriage is an exchange between families or lineages—hence depends on the opposition between wife-givers and wife-takers—it was quite stunning to see this distinction played out in the division of voices in a context such as this one rather than in the context of ritual prestations where its salience is taken for granted.

17. The condition in institutions for treatment of psychiatric patients was indeed dismal until a number of public interest litigations led to the Supreme Court's injunctions for improvements in these institutions. The best description of changes in the law and the various interventions made by the courts for improving conditions in asylums is to be found in Amita Dhanda (2000).

and because he was noncompliant and had shown violent tendencies, it was not possible to care for him at home and that hospitalization was recommended. Armed with this referral, we returned to their home.

Swapan's paternal aunt agreed that they should try to get the men of the family and some neighbors to take Swapan to the hospital, if necessary, by force. She said, her brother (i.e., Swapan's father) and she had no objection to this course of action. "Be certain," said the mother's sister, "later don't tell me that you took away our son, a 'boy' of our house, into an asylum." "No, no, do what you wish"—thus the paternal voice embodied in the father's sister was allowed to serve the paternal function of decision maker. Both genealogy and carnality had been taken into account.

The next day we got a phone call from Swapan's sister, Gudiya. Her paternal uncles had come in the morning. Her uncle (her father's brother) had explained to Swapan that no one was abandoning him, that he needed treatment and that as soon as he was better, they would bring him back home. He was taken to the hospital and admitted. He did not resist admission or treatment anymore. Swapan was put on medication and was discharged after a month. In this period, Rajan and Simi visited him once a week, but I had to leave for the United States soon after. When he was discharged from the hospital, Swapan was told that he must attend OPD (the outpatient department) once every two weeks. He would receive medications for the nominal price of Rs. 10 (approximately 25 cents in 2004) per visit.

Excerpts from a letter written in Hindi on the patient sheet by Swapan while in hospital (my translation):

Deservedly worshiped[18] Mummy and Papa,[19]

I want to say this to you. Now I have no complaints against Mummy, Gudiya, and Nitin [his brother]. Now I, love you all very much. . . . I pray that mummy and papa must come here (to visit). If they come, I will be encouraged. By their not coming I will be broken. To mummy, forgiveness from me—I want to be (stand) defeated by her—I also pray to Gudiya that she should forget my beatings and forgive her brother.

18. This is a standard form of address to parents and elders.
19. Mummy and Papa are the ubiquitous forms of address for parents in these areas, as in most other places in urban India and have completely replaced the use of Hindi terms such as Mata Ji and Pita Ji.

I don't draw attention to this letter to say that finally the tensions were resolved, but to point out the ambiguous way in which Swapan gestures toward the crime of the mother as being both the one from whom he seeks forgiveness and the one he forgives. The juxtaposition of the sentences—forgiveness *from* me as well as I stand defeated—point not to a resolution but to an uncertain future.

Notes on Rehabilitation

Swapan now began to eat regularly. He put on weight. When I met him in the summer of 2004, he told me that he was assisting at his father's shop in the morning and his uncle's shop in the afternoon. Each gave him Rs. 10 as pocket money. "That is my income," he told me with exquisite irony. He was taking medicine from the OPD but insisted that since I was leaving for the United States, Rajan or Simi must accompany him. The agreement with the parents was that after a couple of weeks they would accompany him to the hospital, but we found that his family somehow managed to always "forget" to take him, and no one was sure that he could navigate the distance by himself in the bus.

Toward the end of the month after his discharge from the hospital, Swapan had an adverse reaction to the drugs he was given, and his tongue started swelling and hanging out. He was taken to a local practitioner, who adminis-tered an injection. Swapan got better but now decided on his own to take only one medicine among the prescribed ones. When I learned this, I told him that we must talk to the psychiatrist at the OPD. Simi was with him at the OPD the next time, and she asked the attending psychiatrist why Swapan was not receiving psychotherapy since his discharge note had said he would be receiv-ing counseling. The attending psychiatrist looked at the file and said, "But this is the wrong file." Another file was summoned. Swapan was taken to another psychiatrist. Another set of medicines was prescribed. I was truly dejected as I thought that they do not tie up patients and beat them anymore, but with three minutes per patient in the crowded OPD, mistakes will happen. Swapan, Rajan, Simi, and I planned to see whether he could be enrolled in Open School and pass tenth grade.

On my last visit to his house that winter, Swapan said to me—"Aunty, do you have a PhD?" I replied, yes, and was intrigued. He said, switching to English, "You must be good in studies." I had never spoken to Swapan in

English—never assumed that he could speak English. So I said, "Swapan, you are speaking in English!" He replied proudly, "Yes, in the hospital I met a professor like you. He told me my English is good, and in the hospital, I was speaking in English and he helped me." Then after some reflection, he added, "Perhaps now my career will be made."

Swapan was admitted to a neighboring coaching and tuition center. I agreed to pay the school fee to get him started, but within a year he dropped out, stopped taking medications, and on my last visit to his house, he was busy committing words in an English dictionary to heart because he told me that that was a much better way to educate himself than going to school. The big success story the parents told me was of his sister Gudiya, whose marriage was arranged, and the boy was from a good family. The mother said that she was very relieved that the daughter would be safely married. Soon after, the family moved to another part of Delhi, and we were not able to maintain contact with them.

Commentary

What can anthropology contribute to the question of the challenge of psychopathology to narrative theories of the self with which this chapter started? What does this story of one boy and one family struggling to deal with mental illness and unstable financial conditions tell us about madness in the context of urban poverty? I suggest that Swapan's encounter with illness teaches us that what is at stake is not narrative theories of the self per se, but how we place his words in the world. In one of his formulations on knowledge and the living, Georges Canguilhem, speaks of the creativity of pathology and offers a marvelous distinction between the pathologically normal and the normatively normal (Canguilhem 1991, 1994, 317; see also Margree 2002). In the case of Swapan, as in the cases of many other young persons in the area, I detect the refusal to accept the normatively normal. I saw too much suffering and violence to say that mental illness is all a matter of social construction or that symptoms are only forms of resistance. Instead, I offer the idea that the illness resides in the network of relations, in the movement over institutions, and that the pathology is struggling to find an environment in which it could reestablish new norms.

In his work on psychopathology of the marginal and the abandoned, the anthropologist João Biehl (2005) has shown that when you begin to assume that the words that are spoken in the context of madness need to be brought back to the world, something about the environment in which these words were grown is illuminated. Thus Catarina, the protagonist of Biehl's powerful book on her life, was disabled and abandoned, but she was engaged in the task of completing a dictionary of words that were meaningful to her. Taken by the experts as a sign of her dementia, her words in the institutional context in which she lived were witness to her madness. By tracing her words back to the communities from which they were grown, however, Biehl showed that the words that appeared to be completely incoherent at first sight, in fact, embodied the fractured and painful experiences of Catarina—that the "dictionary" was her record of abuse and the mental institution's investment was in what he calls "pharmaceutical hope." Caterina's story is a story of a zone of abandonment, but the complex telling by Biehl does not allow an easy separation between good and evil. Yet by taking the abandonment of Catarina as the only vantage point from which the ethnography could be conducted, Biehl is unable to access any other shades of the story from others' points of view. The stance of accusation from which he views all other relations in which Catarina was involved gives a highly teleological bent to the direction of the story he tells.

To say that psychiatric illness grows in specific ways in specific social worlds, Biehl argues, is not to opt for a completely constructivist view of mental illness or deny its reality altogether. As I show in Swapan's case, the recognition that the illness is real is at stake in saving him from life in prison, but the trajectory of the illness cannot be separated from the failure of institutions in his local world or the manner in which wild hopes are invested in some kind of lure of modernity.

So when and how do words mean? Cavell says, "Whether our words will go on meaning what they do depends upon whether the other people find it worth their while to continue to understand us—that seeing a better bargain elsewhere they may decide that we are no longer of their world, as if out sanity depended upon their approval of us, finding us to their likeness" (Cavell 1979, 179).

Swapan's story, it seems to me, is not a story about loss of self or of narrative discontinuity so much as it is a story of finding that his many exclusions—from family, from productivity, from genealogy, from intimacy, and ultimately from a human form of life—mean that his words are not found meaningful by others. That ultimately he finds his voice, even if temporarily, literally in a foreign language and in a hospital setting away from home shows that forms of life grow words in complicated ways. There is a phantasmal modernity in his desire to master the whole world by memorizing words from an English dictionary—but there is also that moment of coherence when the collaboration with the mad professor lets Swapan experience himself as the agent of his own actions, as in the letter he wrote to his parents.

The possibility that the illusory qualities of modernity for the poor in places like Delhi may lead one to experience oneself as if one has been made into a ghost is surely a part of that experimentation with life, but not one that can be assumed hastily or without first exhausting other possibilities. In Swapan's case the family could not or would not invest material and emotional resources in him. His sister had far greater luck in that she could complete school. Though she could not find a way to fulfill her dearest wish, which was to experience life in college, she did find a salaried job, and her family was invested enough in her to get her married. Paradoxically, it was easier in terms of family honor to abandon the son than the daughter, but we could also see the beginnings of a new kind of rationality emerging in which an income-earning daughter was valued over a nonproductive son. The complex borders between normality and pathology, between whose life is to be enhanced and who is to "let die" in the context of urban poverty and its experimentation with modernity of a certain sort, call for theoretical humility, which is why I can go this far with this story and no further.

A Believer in Hope

Let us turn to one other family in a similar neighborhood and one other scene of a psychiatric diagnosis. Vidya's (the name indicates knowledge) story follows a different trajectory and a different resolution, though her life too passes through the same trajectories of psychiatric institutions, diviners, exorcists, and psychotropic medications. She too becomes a nodal point of family politics. Yet it may help to see the subtle variations on how her supposed illness unfolds and how she establishes some control over the ability to tell her story in her own words.

Vidya's family was one of the earliest contacts I made in Jahangirpuri, a resettlement colony that arose during the National Emergency in 1975 (see Tarlo 2003). This was the phase of my work in 1999, when ISERDD was yet to be born and I had made initial contacts in a few localities that were eventually to become the study sites for ISERDD. Vidya was fourteen years old and said to be brilliant in her studies. Her father, a tailor, was doing well in his business, and his wife, Vidya's mother, had opened a small storefront in which she stocked small quantities of various food items. There was also a telephone on which various neighbors could make calls and receive calls for a small payment. Unlike today in 2013 when almost everyone I know in this area possesses a telephone and the houses show visible signs of a new affluence as land prices have risen due to the metro station that has been built—then, the sense was of a cautious hope as residents were showing signs of upward mobility. As the eldest daughter, Vidya was assigned responsibilities of taking her two younger siblings (a younger sister and the youngest brother) to school, helping her mother with the shop, and doing other sundry chores.

Vidya's grandmother (her father's mother), who lived with them, was obsessed with the grandson, and I was forever hearing about his ailments, for which she would drag him from one local practitioner to another. She sometimes blamed her daughter-in-law for showing too much leniency toward the girls. Around the time that Vidya turned seventeen and was in eleventh grade, she became the object of close surveillance by her father and her grandmother. I am not sure if there was any particular event that triggered this response. But she was said to have changed from a docile and lovable child to a defiant girl who answered back, was secretive, and resented having to do so many household chores. I heard from neighbors that her father was often beating her up. On the surface her grandmother was full of pity for Vidya—poor girl, her father beat her so mercilessly—but she would simultaneously manage to convey that the world was a dangerous place for growing girls who hardly know how to distinguish good from bad; that the environment of the neighborhood was "bad"—*mahaul kharab hai*—and if a girl lost her footing once, there was nothing to redeem her (an oblique reference to desire in young girls and the dangers they pose to family reputation—the stuff of soap operas on Indian television).

It was true that Jahangirpuri was getting the reputation of being a wild place. There were a number of cases of elopement, which parents often referred to as "abductions." Violence was always in the air, as fistfights could quickly turn into lethal attacks with knives. Girls often complained to me that the groups of young men who hung around in street corners passed lewd comments and that they could not move around freely for fear of being teased or harassed.

Vidya had become completely withdrawn. The women in the immediate neighborhood were very worried about her father's uncontrolled rage. Her own mother, while often visibly upset, could not articulate any opposition to her husband or mother-in-law. Whereas a man might claim rights over his wife to even hit her, according to the norms of Hindu patriarchy, a daughter must always be thought of as a gift, who is only temporarily in her father's house, and thus is to be cherished and loved. It is not that this stated norm is always followed. Neglect of female children is common. But whereas mothers might slap a daughter or hit her, it is rare for fathers to beat their daughters unless the girl has caused irretrievable loss of honor. Some elderly women tried to mediate with Vidya's father to say that it was not so much that Vidya had become defiant and wayward but that she was possessed by some unnamed spirit who made her say things which she was not in control of. This was an interesting way of acknowledging the father's authority while reframing the event within a different narrative structure. Thus instead of saying that the father's rage was the sign of a demonic possession, it became the daughter's behavior that was made to stand in need of explanation. According to the local understandings of available trajectories of healing, local diviners and exorcists were consulted, but these strategies did not work, though they allowed Vidya's father's anger to be cooled somewhat. Vidya agreed that after her school finals she would agree to submit herself to an exorcism at the famous Balaji temple, to which, as we might recall, Swapan was also taken for a healing session.

While Vidya was hard at work mastering her textbooks for the final exams, her grandmother continued to poison the atmosphere with little jibes that if girls studied too hard, their brains got heated—*zabardast padhai hai—ladki ka dimag komal hota hai, sah nahin sakta*—a free translation would be "studies are like confronting a powerful force and a girl's brain is delicate; it cannot bear such force." Or the grandmother might say, "Poor Vidya, her father beats her so mercilessly, but she is so stubborn—she will not let a cry escape—how can a young girl bear such heartrending beating? I cannot even bear to witness it." The ambiguous statements—with the overt expression of concern and the concealed message that only a demon in her can be making her so strong—are part of the politics of the family, especially when it comes to gendered speech, as I have described elsewhere too (V. Das 2007). I noticed that Vidya's mother was not able to speak or offer any other version of the events in the presence of Vidya's grandmother, so dominating was the voice of the older woman. There was no question of my being able to find Vidya alone and talk to her in the tiny, crowded two rooms in which they all lived.

Right after the state-level school-leaving examination was over, Vidya was taken to Balaji, but according to her mother, despite the powerful rituals to identify which spirit had taken hold of Vidya in order to exorcise it, the priests could accomplish nothing. At this stage another neighbor, one who had been suffering from depression and insomnia and who was being treated in the outpatient department of a nearby government hospital, came up with the suggestion that what Vidya was suffering from "tension" and that it was a treatable disorder. She herself had found considerable relief from insomnia and general debility with medications. At this stage exhausted, I think, with the daily battles in the family, Vidya's father took up this suggestion and took her to the hospital for consultation. After spending five minutes in the doctor's office they came back armed with lithium to be taken for six weeks, after which the "patient" was to report for further evaluation and adjustment of medications. (Over the next two years, I met them sporadically and learned that Vidya's father or her brother would simply go to the hospital and have the prescription refilled. As far as I know, the doctor never demanded to see the patient or check on her symptoms.)

After the end of the long summer, the results of the state-level examinations were announced. Vidya had passed with glowing results, securing a first division, Given the dismal state of teaching in many government-run schools, this was a miracle. In a class of fifty children she was the only one to have passed with such high marks. Yet if she wanted to continue her studies at a public university such as the University of Delhi, she could do so only as a noncollegiate student since admission to regular classes demands more than 80 percent marks—such is the discrepancy between demand and supply. Despite her success in the examinations, the bureaucratic processes of getting forms and filing the application were too intimidating for Vidya's parents, and they did not trust her to go to college by herself. Fortunately, they agreed to accept my help, and I was able to get her admitted as a noncollegiate student. I accompanied Vidya to the college to introduce her to the college environment and give her some confidence that she could navigate the demands of the weekend classes that were offered to the students.

On our way home I offered to take her to a café where we could have a snack, and the girl who had avoided me through the last two years burst out with her story in response to a simple question of whether she was feeling better. "But Aunty, I was not the one who was ill. It is my father who needs treatment. They took me to Balaji to have a spirit exorcised. But what is it that I had done? My father had created such a situation that every one was watching me all the time. If I was late returning from school by even fifteen minutes because I had stopped to chat with a friend, then I would get a beating. If I wanted to study late at night, then I was wasting electricity. If I wanted to borrow a book from a friend and needed to go to her house, my father would accuse me of brazenly trying to meet a boyfriend. I was always the accused— no proof of anything—just suspicion, accusations—but you know I am very stubborn [*ziddi*]. I said whatever you can do to me—do it—you will not break my resolve to study." I asked what happened at the Balaji temple. Her response was very simple. "They tried to get the spirit to speak. Now I do believe in the existence of such spirits, but since I did not have any such thing in me, who could speak? They had lamps with some kind of smoke which is supposed to be unbearable to the spirit, but all it did to me was make me drowsy." Then reflecting on the medications she was taking, she said , it is not that I was possessed by a spirit or that I have a mental illness, it is that I had become a "believer in hope" (*ashavadi ho gai thi*).

I never found such moments of intimacy with Vidya again. She graduated from college, and though she did not become a teacher as she had wished to be, she worked in a gas agency for some years, earning a decent income. The conflicts around girls and their education was resolved for this family as her younger sister graduated from high school and went on to college without the kind of trials and tribulations that Vidya had endured. What the psychiatric diagnosis accomplished in this case had nothing to do with therapy, but it did buy the peace that Vidya craved and allowed her to move on with her life. Like Swapan, Vidya too refused to accept the normatively normal, but their trajectories went in the opposite directions. It is when Swapan accepted his illness and the necessity of medicine within the hospital setting that he found a measure of peace. In the end it was not he who failed the institution but the institution that failed him. In Vidya's case, it was her ability to retain a sense of her own autonomy that made her endure the hardships that her father and grandmother imposed on her. We may say that in one case there was an illness that craved recognition, whereas in the second case illness was a fiction created within the network of relations that kept Vidya's father's anger in abeyance. But both cases show how diagnosis becomes dispersed over a range of narrative accounts crafted through the interactional contexts in which ongoing narratives are created within the upheavals of social life.

A Possible Conclusion

Is this chapter "about" mental illness or urban modernity or poverty or kinship? It is hard to say. Each of these objects is created through the relationship with the other. Sometimes illness is in modernity, and at other times modernity is in the illness. The desire for English, for autonomy, and for being able to escape the stifling constraints of gender or kinship norms are evident in both cases, but these desires are not always decipherable to the senior generation. There are times when the younger generation who is getting educated shows utter contempt for their elders, but we don't get the sharp lines of distinction between tradition and modernity that are evident in Pandolfo's descriptions of the clinical encounter between a patient, his mother, and the psychiatrist (Pandolfo 2008). In that case the son makes contemptuous references to the mother's tradition-bound ideas and deliberately resorts to speaking in French, thus snubbing his mother whose language is Arabic. Similar to the divide between Arabic and French that Pandolfo describes within this clinical scene, there is a tension between Hindi and English in the two families I described—but the pursuit of English for the young is more like the promise of modernity that is never fulfilled.

In her descriptions of the experiences of patients with psychosis, Ellen Corin (2007) argues that such experiences remain at the fringe of biomedical discourses. Scientific discourses and rehabilitation practices, she says, are the "public face" of mental health problems and difficulties. The experience of patients who make a claim to normality, with which I started this chapter, draw our attention to the fact that the normal and the normative remain the most elusive concepts to pin down ethnographically. Corin argues that patients with psychosis will often resort to religious signifiers to express their experiences of feeling marginal or isolated but that they use these religious symbols to express and tame feeling of strangeness, which elude description because they are marginal to biomedical discourse and also to the religiously bound community. In contrast, in the contexts I am describing in which the status of biomedical knowledge is itself in question as psychiatric practice is embedded within the general practice of treating patients on the basis of symptoms rather than diagnosis, illness takes its meaning or loses its meaning by the putting together of different kinds of parts and wholes in which the biomedical discourse penetrates familial discourse and is penetrated by it. Hence I agree with Good (2012) that instead of a coherent unitary subject of psychiatric discourse it may be better to pluralize what we call illness, health, normality, and pathology. This, of course, makes it very difficult to think of some magic-bullet solution to the kinds of problems that I have described here. I did find that sometimes the imperative to act will overrun the imperative to understand, as was the case when Swapan's mother would drag me into trying to find a solution to her problems. But apart from showing that one is there to receive the words and act when one can, I see no smart, conclusive way of finding closure. The fact is that I would repeatedly console myself with the verse from the Bhagavad Gita, *karmaniyeva adhikaras te ma phaleshu kadachan* (you have authority only over your action, never over the consequences). I have to confess—my spade is turned—and I hope that others will pick up where I have stumbled.

FOUR

Dangerous Liaisons: Technology, Kinship, and Wild Spirits

As the illness biographies in the last two chapters show, the severity and the course of illness are strongly influenced by conditions of poverty and by the local ecologies of the neighborhoods in which the poor live. However, it is also the case that the existential pressure that illness exerts on the person suffering, and on the caregivers too, goes beyond issues of poverty and resource constraints, though these conditions can never be simply bracketed. Swapan's case brings home forcefully the fact that in such cases as that of madness, we are faced not with the epistemic question as to the problem of the Other, but with the struggles over a concrete other whose illness cannot be absorbed into everyday life. As in Swapan's case, when the other presents himself in a mode such as that of madness, the process of "letting die" happens through a number of dispersed institutions, diffused forms of neglect, and a braiding of small and large events spread over several years. Abandonment here is not so much an act of the will resulting from choice but an exhaustion of the will and the capacity to marshal yet more energy, yet more love, to be able to offer care. Recall the words that were wrenched out of Swapan's mother, Rajkarni, when she said that her son had remade his own mother into a demonic being who could wish death upon the same son that she had borne and given birth to. Reflections on what it is to be human are expressed in several such moments in this familial drama, but it would be a misreading to imagine that in giving a place to these expressions in my analysis, I am simply calling on some intrinsic human quality that will allow one to connect to any of the protagonists of these accounts in an unmediated manner through cultivation of sympathy or empathy. For starters, the experience one has of grief or of somehow falling out of the taken-for-granted routines of everyday life is not transparent to oneself. Ralph Waldo Emerson (1844) in his marvelous essay on experience expresses this inability by the idea that the death of his son taught him that grief has nothing to teach him. One cannot even touch experience let alone grasp it in a case of massive loss. I have sometimes accordingly thought of the condition of human beings in their everyday existence as that of being not quite alive to themselves or, as Stanley Cavell (2005, 214) put it, "as not awake to their lives." This is a description of both what it is to inhabit the world with the other and a reflection on a particular aspect of the everyday. Pursuit of the moral within the trancelike quotidian might be thought of as being called to awaken from forgetfulness.

In this chapter, I evoke the complexity arising from being called to awaken by another in the context of competing obligations to the living, the dead, and the dying. Lévinas's (1989) signature theme of the face as the emblem of the other, along with his idea of the asymmetry of my relation to the other standing in an accusatory or persecutory relation to me, suggests some of this experience. From the infinite and the completely unknowable other to the concrete other in the figures of the widow, the orphan, and the stranger, Lévinas recognizes that a violence occurs in opening to the claims of the other. This violence comes from outside us, as Cavell (2005, 145) notes in discussing Lévinas: "Lévinas's idea is that my openness to the other—to a region 'beyond' my narcissism—requires a violence associated with the infinite having been put into me: he speaks of this intervention or aggression in images of trauma, breakup, monstrosity, devastation. This event creates as it were an outside to my existence, hence an isolated, singular inside."[1] From here Cavell reformu-

---

1. In the essay "What Is the Scandal of Skepticism?" Cavell (2005) discusses Lévinas and these ideas. For a good introduction to these issues through his own writing, see Lévinas (1989).

lates the problem of responsibility to the other as originating not in the recognition of finitude in relation to the infinite nature of the other, but in the recognition that the particular other who is part of my existence is also completely separate from me. "The extravagant intimacy at stake in these relations [i.e., of Shakespearean characters such as Hamlet and his mother and Othello and his wife] suggests that the 'proof' of the other's existence is a problem not of establishing connection with the other, but of achieving, or suffering, separation from the other, individuation with respect to the one upon whom my nature is staked" (Cavell 2005, 146). Taking a cue from Cavell, then, I suggest that the issue is not the intuition of the infinite involved in this trauma, but rather the recognition that my responsibility to the other can be only a finite one. Limiting the desire for infinite responsibility to the other is paradoxically what might attach one to life itself. It explains to me my own sense of the moral as a move, not toward the transcendental but toward an awakened everyday from the rote everyday: not an escape from the everyday but an embracing of it.[2] Or to use one of Cavell's intellectual insights, it is the relation we establish between the actual everyday and the eventual everyday.[3]

2. I cannot take up in any detail here the kind of misreading done by some scholars who have a rather simplistic idea of language as that which is only available as actualized in conversation. Thus, for instance, Michael Lempert (2013) happily puts Wittgenstein's philosophy as that of the "old" ordinary language philosophy as if the work of philosophers who have interpreted Wittgenstein to argue that what is at stake in his philosophy is not some simple idea of "ordinary language" but of the philosophical status of the *ordinary* as shadowed by skepticism, or the work on third Wittgenstein, does not exist. On my notion of ordinary ethics Lempert claims that Das narrates how small acts can do large things from care to harm without ever announcing what they do, I can only respond as follows. In my book, *Life and Words*, I show that small acts such as sitting in silence in the street in which more than three hundred men were burned alive, refusal to bathe, or to allow traditional laments to escape from the body—thus embodying pollution publicly—which women did in 1984 in Delhi, was about proclaiming the terrible crimes of the state, and also making room for life to be knit together again in slow rhythms. Perhaps in Lempert's world this work amounts to "doing nothing," but in the worlds I am familiar with, this is what doing something means—it is the braiding of action and expression, of making such deaths count (see Das 2007, 2014a, 2014b).

3. This theme is especially poignant in Stanley Cavell's understanding of America as a country that has not found its voice, philosophically speaking. This idea is found in several of Cavell's books but especially in Cavell (1989). Among his many commentators, Simon Critchley and Sandra Laugier are especially attentive to this strand of Cavell's thought. Critchley writes about the attempt to recover the American romantic tradition and the sadness of

I wonder how this idea was planted in me in my relation to these ethnographic sites. Scenes of visitations from the dead involve this question of responsibility to the concrete other, and thus also further the conversation between the finite limit of relations and the desire for the infinite. It is evident from the earlier chapters that the urban neighborhoods in Delhi are composed of various kinds of beings. Life is not simply the relations humans have with each other, but also how the inhuman—as animal, as machine, as ghost or as spirit—is, or becomes part of, the social and cultural milieu within which human beings are thrown together. According to many people from these neighborhoods with whom I have conversed, forms of gods and goddesses dwell there as well as ghosts, jinns, visions of people with light dripping from their faces (lit., *noor tapakta hai*—a reference to the quality of light that angels have), and, of course, the recently dead, who can be sensed only through calling on the inner senses. The commerce between such forms of life is not bound by caste or sect or language. The human body and the human senses receive these neighbors in an astonishing multiplicity of forms.

In the case studies of illness and institutions in the preceding three chapters, we saw the ambiguous nature of kinship relations, but this is not simply a proposition about the innate nature of kinship. The dilemmas a family faces when looking after a terminally sick relative are also dependent on the resources it commands and their allocation. Families that live at the margin of economic survival have to constantly negotiate how to balance different claims. However, the specificities of the scenarios in which families struggle with illness and poverty and the dark side of care are not confined to the poor, as revealed in Arthur Kleinman's (2009, 2014) extraordinary writing on the divided self of the caregiver in the case of the terminal illness of his wife, Joan, and John Bailey's (1999) memoir of life with his wife, the philosopher Iris Murdoch, toward the end of her life.

As medical technologies advance, the pressure to expand one's obligations toward kin for seeking more options in cases of illness also goes up. When the latest technologies (such as CT scans and MRIs) are touted in the low-income neighborhoods, poor families can incur heavy expenditures, but the failure to treat people with appropriate medications for less complicated diseases that

---

"an unworked America that hesitates in the tension between nihilism and its overcoming; between the actual everyday and the eventual everyday." See Critchley (2005, 7). See also Laugier (2005) for rethinking the notion of the ordinary.

could nevertheless grow into life-threatening conditions results in a sort of incoherence in the lives of the poor. Acute observers of this scene of incoherence such as Lawrence Cohen (2005) have shown how transplant technology creates not only conditions in which the bodies of the poor become "bioavailable" to the rich but also a social imaginary in which "selling one's kidney" or "renting one's womb" to pay off a debt or to arrange a marriage comes to be seen as part of kinship obligations.

What happens when one feels deeply ambivalent about such obligations to one's kin? Cheryl Mattingly (2012) offers an elegant analysis of the moral scenes within which the self is sought to be constructed in the case of caregivers of children with terminal illness or severe disabilities. She summarizes these scenes through the spatial imaginary of being in different setting—a courtroom, an artisan's workshop, and a laboratory. In the first case one is asked to give an account of oneself as if one were an accused in a court of law (see Butler 2005). In the second case, one crafts oneself as if one were an apprentice in a workshop, and in the third case one constructs oneself in an experimental mode much as a scientist might construct objects in a laboratory. In the first case the subject, for Mattingly, comes into existence in response to an accusation, and an ethical self is created when one steps out from the flow of relations and looks retrospectively at one's life through the eyes of another. In the second case, she says, there is an element of experiment in the making of the self and a picture of being oriented to the future, but learning happens in a scene where some notion of tradition sets the moral compass. In the third case she contends that the narrative understanding of moral experience is neither seen in terms of defending oneself after the fact, nor aligning oneself to the cultivation of virtues that are named and understood in advance, but rather of experiencing oneself to be living, as Mattingly states it, within possible narrative plot lines. Said otherwise, the laboratory analogy allows a privileging of a fragile "I" that is in the making rather than a fully constituted subject who confronts a moral decision from a position of the sovereign self.

In my own recent writing on ordinary ethics I have also thought of the attentiveness to the other within the small events of everyday life as the expression of the moral. Instead of a sharp contrast between obligation and freedom, habit and innovation, I have argued that habit itself is the place in which the creation of the ethical subject happens, provided we pay attention to the potential of both good and evil within these small events of the everyday (V. Das 2012). Similarly, Michael Lambek (2012) has argued that ethics is intrinsic to human action. Whereas for Mattingly these three modes through which the subject comes into being are in opposition to each other, I hope to show in this chapter that one cascades between these different modes—now incorporating the voice of the accusing other, now aligning oneself to traditionally defined ideas of virtue, now finding it necessary to innovate. A further issue for me is that the ethical experiments do not happen to an isolated individual but to someone who is already within a web of relations with both humans and nonhumans.

My specific form of argument in this chapter is to take questions about human life away from, say, a theory of virtue that would think of morality as some kind of rule following. Otherwise said, I am suggesting that whereas a common conception of morality along Kantian lines would have it that any satisfactory account of morality must take our intuitive understanding that moral judgments are both "objective" and thus held to be universally valid *and* that that they are intrinsically practical,[4] the scenes of moral dilemmas that I encountered such as the one I describe in this chapter were those in which one's entire life could be put into question. In my fieldwork such moments of self-interrogation often included the mediation of a nonhuman form of life into the rhythms of the everyday. Sometimes a deity might come and possess someone, making them give expression to desires they had never known to be theirs. At other times, beings that dwell in the world with humans even though they might possess only a virtual existence—beings lost through death or betrayal or sheer forgetfulness of their existence— make themselves present in ways that press upon humans to attend to relationships they think are best forgotten. Heonik Kwon's (2008, 2012) stunning work on the way ancestral cults were bent slightly in the Vietnamese village he studied to make place for the unclaimed dead on the enemy side and errant ancestors on one's own side after the war with the United States was over is one example of the navigation of memory and forgetfulness between the living and the dead.

The protagonist of the story in this chapter is a man called Billu.[5] I see Billu's existence as a conjugate of man and machine within which the media-

4. For a concise account of this conception and its critique, see Crary (2007)

5. To the person I call Billu, his family, and the household in which he worked and to whom he introduced me, I am grateful for discussions on how to raise resources for such contingencies as he faced. Almost all the interviews took place within that frame of discus-

tion of a spirit reveals what I call, after Cora Diamond (2008), a difficulty of reality. Everyday life in this case secretes a dimension of reality in which Billu finds himself suspended between the hold of the past and the demands of the present. He nearly loses himself with the deaths of his brother and his new-born son within the same month. What finally reattaches him to life is not a grand resolution of the problems he faced but his acknowledgment of a limit through the force of the spirit.

In contemplating issues such as the ones Billu faced about the claims of his sick brother on him I was initially attracted to Lévinas and his grand vision of infinite responsibility to the Other whose nature cannot be known to me. But I have been compelled to ask, as has Clara Han (2012) in her deep engage-ment with the lives of the poor in a neighborhood in Santiago, Chile, what does this infinite responsibility mean when the other is not a distant God but a relative or a neighbor, for whom one does what one can—yet the conditions of poverty, addiction, and everyday violence simply will not allow obligations to be fully sustained. Cavell (2005) is helpful here. Cavell, above all the scholar of acknowledgment, cautions us that the problem of human existence is not primarily that of establishing connection with the other but of *suffering sepa-ration* with respect to the one "in whom my nature is staked." I find it import-ant without yet being able to say how, that this acknowledgment of separateness in Billu's life was imbued with the color of failure, perhaps a "bitter compro-mise" (Diamond 2008) with the fact of having to live this kind of life and not another; suffering not only the separateness from the other but also an implicit indictment of himself and the spirit he came to listen to even if he did not trust her fully. His relation to the spirit as well as his relation to technology was suspended, as we shall see, between trust and suspicion. In the works of Stanley Cavell and Cora Diamond, this might be thought of as the condition of skepticism against which one is neither allowed to win nor lose (Cavell, Diamond, McDowell, et al. 2008).

---

sion as I also helped Billu write applications and find addresses. I also put him in contact with other patients awaiting kidney transplants so that he could learn what this surgery entailed. I continued to run into him whenever I visited his neighborhood so that the con-versations continued over one year. However, it would have been very difficult for me to write the original paper on which this chapter is based if Susan Lloyd McGarry at Harvard University had not given her input into developing the argument and encouraging me to clarify some of the issues. I am indebted to her more than she knows.

Bio-exchanges

There is a growing literature on bio-exchanges that brings to light the inequities, and even violence, involved. Thus both Nancy Scheper-Hughes (2009)
and Margaret Lock (2001), two of the most influential authors in the field of
medical anthropology, have shown that the movement of organs from the
poor to the rich creates new perils for the poor who are organ donors even as
it enhances the life of the rich. In an important intervention in this debate
Lawrence Cohen (2005) draws attention to the panic-producing language of
moral outrage in much of the debates on organ exchange and offers a more
nuanced concept of "bioavailability." Cohen hopes that the concept of bioavailability would help bring forth the imaginaries of the body as a resource
for supplementing other bodies, thus allowing various new political and ethical formations to be generated. The concept is flexible enough to cover both
forcible extraction of organs and processes through which the poor might
themselves participate in sale of organs (their own and their family members')
as a form of ethical self-making. Productive as these thoughts are, the ethnographic details in Cohen's analysis are somewhat sparse; thus the full geography of the relations brought about by the possibility of organ exchange is not
developed. The work of Jacob Copeman (2009) on blood-donation camps
organized by two important religious sects is ethnographically rich and theoretically innovative, but the emphasis in this work is on anonymous blood
donations as a public gift and relationships created at a distance. I hope to
show instead what happens to one's close relationships once the possibility of
a new technology is introduced and what this can tell us about the human as
embedded within a specific form of life and its kinship with the nonhuman as
machine and as spirit.

Billu, His Brother, and His Son

Billu lived with his wife and two-year-old son in a rented room in one of the
low-income neighborhoods in our study. The street on which he lived was
overcrowded with poor facilities for water and sanitation. He worked as a
part-time gardener who tended the grounds around a nearby factory and sup-
plemented his income by doing domestic work for a middle-class family.
Unlike other households similar to Billu's in which women were able to sup-

plement the family income by either part-time work as housemaids or by making small products at home which they then provided to shops on piece-rate basis, Billu's wife could not engage in any income-generating activities because she was sickly and often required attention for varied medical conditions. Over the years Billu had accumulated massive debts due to medical contingencies as well as his desire for new commodities. It was not that he never accumulated any money, but he could never retain any savings. Growth of markets for goods in low-income localities that offer ready credit has meant that the poor are being reconstituted as consumers and often lured into buying television sets, refrigerators, or other commodities on hire purchase—schemes that inevitably lead to serious indebtedness. Since it is hard for the poor to borrow from formal institutions, they end up either relying on ties of kinship or borrowing from informal credit markets at extremely high rates of interest. Billu too had fallen into the cycle of buying an attractive commodity with a down payment, getting into debt, paying high rates of interest, and ultimately forfeiting or selling off the commodity. This is not the place to give a full history of his financial transactions. The general observations I offer, however, are drawn from a detailed record of such transactions in several cases. Here I offer one or two examples of the pattern of income and expenditures and the modalities of decision making in Billu's household.

Because Billu had worked with the same employers for more than ten years, he could mobilize them through appeals for sympathy with his situation and the hardships he faced. Sometimes his employers would give him outright loans of money without interest that he promised to return but never could; and at other times, during particular crises, he received monetary help to tide him over. These were not his main sources of credit, but the help provided by his two employers was not negligible either. The pathways he followed had the character of contingency—he might be able to get some money from one or other of his superiors at his workplace or from the household in which he did part-time work, but there were never any guarantees. One could describe him as following the moves of a gambler, not infrequent in the economic circumstances of many residents of low-income neighborhoods (cf. the playful description of the swirling affects and the changing intensities of hope and disappointment among the urban poor youth in urban Mongolia by Morten Pedersen [2012]) . For example, through regular savings in a bank that his employer (the head of the household he worked in) had insisted he deposit every month under a small savings scheme, he had saved enough money over four years to begin to pay off his debt. But instead, he bought a jhuggi (shanty) on the border of Delhi and Uttar Pradesh. Over one year he made gradual improvements—a tin roof and a door, which his employer had discarded. He was planning to convert the jhuggi into a brick and cement dwelling when all jhuggis in that locality were declared illegal because the builder who had sold them apparently never had the legal rights over the land. Billu had to move back to a rented one-room windowless dwelling after losing all his invest-ment. There were other occasions when the moment he had accumulated a little money someone from his village would fall ill, or he had to contribute money toward a wedding or a funeral in the village. The combination of factors that allow people like Billu to survive, living from one emergency to another, are made up of a complex formation of the employer's needs for trustworthy labor, especially domestic labor; some ideas about charity (*dana*) that lead employers to dispense money that stands somewhere between debt and charity; and shadows of old patron-client relations that continue to oper-ate even within the informal cash economy. As Collins, Morduch, Rutherford, and Ruthven (2009) argue in their work on the portfolios of the poor, such strategies are frequently used by the poor to meet their consumption needs, but these have not received sustained attention because scholars have never taken the financial instruments the poor use to be worthy of serious attention.

A crisis Billu recalled as the worst crisis in recent memory had to do with his brother. His elder brother, Ramvilas, who worked as domestic servant in an affluent household, as cook, odd-jobs man, and cleaner for their bachelor son, who had set up a separate establishment, fell ill with what initially looked like a viral fever. Ramvilas bought some analgesics from the local pharmacist and continued to work, since his employer was not inclined to give him leave for what the employer thought was a minor seasonal fever. The fever turned out to be a hepatitis infection. Ramvilas's condition deteriorated rapidly, and by the time his employer paid serious attention to the illness, Ramvilas's kid-neys were adversely affected. His employer was quite distraught and perhaps felt guilty over the condition of Billu's brother. Through personal contacts he was able to get him admitted to a private hospital where a well-known trans-plant surgeon agreed to perform a transplant operation free of cost. As I shall explain later, this is less surprising than it seems at first sight since many pri-vate hospitals that have been given government land on subsidized rates in Delhi are under contractual agreement to provide facilities for treatment to a small number of patients from low-income families . Since Billu's brother's employer was an influential businessman with political connections, he was able to get him admitted to this hospital under the quota reserved for the poor. However, those admitted under this provision did not have access to other services free of cost.

While Billu's brother awaited his turn for a kidney to become available, he had to be put on dialysis. His employer, having already spent a good amount of money on him, agreed to pay part of the costs but asked that the family contribute some part of the expenditure. Billu's brother had no one else to turn to, so Billu ended up borrowing more money from his own employers to meet this contingency. He showed them the various hospital records and even took his brother to their house so they could see for themselves what a pitiable condition he was in. Such "showing" of one's economic condition in order to elicit charity or to borrow money is encountered in other studies and is part of the performance of aggressive dependency that James Wilce (1998) has explored in his work (see also chapter 2).

Some of Billu's neighbors tried to persuade him to send his brother to an *ashram* in the pilgrimage city of Rishikeh where he would be looked after, advising him that he might not be able to sustain the medical expenses over time. Billu's employers also tried to make him aware of the exorbitant costs of postoperative care and immune-suppressant medicines and to urge him to think beyond the actual surgery. But what weighed most heavily on Billu was his brother's heartbreaking pleas that he "wanted to live." "I could not turn away from my brother," he told me, "for, I thought—what happens later, one can only wait and see [lit., *ham ne socha baad ki baad mein dekhi jayegi*]." This relation to temporality in terms of immediacy, leaving the distant future to take care of itself is an important part of the way in which the poor inhabit the world. As it happened Billu's brother died before a suitable kidney could be found. I think it is possible that Billu was secretly relieved that he turned out to not be a good match for a transplant—otherwise he might have had to donate a kidney. His brother's death also solved the problem of how to raise more money for postoperative medications even if the operation had been successful.

I have had to tell this story in straightforward, linear terms as the first approximation to something akin to a plot of the story. However, Billu told me the story as it unfolded over three months in bits and pieces—hence the plot is my construction, retrospectively imposed on the fragments of narration that I actually encountered. Finally, there is another event and a different set of constellations that appeared in the telling of this story, which surfaced only toward the end of the episode, though it must have been present in Billu's consciousness throughout the time that he was dealing with his brother's illness. This final burst of revelation as I will describe later, seemed to suggest that the event of the brother's death was shot through with another experience of death for Billu about which he was very reluctant to talk.

Another Event Casts Its Shadow on Billu's Story

At the first instance it might seem that this is a simple story of kinship obligations and the normative force of kinship in the lives of the poor. However, not all his relatives exercised the same pull on Billu. Furthermore, while kinship is a source of solidarity and social support in many cases, kinship relations, especially between brothers, are often fraught with conflict . So we would have to go beyond general appeals to kinship norms to understand Billu's desperate desire to help his brother. What was the texture of emotions that bound the two brothers? Billu had come to the city when he was quite young to work along with his brother. His father had died when he was barely five years old, and with a very small plot of land and six children to feed, his mother had found it very difficult to provide for them. So though Billu was only eleven or twelve years old at that time, he came to the city and got employment as a domestic helper.

Billu told me that though his mother had sent him off with his brother and in a way abandoned him, she and his other siblings had often turned to him for his help once he started earning. It is hard for me to discern what he really felt for his mother—his characterizations of her were often contradictory. He felt she was taking advantage of him and yet that she was his mother, and a son who abandoned his mother could find no happiness in this or any other life. Like many other migrants to the city, Billu would sometimes attempt to hide his money by keeping it as credit with his employers, but he often gave in to his mother's pleas for help. It was not simply that he considered it a moral obligation to help his extended family, but he also felt the attraction of being recognized as a dutiful son and a man of means back in the village. Yet Billu recognized that this effort drained him of any possibility of building a reasonably secure future for himself. His brother had been his biggest support in the city—in a way the only close relative he had known in his childhood—so he felt a special bond to him. When his brother died, Billu felt the force of his own failure mixed with helplessness but also a sense of relief. This mixture of emotions animates the story. He could articulate how he had failed his brother but could never say how his brother's life might have drained him of his own life. A straightforward narrative in terms of plot and characters is likely to leave out the force of that which remained mostly unsaid in his story and that which burst out on occasions without ever being integrated into the story he was ready to tell of his brother's death.

For all the love Billu had for his brother, there was one event that could enrage him whenever he talked about it, even after many years had passed. This was a marriage his mother had arranged for him in the village in which his brother had apparently connived. Lured by promises of a dowry, Billu's mother had arranged his marriage when he was barely fifteen to a much older woman. Soon after the marriage this woman ran away with another man, alleging, falsely according to Billu, that he was "not a man." Billu refused to return to the village, even for occasional visits, after that episode and for some years did not even talk to his mother and brother. Subsequently, he arranged for his own marriage through a neighbor. The girl, his present wife, turned out to be older than him and sickly, but he was determined that he would make a "good life" with her. The marriage cost him a fair amount of money, since the bride's parents begged him to bear the expenses of the bridal meal and later refused to reimburse him for it. Nevertheless, against the usual aura of superiority that wife-takers maintain in Hindu marriages, laying all problems in a marriage to the door of wife-takers, Billu could not bring himself to blame his wife.[6] He repeatedly reiterated that it was not his wife's fault that her parents were so mean. "I have never eyed anyone's money," he told me. From my experience of years of hanging out in this and similar neighborhoods, I can vouch that this was not the usual rhetorical stance through which moral claims are made by everyone from local politicians to the shopkeepers who fleece those in need by the high rates of interest they charge. Instead, his claim of caring for his wife and not for the material goods she came with was grounded in the small everyday acts through which he performed his love and care for her. I have seen him cook early in the morning before he goes off to work,

---

6. Although there have been considerable changes in the rules of marriage, the superiority of wife-takers relative to wife-givers continues to be an important feature of marriage exchanges. See Raheja (1988). See also Charsley and Shaw (2006).

fetch water from the municipal tap since water supply is very irregular, and try his best to comfort his wife during her frequent episodes of illness.

Two years after their marriage a son was born to them, but he died within the first month. From Billu's descriptions of the symptoms I suspect it might have been a congenital heart condition that remained undiagnosed. Billu used the term he often uses to describe how he cared for someone by saying "*bahut seva kari, jitna ho saka seva kari par nahin baccha paya*"—I served him a lot, as much as I was capable of serving him, but I could not save him.

After his son's death he began to have visions and dreams in which a woman in white beckoned him to come to her. He was frightened by this woman but could not decipher what she wanted. After many consultations with the local *ojhas* (diviners) he understood that the woman in white was a form of the goddess of the village (*gramdevata*) who blamed him for having forgotten the village. Billu arranged for a propitiation ceremony to placate the goddess, but in turn he set the condition that he would visit the village only after he was granted another son. The woman in white advised him to establish a silver idol of baby Krishna and also to make a pledge to perform *karseva* (acts of service such as sweeping the floors) at the local Gurudwara (Sikh temple) and especially to accept Guru Gobinda of the Sikh faith as his own guru. This complicated nexus of sacred beings that cut across caste, sect, religion, and locality to create a singular sacred being with whom the devotee enters into a completely individualized relation is not at all uncommon for the Hindus. In this case it draws from etymological connections—one of Krishna's name is Gobinda, referring to his pastoral past. Connecting this with the Sikh guru on the basis of a common name participates in a form of reasoning prevalent in these neighborhoods in which similar names are made the basis of a mystical, hidden connection. (Sometimes children who have the same name will call each other *sahnam*—the one bearing the same name rather than use the proper names.) So on the behest of this goddess whose identity remained obscure to Billu, despite the *ojha's* divination, he became a devotee of the child Krishna and a regular attendee in the local Sikh temple. He also pledged that if he were granted a son, he would call him Gobinda.

Billu's efforts to placate and please the various figures mentioned here bore positive results, and a second child was born whom he duly named Gobinda after the baby Krishna and the Sikh guru. The silver idol of the Krishna figure had been established in the house, and Billu went with his wife and newborn child to the village to offer thanks as he had pledged to the unnamed goddess in white.

It was about two years after this event that Billu's brother felt sick and died, leaving him very sad but also guilt-ridden that he had not been able to do enough for his brother. Although Billu did not mention this while he related this story in bits and pieces whenever we met, it turned out that at this time his wife had become pregnant again. In the process of running around between hospitals, his work, the various local diviners, and various agencies from which he had tried to get charitable donations for his brother's treatment, Billu just could not find the time to attend to his wife. Unlike many other women in the area who are quite resourceful in accessing locally available medical care, Billu's wife, though born and bred in the city, had never been able to care for herself. At the last moment, Billu got a locally trained midwife at the time of delivery, but the newborn son died of an infection the next day. This event occurred about one month after the death of his brother, though Billu brought it up only much later in a casual way in a conversation when I happened to ask him how his wife and children were doing. Having moved to the United States, I had not been able to visit him for many months after his brother's death and thought I would check out how his family and he were doing.

Billu told me that after his brother's death he had started having visions and dreams in which his brother would appear to him and accuse him of not caring for him. Billu always woke up frightened—the dreams he said were like coming face to face with an accusing figure he hardly knew rather than the brother he had known and loved, however ambivalently. He became convinced that the newborn child had been a reincarnation of his brother, but that in his anger he had refused to make life together with Billu and to accept Billu's service (*seva*). This is why the brother/son had decided to die. Once more, I note the cultural resonance with the widely held ideas that a newborn has to be persuaded to make life with the family he or she has been born into since the soul of the newborn is still attached to the life it left behind. There is also the idea that the recently dead are so attached to the living that they will try to take one of them on their new journey. What is specific to Billu's visions is the manner in which the possibilities of modernity fold into his life—new technologies such as transplant operations are both within reach of the poor now and yet out of reach. These create the singularity of the inner in which the responsibility for the concrete others expands in a manner that can rarely be fulfilled. For Billu the matter was laid to some rest by the vision of the woman in white who appeared to him and admonished him for not accepting the conditions she had placed upon him. This is how he said she admonished him:

> I told you that I would give you a son—that he would be blessed, for he would carry the blessings of the baby Krishna and of Guru Gobinda. I did not tell you that you could now call upon me to deal with every misfortune. Anything that takes you away from serving that son—my blessing, my *prasad* [an offering made to a god or goddess and returned to the devotee with his or her blessing imbued in it] in your house—the son who is yours only so long as it pleases me—anything that turns you away from him will incur my anger. I took responsibility only for him—not for anyone else—go and serve him.

Billu said he felt truly frightened of that figure, but perhaps the admonishing figure gave him some peace too. He repeatedly said that he could not understand the woman/goddess in white. If she is a goddess, he said, is she asking me not to pay attention to the needs of my mother or my brothers who are my blood, who gave me life? She is the one who took me back to the village, and now is it her desire that I serve her only through the medium of my son?

Questions and Reflections

What is the pressure that a case such as this might put on us? In thinking about Billu's story and its implications for understanding the human, I turn to the philosopher Stephen Mulhall (2009, 31–32), writing on the theme of the human and humanity:

> Our concept of a person is an outgrowth or aspect of our concept of a human being; and that concept is not merely biological but rather a crystallization of everything we have made of our distinctive species nature. To see another as a human being is to see her as a fellow creature—another being whose embodiment embeds her in our distinctive form of common life . . .
>   . . . Nonhuman animals too, can be seen as our fellow creatures in a different but related sense of the term. Their embodied existence, and hence their form of life is different; but in certain cases the human and the nonhuman form of

creaturely existence can overlap, interact, even offer companionship to one another, and in many cases nonhuman animals can be seen as sharing a common fate with us.

For Mulhall, we can see our connectedness to the nonhuman forms of life because of our embodiment: We share with animals the facts of a creaturely existence—susceptibility to pain, disease, and death. Embodiment, however, is no guarantee of understanding. In Wittgenstein's famous formulation, if a lion could speak, how would we understand what he had to say?[7] We share our vulnerability to death and disease with animals, but another vulnerability sets us apart from animals—our vulnerability to language. What if certain forms of nonhuman life that we imagine are embodied differently from humans and the language such beings use to express themselves partakes of our language but is also strange to it? Anthropologists have often imagined[8] that our kinship with animals expresses our kinship with gods and spirits, unlike the metaphysical imagination of Descartes in which our turning to the divine is a turning away from our animal nature and relegating the body to being a mere machine.

Billu's story suggests that the inhuman or nonhuman might teach us ways of being human in a spirit of wakefulness to ourselves and to others. Mulhall's quotation comes from his consideration of J. M. Coetzee's literary figure, Mrs. Costello, and the issues raised there on the condition of humans and of animals. In Coetzee's *The Lives of Animals* and *Elizabeth Costello*,[9] the main character, Elizabeth Costello, is a novelist and animal rights activist who appears to us mainly through a series of lectures and the events surrounding them. She suffers and expresses that suffering. Response to Coetzee's work has produced a stunning set of literary and philosophical reflections on how human beings wound each other in the course of their daily living (Cavell, Diamond, McDowell, et al. 2008). These deliberations compel us to ask how our companionship with each other and with nonhuman forms of life might be acknowledged despite or along with this wounding. The dominant sense on

7. Many writers on Wittgenstein refer to this lion. See, for example, Simon Glendinning (1998, 71) or Brian McGuiness (2002), especially the chapter titled, "The lion speaks, and we don't understand."

8. The classic position on this might be said to be that of Émile Durkheim ([1912] 2001).

9. See Coetzee (2001, 2003).

reading these musings by some of philosophy's most accomplished writers remains what Cora Diamond calls the "difficulty of reality" (Diamond 2008). There is something resistant to thought when we try to imagine the condition of being wounded that Mrs. Costello experiences when she sees ordinary and apparently nice people indifferently consuming animals killed for food. Something other than rational argumentation is called for in the face of this condition, not simply emotion or empathy as opposed to reason, but wakefulness—the state Billu reaches after the woman in white speaks to him about his duty to his son and the state in which we hope to listen to his story.

Cavell might say that Billu experienced finite responsibility—the spirit's command to care only for his son—as further wounding that forced him to reside in the ambiguities of wakefulness after the initial wounding of caring for others such as his brother. The events that cause his life to become a question to him include human and nonhuman forces, both the potentiality of organ transplant and the commands of the lady in white. Through her, we recognize that the desires that move beings such as gods, goddesses, ancestors, or jinns implicate human beings in their fulfillment but also pose great risks for the humans involved. Some concerns about the desires of the spirits are related to specific traditions that Hindus or Muslims evoke within Hinduism or Islam, but frequently divine desire crosses both social boundaries and boundaries between life and death. In his visions, Billu was confronted with two different modalities in which the occult world made its presence felt in the world of the living. In one modality, the dead seem to have entailments in the actual world: They had a history that connected them with the living in which love, betrayal, failed promises, and unrealized hopes provide some guidance to the living on how to interpret the sightings or hearings with which the living are confronted. Error and doubt are as much a part of this experience as belief, a reminder of the vulnerability to which human action is subject—mistakes made, excuses offered, guilt for failures in relationship. Such interpretations have most often been brought to mind when a dead relative returned. Although in Billu's case he was the one who stood accused, in other cases the dead themselves seek forgiveness. For instance, a father who had been unable to marry off his daughter because he had been too proud to accept any of the offers that came for her hand would appear in her dreams to seek her forgiveness so that he could be released from the sin of failing to perform the most sacred duty a Hindu father is expected to perform for a daughter. In either case there is a history to the relationship in which the possible world in which the dead now live carries with it memories of the world in which actions were undertaken, often unsuccessfully—a past imperfect that continues to impinge on the possible world in which the dead are imagined to be now having a life.

The modality of the lady in white was different. Her initial actions in insisting that Billu return to the village to placate the local goddess revealed her to be that local goddess but displaced from the village. At one level she created conditions for the continuity of Billu's relation to the village. Yet as events developed in Billu's life, she insisted that Billu limit his sense of infinite responsibility to the relations that were devouring him and commit himself to ensuring the survival of the child that he had received as her blessing. A simple explanation might be that her appearance authorized him to separate himself from the terrible responsibilities for the village that he was unable to meet and that this vision was a rationalization of his desire to dissociate himself from his past. There is surely some element of truth in such an explanation. However, the goddess in white belonged to a class of beings who could not be fully assimilated with gods, goddesses, or spirits whose mythologies, forms of rituals, or character were fully known. In this sense these emergent beings were like the emergent technologies whose form was transfigured as they were detached from the places in which they properly belong. Yet these two emergent entities took different lines of flight. The technologies expanded hope invested in the idea of the body as a machine while expanding the scope of obligations to kin to such an extent that the immediacy of material conditions and their limitations disappear from view. Conversely, the goddess in white attached Billu to his immediate life and asked him to saturate his immediate surroundings with care and love and make it livable. Two forms of the inhuman then conjugate with the human, one drawing the human figure toward kinship with machines and the second toward a relationship with beings of the occult world. The person then is an aspect of this conjugation of human and inhuman rather than an aspect of humanity as an abstract concept.

These relationships also draw attention to the capacity of human beings for displacement. Although well-defined ritual procedures might be described in terms of the felicitous conditions for illocutionary acts enumerated by J. L. Austin ([1962] 1975), especially the importance of first-person-singular utterances such as "I promise" or "I declare" and the stability of context, the visions and dreams that Billu and many others described to me might be thought of as improvisations on traditionally stable ritual acts in which the addressee is singled out and known as the recipient of the command/desire of the being that has chosen to speak, but the being itself has no clear standing. Billu did not recognize the lady in white. Initially she established her position by making him see what he had ignored, his obligation to the village. Then she freed him from that very same obligation: the past which was taking away his capacity to live in the present. Meanwhile, she also managed to establish herself as a goddess to be worshipped. Walter Benjamin (1986) famously distinguished between mythic violence and divine violence and saw the former as establishing the subject as one bound to the law while the latter struck against the injustice of law itself. Although many criticize Benjamin for not distinguishing sufficiently between the law itself and the injustices of certain laws (see Tuitt 2006), Benjamin's insight forces our attention to the idea that law as rule following might drain us of life, in the sense that our life might become machine-like. One reading of the bitter compromise or the difficulty of reality that we see in Billu's life is that, in his return to the everyday, he acknowledged the limits of his flesh-and-blood human self.

Carrying further the thought of how illness and misfortune connects humans to other modalities of being, we will meet Hafiz Mian who is a well-known amil (Islamic healer) in a neighboring locality in the next chapter. Through his life, I hope to show the burdens that healers bear as they confront everyday forms of suffering, the indecipherability of illness, and the marks of violent histories on their bodies and souls. If patients often experiment with disease to find the limits of the normal, healers (both recognizable as modern and as folk or traditional) too might be seen as those whose moral selves are defined by the stance they take toward the disorders with which they must establish an intimacy as a condition of their modes of being. Yet we cannot settle into a single, stable position with regard to what is the moral life of the healer in these neighborhoods. The encounters between healers and those they serve might carry the profound weight of an exchange of life forces, or they might turn out to be just a market transaction over a few pills. The next two chapters (5 and 6) take us into these uncharted territories.

FIVE

The Reluctant Healer and the Darkness of Our Times

The national newspaper the *Indian Express* reported on September 24, 2003, that a minister of state for human resource development, Dr. Sanjay Paswan, had honored fifty "traditional healers" in a function in Patna, capital of Bihar in east India. Wearing two coiled cobras around his neck, Sanjay Paswan is reported to have danced onstage and walked on fire to the rhythm of beating drums and ritual chanting. In explaining his actions, he said, "This is all futuristic science and hence needs promotion by the state, media and the civil society," and he added, "I am saying this with conviction, not politics on my mind." There were immediate demands for his expulsion from the ministry for "promoting superstition," but it was not easy to put the minister in any preexisting slots, for he held a PhD in physics from Ranchi University and was a Dalit, who had also produced an *Encyclopedia of Dalit Studies*.

I wish to take up the theme of the proximity of magic and medicine, not as cognitive categories but as embedded in practices. However, I start with this scenario to say that the healers who fall within the category of "traditional healers" or "practitioners of the occult" are not always separable from each other. What was "knowledge" for Dr. Paswan was "witchcraft" for his detractors. Occult practices evoke a sense of the clandestine but the ambivalence with which they are regarded is not purely a function of modernity, as many have assumed. Such practitioners of the occult are transgressive figures within both tradition and modernity, yet they are widely sought as we saw in the case studies. Curiously, our surveys did not capture this aspect of health-seeking behavior because people seemed to have assumed that while going to practitioners with degrees in Ayurvedic or Unani medicine constituted the kind of access that could be reported to investigators with survey forms in hand, the urge to seek remedies from *ojhas*, *bhagats*, *tantriks*, *amils*, and *maulavis*—all different kinds of occult practitioners—could not be reported until intimacy had developed between the researcher and the respondent.

Although I came to know several such practitioners over the course of time, there was something that remained veiled in our encounters. I did get to know Hafiz Mian, a Muslim healer, quite well, and it is his story I share in this chapter. I think Hafiz Mian felt a particular affinity with my life as an anthropologist, and my interactions with him gave me a glimpse of the complex lives and the burden of suffering that many healers bear. Because I am critical of the poor quality of care provided by practitioners in the low-income neighborhoods and I unblinkingly endorse the finding that people are put into grave risks by the modes in which medicine is practiced in these areas, I also want to acknowledge a strong need to understand the moral lives of the healers rather than simply condemning them for the failures of medical care in these neighborhoods. I cannot resolve the ambivalence I feel toward this issue, nor can I iron out the contradictory affects that run through this and the next chapter. The best I can do is to allow this ambivalence to be fully expressed.

The Amil and the Anthropologist

This chapter starts with a dream that happened to come up suddenly between us—Hafiz Mian and me—as unbidden thoughts often do, on one sunny afternoon in a small room in Jahangirpuri. Hafiz Mian is a Muslim man known in the neighborhood for his piety. He had performed the *haj*, was actively engaged in local politics, and defined himself as a healer (*amil*) who used forms of occult knowledge within the bounds of legitimate practice as set by the

Qur'an and the *hadith* (the sayings of the Prophet). Hafiz Mian had often shared with me his concerns over how to maintain the purity of Islamic teaching in his life and especially in the healing practices he employed to cure the many ills caused by beings of the unseen world. The term for the unseen world is *neadeeda duniya*, that which one cannot see with the eyes. It refers to beings of the occult world whose presence can be sensed with other organs such as those of hearing and touch, even if they cannot be seen. Several Hindu figures also emerged in this story that started with my dream and unexpectedly elicited Hafiz Mian's own travails over the practice of *amiliyat* (the knowledge and status of amil).

Hafiz Mian puzzled over the question of whether signs and symbols in dreams of a Hindu man or woman could be regarded as the secret working of Shaiytan (devil), as some passages in texts on interpretation of dreams within Islam might be read to mean. Guru Maharaj, a Hindu guru (spiritual guide), who remains unnamed in the story—a figure of imagination—appeared at an odd moment in Hafiz Mian's stories though his actual relation to Guru Maharaj, or for that matter, any other guru or any Hindu deity, never emerged clearly. Unlike some other figures in Hafiz Mian's narrative, such as "the priest of the black knowledge [*kale ilm ke pujari*]," Guru Maharaj could not be characterized as "evil," though he had, of necessity, to traffic with evil. Hafiz Mian's narrative managed to unsettle notions of clear boundaries between Islam and Hinduism, or between physical ailments and spiritual malaise.

Let me return to the dream that provoked some of this discussion. Sitting in the tiny *baithak*—a small room at the entrance to his house where he received visitors and clients, I saw that Hafiz Mian had acquired a copy of an Urdu book on dreams, titled *Khwab aur unke Tabir,* that claimed to be based on an authoritative book on dream interpretation, titled *Kamil Al-Tabir,* by Abu al-Fazl Hussain Ibn Ibrahim bin Muhammad al Tiflisi.[1] Because I had been allowed to spend some time with another healer, a low-caste devotee of Shiva

---

1. There are many popular books and pamphlets in Urdu on the meaning of dreams that circulate in Muslim localities. Scholars too have been fascinated by the textual tradition of dream interpretation in Islam (see Al-Bagdadi 2006; Blad 1856; Gouda 2006). Amira Mittermaier (2011) has provided an important analysis of the actual practices of dream interpretation on three different sites in Cairo, Egypt, that takes up the question of imagination in everyday life. None of these texts, though, asks questions about what it means to confront symbols of other traditions in one's dreams.

in his terrifying aspect (*raudra roopa*), I was aware that some people seeking a cure would bring up dreams or hallucinatory experiences during the healing session. What Hafiz Mian seemed to be seeking was the authoritative discourse on how to interpret dreams.

The preface to the book asked, "What is a true dream [*saccha khwab kya hota hai*]?" and went on to describe three types of dreams—first, a dream caused by purely physiological reactions of the body; second, a dream sent by Allah; and third, a dream sent by Shaiytan.[2] The first of these was not to be regarded as a dream at all because it did not convey news of another time or place.[3] The second was a true dream since it was sent by Allah and gives indications of what is to come. The third was a dream meant to spread confusion in the minds of the faithful and hence was to be regarded with great caution. Hafiz Mian told me that though his expertise was not in dream interpretation, his close engagement with practices of healing against the troubles caused by occult beings put him in special danger from the guiles of Shaiytan. Hence he was mindful of what dreams might tell—especially, as dreams were the only part of revelation left to humankind (to speak precisely, dreams are one forty-sixth part of revelation as per the Islamic tradition).

At this point, I mentioned that I had a recurring dream that left me somewhat bewildered because I could not fathom from where it could have come. This was the dream.

> I am going in a train but this is some earlier period of history. (It is not clear to me who the young woman I am calling "I" is in the dream. She certainly bears no resemblance to me as a visual image.) There are some British soldiers who come

2. I note here that according to some other amils, there are specialized angels and jinns who are responsible for sending good dreams and bad ones.

3. Naveeda Khan (2011) considers such dreams as manifestations of the concerns, anxieties, and weaknesses within the individual, expressions of the *nafs* or earthly spirit of the individual. These dreams, she says, are not the sites of psychic battles internal to the individual but of a self revealing its weaknesses to itself. Hafiz Mian was dismissive of such dreams as of no importance whatsoever. They were caused, he said, by gas or pain or numbness caused by sleeping in a wrong posture; you just need to turn over and the dream will disappear, he said. For Hafiz Mian true dreams were those that carried some intimation of the future —"*bisharaton ke siva, nabuyat ki koi chhez baki nahin*—except for the potential for intimating the future [in dreams] there is nothing left of prophecy in this world."

into the train. I know that an Indian revolutionary in the nationalist terror movement is in the train disguised as a Sikh, and it is my work to distract the soldiers so
that they do not discover him.[4]

The rest of the dream was completely confused. I know that the train kept
moving but never reached anywhere. I kept trying to engage the soldiers in
banter. There was a feeling of dread that pervaded the dream—dread that we
will be discovered at any moment, but all I knew was that the train kept moving. Nothing in the dream was ever resolved.

More than twenty years ago when I was working on militancy in the Punjab, I told this dream to Audrey Cantlie, who famously brought psychoanalysis
into anthropological work (and also the other way round) (Cantlie 1993).[5]
Audrey told me not to look for any deep meanings; according to her, my
dream probably meant that I knew in my heart that I was not able to understand terrorism. I did not offer this insight to Hafiz Mian, but my recurring
anxiety that I might be misrepresenting people I came to know intimately in
my ethnographic work because they were not really comprehensible to me
probably found expression at moments such as the one I was sharing with
Hafiz Mian.

Hafiz Mian first cautioned me that it is not so wise to tell one's dreams to
"just anyone" because if told to a person who did not know how to interpret
it, the dream could have dangerous effects in the world, transforming what
could have remained hidden and latent, into reality.[6] This was especially true
for the dreams sent by Shaiytan. He then pronounced that the fact of moving
away could be a harbinger of good news if you were going toward, say, a place
where you could see a *basti* (a settlement) with a market, a mosque, or other
signs of peaceful activities—on the other hand, going toward a wilderness
was not a good sign, though seeing green grass or trees was again a good sign.

4. My use of the terms *revolutionary* and *terror* captures the sense of how the person is
characterized in the dream—it is not a deliberative statement.

5. Audrey Cantlie was closely associated with THERIP, The Higher Education Network
for Research and Information in Psychoanalysis.

6. The hidden or latent does not refer to the latent content of the dream as in Freud
(1913) but to latent aspects of reality. In other words, telling the dream to the wrong person
could make what was only potential come into being in the world. Such dangers did not
attach to the good dream, but a dreamer cannot decipher what is a good or bad dream
without the help of an expert.

What was important, he said, was not what one saw but the feeling of dread (*khauf*) that I described. He feared for me since the signs of the dream were not clear. Perhaps a Hindu healer or a diviner would be better able to tell what such a dream meant and help me take precautions. I said that I had my own *ishta* goddess (beloved or chosen goddess) and that I left all to her wishes. The conversation moved to other things.

It was some time after this conversation that a woman from a Hindu family in the neighborhood who had been facing many difficulties persuaded me to accompany her to a local, well-known temple of the goddess Santoshi Ma which had gained a steady reputation for its miraculous powers in the last twenty years or so. One of the priests in this temple, she said, manifested the divine presence of the goddess in his body every Thursday. The common expression for the event is "*unki chauki lagti hai,*" which is hard to translate. Literally, it means he establishes a "*chauki*"—where we could think of *chauki* as a protected and sacred square space within which a ritual takes place for a limited duration. The term has migrated to other spheres so that a police picket might be referred to as *chauki*, and the term *chauk*, a masculine form of *chauki*, is the public space for a market or a public event. My Hindu friend told me that many people in the area had received solace and direction from this manifestation of Santoshi Ma and now regarded the priest as a guru to be consulted in the face of difficulties even when he was not possessed by the goddess.[7] Whereas on Thursdays the priest was to be approached as the goddess, on other days he was treated as a guru. As the goddess, he had special powers of divination, but when he came out of his trance as the goddess, he had no memory of what he had said but could give advice on how to follow what the "goddess" had said. My friend told me, "When you are presented before the goddess—you are not allowed to say anything except affirm what she tells you. Under no conditions must you say no." Hafiz Mian, when he heard that I was going to visit the temple and the injunction not to speak, said that indeed, the manifestation of the goddess might be able to discern my dream and what lay ahead since the proper thing for a healer was to be able to infer the true desires of the disciple without anything having to be told.

My visit to the temple was a bit of a fiasco, but to my astonishment, my Hindu friend just shook off the event by saying that the present priest had just

7. On the emergence and popularity of the goddess Santoshi Ma, see Das (1980) and Lutgendorf (2002a and 2002b).

inherited the *gaddi* (the seat) from his father and was perhaps not so adept. What happened in the temple (where most devotees were from the adjoining low-income areas) was, that despite my protests, I was ushered to the head of the queue of devotees standing before the divine presence. The attendants had warned me that the goddess knows all, and she would tell me why I had been brought in her presence. "Whatever happens, do not speak—you can only nod your head in the affirmative."[8] The priest as the manifestation of the goddess spoke in a falsetto, presumably, feminine voice, and pronounced: "There is a problem with your business—the profits are not coming." I remained mute—she quickly moved to another direction: "Ah, I see—someone is ill—do not worry; he will be cured." I was still mute—"nod your head," the attendant said to me, but I could not affirm this assertion of what had brought me there. After two more attempts, the priest/ goddess was a bit exasperated and asked, "So what is it that you want?" And for some reason, much to my own embarrassment, I blurted out, "*Gareebon ki seva karne ki ichha hai*—I desire to serve the poor." Promptly came the reply—"*Langar lagva denge* [we will have a *langar* (free public feeding) in your name]." I will not pursue the absolute tangle I had created. I could see as I waited for the details of the langar to be fixed that the priest/goddess did not have much difficulty reading the desires of others assembled there. This child looked sickly, so she would take the child in her lap and command, "Bring him again next week." This one needed a job; that one required the goddess to assure that her husband was released on bail. I felt a bit ashamed. If the unwritten contract here was that devotees came with desires that could be deciphered within this local moral world, I had failed the test as an ethnographer. But I could not have found a way to bear false witness to myself in the presence of the goddess in whatever form. My behavior closed some doors for me, but it opened other unexpected ones. Most important for me was that it crystallized a question: What regions of language were indicated by the two experiences I described? And what connection did they bear to forms of telling in relation to illness or

8. I might mention here that in the Vedic texts, gods do not speak to humans directly. Although the manner in which gods and goddesses speak to humans undergoes considerable transformation in later Hinduism, the appearance of fragments, rather than whole sentences, is a sign of divine speech such as the one I describe in this case and seem like traces of that past. I thank Charles Malamoud for pointing this out to me. This aspect of the speech of gods is described with great finesse in a conversation between Malamoud and Marcel Detienne (see Detienne 1995).

misfortune? First, there was Hafiz Mian's warning that telling a dream might make the latent possibilities of a dream real in the material world. The second was the expectation that the priest/goddess's speech would just emanate from her and would decipher desires without the devotee's having to express them in language. From both perspectives, it seemed that I had said too much. I wondered if this reluctance to put into words what would be a closure or an authoritative statement on oneself—that is, saying clearly what one wants—or making a dream come into the world by relating it—influenced everyday interactions around disease (a point I take up in the next chapter). I was yet to learn what it is to say too much. But this very failure on my part allowed a new conversation to emerge with Hafiz Mian.

Whose Dream Was It Anyway?

The next time I met Hafiz Mian, he told me that the text on dream interpretation that he was reading was very good because it was fully alive to the dangers that the Shaiytan posed; for Shaiytan cunningly manipulated the close relations between dreams and prophecy. One problem with our present understandings of such texts, he said, was the emphasis people placed on the faculty of *seeing*. Dreams, he explained, are partly about images that come to you unbidden (see Khan 2011) but also what you hear and what you sense.[9] Did you, for instance, *see* the figure of the revolutionary (*inqalabi*) in your dream? Did you *see* the figure of the British soldiers? I realized then that I had not actually *seen* who was hiding in the train; I had just known. Sometimes, said Hafiz Mian, there are people who appear in your dreams—and even when you are awake you can sense someone to be around you—who are figures from some other past (*kisi guzre zamane ki hasti*), but they have reality (*unka wajud kayam hota hai*).[10] He then proceeded to tell me the story of his own ancestors and how he had come to inherit the knowledge of an amil and how

9. Mittermaier tells a story about Ibn Sarin, the famed Arab writer on dream interpretation: He gave two different interpretations for the same dream because he "read" the faces of the two different men who told him about that dream differently. Mittermaier concludes, "According to this story, it is essential for interpreter and dreamer to meet face-to-face" (Mittermaier 2011, 62).

10. Compare Maurice Blanchot's (1982) formulation that the dream is the premonition of the other, it is not becoming another. See also Farbman (2005).

it made him walk a tightrope between *nuri ilm* (luminous knowledge) and *kala ilm* (black or dark knowledge) (see Ewing 1997; Flueckiger 2006, 119). I give some parts of this story to show how another figure—that of Guru Maharaj, a Hindu guru—found a place in this narrative and ultimately provided a clue to Hafiz Mian's concern that I might harm myself if I said too much, as I had on both occasions. Incidentally, it seemed like a good diagnosis of my many troubles.

Ancestral Memories

Hafiz Mian did not remember his grandfather or what he looked like, but he knew a lot about him. He told me about the life of his grandfather in a pretty straightforward way, but it is obvious that this narrative was stitched together out of many different stories he had heard from his aunt and his mother. Though voiced by a male amil, we might consider the story as a braiding of childhood memories with sediments made up of women's voices that convey dispersed experiences of affliction, terror, and healing. I use the indicative tense in what follows to convey that Hafiz Mian, in his telling, bestowed these stories with a kind of facticity. Toward the end he introduced a twist that might encourage us to reread this account a second time in a subjunctive mood—expressing wish, emotion, and possibilities rather than actualities. We might also learn from this play between actuality and potentiality to pose a question I have refrained from asking until now—namely, what is the mode of existence of illness and misfortune? The question is deeper than asking how we represent illness or even what the meaning is of illness and misfortune. Although I cannot resolve the question with some definitive account of the boundaries between illness and misfortune, what healers know and what patients know, I hope the discussion in this and the following chapter will take us to thoughts that touch each other on these issues.

Hafiz Mian's grandfather Nihal Shah was a chowdhury (leader) of a group of villages in the Sardanha Estate in the former North-West Provinces. The family, according to his account, belonged to a minor branch of the Muswi Sayyid family, the rulers of Sardanha, who claimed descent from Ali Muswa Raza, the eighth Imam, and had originally belonged to Afghanistan. Because of their closeness to the British and the services they had rendered during the historic Kabul mission of 1842, the Muswi Sayyid family had to flee their home when the British troops were defeated. They resettled in India and were awarded the Sardanha Estate. After the mutiny of 1857 the title of Nawab Bahadur was conferred on the ruler for his help to the English army. Nihal Shah was a relative by marriage of the dominant clan and was given rights to the revenues of a group of villages in the estate. According to Hafiz Mian, his grandfather was never very interested in either managing his lands or taking part in politics.[11] A different struggle was at stake for him.

11. I have no way of confirming whether the particular ancestry sketched by Hafiz Mian is correct. I found often that dates and names got mixed in his narratives so that names of historical personages and the dates do not always match the historical record. The Sardanha estate has a colorful history, which I cannot fully recount here. However, here is the description given in the *Golden Book of India* by Sir Robert Lethbridge (1900) that gives an alphabetical list of all titles bestowed by the British. Referring to the title of Nawab bestowed on Ahmad Shah Sayyid who succeeded to the estate in 1882, the description says: "The family are Muswi or Mashadi Sayyids, descended from Hayat Ali Musa Raza and originally residing at Paghman near Kabul. On account of services rendered to Alexander Barnes in his Kabul Mission, and subsequently to the English in their retreat from Kabul, they were expelled from Kabul and settled at Sardanha. When the mutiny occurred at Meerut, the head of the family, Sayyid Muhammad Jan Fishan, Khan Sahib raised a body of horses and men, consisting of his followers and descendants; accompanied General Wilson's force to the Hindan; was present in both actions and thence to Delhi where he remained with the headquarters camp till the city was taken when his men were employed to keep order in Delhi. For these eminent services the title of Nawab with a suitable *khilat* [an honorific robe]was conferred on him." Although Hafiz Mian did not know anything about the earlier history of this estate, Sardanha had been awarded as a jagir in 1777 to a German mercenary by the Mughal Emperor along with a title. The mercenary, Walter Reinhardt, variously identified as a carpenter, a butcher, or a gypsy, had arrived in a ship of the French navy that he abandoned and then offered his services to various princely kingdoms as well as to the Mughal Emperor, Shah Alam. He either had a mistress or was married to one Begum Sumroo, widely reported to be a dancing girl, who, at his death, succeeded him as the ruler of Sardanha. The story of her conversion to the Roman Catholic faith as well as the contentious case around her heir, Doyce Sombre, from whom the East India Company confiscated the estate on grounds of his "lunacy" is detailed in Fisher (2010) and Lall (1997). The *Imperial Gazetteer* of 1931 also mentions confiscation of estates that were later granted to Sayyid Muhammad Jan Fishan.

I give this lengthy description to make the point that different neighborhoods in Delhi contain very different kinds of stories. Amils or other kinds of healers and diviners in other neighborhoods have different kinds of pasts that bear on their relation to their practice in significantly different ways. To give one example, Anand Taneja finds that jinn stories in abandoned ruins in Delhi are hooked into the life of the city and its past in a different way than the stories of jinns that will emerge in Hafiz Mian's story, though events crisscross each other in these dispersed spaces (see Taneja 2010, 2013).

Hafiz Mian did not know from whom his grandfather received the knowledge of healing,[12] nor did he know much about the specific techniques his grandfather had used. The two most prominent features of Nihal Shah's life that he gathered from family lore were: first, about Nihal Shah's piety, since he was said to have specialized in reading *vazifa* (ritual repetition of certain texts in Arabic) and, second, that he had a special relation with two extremely pious jinns, Abu-Hassan and Atum. (Here I ask the reader to keep in mind my earlier statement that I render the following account in indicative statements to capture the initial sense of realism that Hafiz Mian bestowed on them.) Muslims consider jinns to be real creatures of smokeless fire, mentioned in the Qur'an and hadith (sayings of the Prophet). Jinns were created before Allah created humans, and just like humans, they are bestowed with free will. As in the case of human beings, jinns too are divided into different tribes, sects, and religions. There are jinns who have accepted Islam, and others who are kafirs (nonbelievers). Although Hafiz Mian did not know how the jinn named Abu-Hassan came to be an associate of Baba Nihal Shah, he had heard that Atum was of Mongolian descent and had taken the form of a child during a period when his grandfather was performing ritual austerities, such as fasting and forgoing sensual pleasures, in the Shavalik hills in order to acquire learning from Baba ji (an affectionate term that Hafiz Mian used for his grandfather). It was only later that Baba ji discovered that Atum was a jinn. Except for one fault—namely, that he had a very bad temper due to the warrior lineage from which he came—Atum was considered dutiful and devoted to Baba ji.

Some jinns like to inhabit the wilderness or are to be found near graveyards and abandoned buildings. Sometimes you can see a snake, and this might be a jinn who has taken that form since jinns can change form at will. Humans often fear jinns for their capacity to cause mischief. Shaiytan (whose Islamic name is Iblis), was a fallen jinn who fell into disfavor with God because he had defied God and had refused to prostrate before man. However, as attested in the Qur'an and the hadith literature, there have been many instances of pious jinns. Abu-Hassan and Atum, came from well-respected and high-status *kabilas*

12. The amils I know distinguish between those who make the ritual *taviz* or *falita*—sacred words or numerals inscribed on paper or metal and worn as protection or in the latter case soaked in water that is then imbibed—and those who help dealing with afflictions caused by occult beings—*bhut, pret, jinn vagerah ki harkaton se nijat dilana.*

(lineages). Baba ji did not call upon Atum very often, but with Abu-Hassan he would discuss matters of faith and events in the world. Hafiz Mian used the analogy of newspapers and said that Abu-Hassan brought news of different worlds since the jinns could travel into the lower skies and pick up news about future events. Though jinns are normally forbidden to take human form, Hafiz Mian said, they can take human appearance in the presence of pious people like Nihal Shah. Unfortunately for Hafiz Mian, these jinns who were the protectors of their family left after his grandfather's death and revealed themselves but once to his aunt, his father's sister. This aunt was the source of the stories of Abu-Hassan and Atum that Hafiz Mian had heard, hinting at an intimacy between Nihal Shah and his daughter that played a crucial role in the transmission of some knowledge of the occult that she acquired, though such knowledge is usually forbidden to women. According to Hafiz Mian, the family had gone into moral decline, and even if the jinns wanted to help, they were unable to do so, because they were not allowed to be present to those who had not observed the strict discipline of the amil. With this background on some of the occult figures (there were others such as *muakil, hamzad,* and various left-handed tantric occult beings that I cannot take up here), I turn to the first Hindu figure whose stories are braided with the story of the moral decline to which Hafiz Mian made an allusion. This segment of the story brings me back to Hafiz Mian's oblique suggestion that in order to decipher my dream I had to first understand how figures from some other past come to haunt one's life. We might also recall the section titled "Deadly Intimacy" in chapter 1, in which we saw how ideas of misfortune were anchored to the proximity of Hindus and Muslims in these neighborhoods.

Princess Padmini: Dangerous Intimacy

Hafiz Mian told me these episodes in the life of Baba Nihal Shah.

Baba ji was often lost in his own imaginary world (*khayali dunia*), but once when he was back in his *haveli* (private mansion with an inner courtyard), he was met by a group of elders from the village who warned him that a member of his clan was conspiring against him and that if he did not pay attention to his lands and to village affairs, then he was in danger of losing his position of authority. Worse, they told him that in his absence, an abandoned temple with an idol of Kali had become the meeting place of many amils of the dark knowledge (*kala ilm*) and that rumors of young girls being abducted and sacrificed were afloat.

Baba ji immediately summoned Abu-Hassan to his side and consulted with him as to what the best course of action would be. The jinn advised him to fortify himself by reading appropriate *vazifas* in a purified state.[13] Baba ji withdrew to his *hujra* (sanctuary and prayer room), made a circle around himself (*hisar dala*), and in that protective circle he meditated on the events in the temple.[14] With his mind's eye he could see that various nefarious things were being done and that even the innocent Hindus of his village were being deceived by the cunning priests of Kali, who, according to Hafiz Mian, was not even a goddess but Shaiytan who had taken that form.

Without describing every move that Baba ji made in countering this evil that had grown right on his doorstep because of his inattention, I will come to the point when Baba ji had entered the temple and gone into the inner sanctum where he found a beautiful young girl with flowing tresses wailing at her fate. The girl told him that she belonged to a Muslim family and had been brought there by guile and was to be sacrificed that night. Baba ji was so moved by her plight that he was about to take her hand into his to assure her that he would rescue her, when suddenly Abu-Hassan zoomed in front of him and forcibly pulling his hand away. He admonished Baba Ji: "What were you going to do, Baba Ji? Can't you see that she is a form created by Shaiytan?" The woman then revealed herself to be indeed a demoness (*rakshasi*) with a terrifying form. Baba ji immediately threw some black pearls he was carrying with him at her and recited some words, and she ran away screeching.

All would have ended well, and Baba ji would have destroyed all those priests of darkness, but he was unprepared for an attack from a host of beings commanded by the priest—including a fierce *kabila (lineage)* of kafir jinns (nonbelievers or those who have not accepted the truth of Islam).[15] He called

13. Vazifa is a practice of recitation of a prayer (*dua*) or of the name of God. According to the more strict interpretations of Islam, it can become *bidah*, or an incorrect innovation (which is a sin), if not performed according to the strict rules of Islam, but I did not sense any such anxiety on the part of Hafiz Mian.

14. It was impressed upon me again and again that an amil never performs any ritual or recites the vazifa without drawing this protective circle around himself, for his work attracts dangerous occult beings often sent by Shaiytan.

15. Like humans, jinns too are divided between Hindu, Christian, and Muslim jinns and perhaps even other divisions.

again on Abu-Hassan, but the jinn at that moment had been summoned by his own master, the sultan (ruler) of jinns, and he could not come precisely at that moment (*hazri na laga saka*).[16] Baba ji was forced to call on Atum, who was, of course, very powerful but not very poised. Seeing the enemy kabilas of the kafir jinns, he got into a fierce battle and in the process managed to also kill the girl.

Baba ji tried to control Atum's fury, telling him that the important thing at that moment was to rescue him from that place and not to get into a full-fledged battle since Baba ji's spiritual force was weakening. The result of Atum's impulsive behavior was that though Baba ji was able to escape from that temple, the soul of the girl who was killed by Atum became attached to Baba ji. That night she came to him in his dream and said, "I am Padmini. For years I was captured by the evil priests and had to do whatever evil tasks they asked me to do, but I have always longed for you. I am your slave. I am still not dead, for in my previous birth I committed myself to fire and was not given proper death rites. I have only one desire and that is to serve you. Please accept me as your apprentice."

To cut a long story short, Baba ji was stuck with the soul of this woman. He began to make her manifest by lighting a fire and reciting some verses so that the smoke would take her form but always within the protective circle. Gradually he became attached to her. Meanwhile under pressure from his family he got married and in the course of the next few years had five children. Hafiz Mian's father was the second, the eldest being a girl who was very pious. Baba ji made Padmini promise that she would always serve his family and would never harm them. None of his family knew about this secret relationship that had grown between them.

Once when Padmini was very adamant, begging and pleading that she wanted to become a proper disciple of Baba ji, he softened and allowed her to come with him to the forest where he was to perform some austerities for a period of forty days (*chilla*). He drew a hisar (protective circle) and began to read vazifa. With the help of a magical fire that he lighted he made a powerful *maukil* appear to aid him. And then he conjured Padmini to appear within the circle.

16. *Hazri* or *peshi* is sometimes used to refer to a trance, as it indicates the presence of a spirit. However, in this narrative *hazri* refers to the jinn presenting himself much in the way office workers indicate their presence by signing an attendance register.

I take a moment's detour to briefly explain the concept of maukil and its appearance at this stage of the narrative. A maukil is a category of angels who are deployed to do work on earth, and one of their main tasks is to protect the words of the Qur'an. Whereas a jinn can be commanded by an amil, the maukil cannot be so commanded. He might come to the aid of an amil but only if the amil is in a pure state and engages in recitation of the Qur'an. Although this much is agreed on in the various texts on amils and their practices, the amils in India, Pakistan, and Iran, according to Hafiz Mian, add another category of maukil because they have experience of this entity—the implication being that Islam in these countries lives in the company of other religions. This is the category of maukils who are guardians of scriptures of other religions and could be of demonic inspiration but are not necessarily so.[17] Finally maukils of each category can be divided between the *jamali* (gentle) maukils and *jalali* (fierce) maukils—corresponding to a division of jamali and jalali attributes of God. Nihal Shah was forced to call on the maukil because the jinn, Abu-Hassan, was not pleased with the fact that he was initiating Padmini into his dearly guarded secrets, and Baba ji wanted to avoid confronting him on this matter. Baba ji was confident of his own spiritual correctness so that he could trust that the maukil was of *nuri ilm* (knowledge on the side of light), for if bad energies flow within you, then despite your good intentions you can bring a bad maukil into your presence. Still, Baba ji would have to be on guard because neither of his trusted jinns was present—Abu-Hassan because of his distrust of the growing relation between Baba ji and Padmini, and Atum, because Baba ji did not trust him to keep his cool.

One strand of the story in the adventures of Nihal Shah that I need to introduce here relates to his having been summoned by the king of Nepal (Hari Singh, according to Hafiz Mian, but since Hari Singh Dev ruled a part of Nepal during the fourteenth century, there is a mix of names and dates). Anyhow, Baba ji had been successful in helping the king sire a son whom he named Shamsher. I cannot go into the manner in which historical references are folded into the narrative, but for the present purposes I only note that this

---

17. The subclassifications among these two types of maukils are subtle. For now, I only note that the maukils who guard other scriptures are not by definition evil but can be made the vehicles of demonic communications, while Shaiytan cannot influence the maukils that guard the words of the Qur'an since the words of the Qur'an are the major shields against Shaiytan.

relation to the king of Nepal appears off and on in the narrative to establish that the Hindu kings were very knowledgeable about the powers of Nihal Shah, gave him honor, and were apparently the source of his later riches. A Dev Shamsher Bahadur Rana did become prime minister of Nepal for a short period in 1901, but the name performs more a semiotic function and is not evidence of a historical connection between the historical Shamsher Bahadur and the baby bearing that name in the narrative,

I return to the moment when Baba ji is in his hisar with Padmini and the maukil. When they were in the middle of the ritual performance, a calamity occurred. Urgent news came that the king of Nepal (Hari Singh) was on his deathbed and had asked for Nihal Shah to be brought there immediately. Summoning Abu-Hassan, Nihal Shah sent him to Nepal to administer some medicines immediately while he followed with the help of Atum.[18] Unfortunately, the shah of Nepal died and Nihal Shah had to stay on for the coronation of his heir, King Shamsher.

It was many months before Baba ji could return to his village. On his return he learned the grievous news that since the hisar had been broken by his leaving in the middle of the ritual, evil spirits had gained access and that Padmini (or her conjured form) was killed magically and her corpse was ill treated—lit., *uski laash ke sath badsaluki ki gayi.* I do not know what the nature of this ill-treatment was. I have learned not to ask certain questions both because of the delicacy of the relationships I have to maintain but also because, frankly, I am afraid to learn.

Baba ji was successful in gaining access to the soul of Padmini, and he knew that unless proper *kriya-karma*—that is, death rites according to Hindu rituals—were performed, her tortured soul would continue to wander and be used for various nefarious rites. It is important to note that the treatment of dead bodies and their proper burial or cremation is a major preoccupation in the world of amils. Hindu corpses that have been cremated but not given proper postcremation rituals and feasts are a source of danger. The amils on the side of darkness can capture their ashes, which carry all the potency of illnesses and misfortunes that the dead man or woman had suffered. Such

18. Here I should note that even though he was an amil, Baba ji was not able to overcome the constraints of time and space whereas jinns, such as Abu-Hassan and Atum could move from one place to another in the blink of an eye.

ashes, known as *masan*, can be fatal if fed or rubbed on someone's body. I draw attention to Hafiz Mian calling the rites *kriya-karma* and not simply disposal of the dead, showing the linguistic and ritual intimacy between Hindus and Muslims, especially among amils and tantrics. I also note that while we would be inclined to think of illness and misfortune as an attribute of the living, for those who deal with the occult the sufferings of the dead are as important to address. This is similar to the idea of Kwon (2008, 2012) that one way in which ancestral cults in Vietnam have mutated is to find a place for the spirits of American soldiers who died in Vietnam and to slowly absorb errant ancestors who sided with the Americans in the Vietnam War. Dealing with turbulent events of the past and their traces in the suffering encountered every day seems to be a task that figures such as the amil and the guru have to perform as a condition of their ability to heal. But dealing with these traces also darkens the soul, as we will see.

I return to Nihal Shah. As he was preparing to perform the rituals for Padmini's soul, she again begged him to let her stay as she did not want to leave his side. Baba ji agreed on two conditions. First, she was never to become manifest unless called upon by him or one of his descendants. Second, she would undertake to ensure that the knowledge of an amil, that he was proud to hold, would never disappear from his descendants. The reason for the second condition was that Baba ji was already apprehensive that his son (Hafiz Mian's father) was not showing any inclination to take on the work of an amil; he was much more interested in horses and in sports than in pursuing the knowledge that Nihal Shah had gathered with such difficulty. "With the decision to believe Padmini, and to spare her soul from total annihilation, my grandfather planted the seed of a poisonous plant in the lives of his descendants," said Hafiz Mian.

The Flowering of the Poisonous Plant

Let us move to the tumultuous years of 1946 and 1947 and the upheaval that the Partition caused in these regions. Nihal Shah had died a few years earlier. The movement of the Muslim families in the villages of Sardanha began with the abduction of two girls from a poor family who had gone out to the forest for daily ablutions during a relative calm and were captured by a group (*jatha*) of young Sikh men.[19] Hafiz Mian's aunt's young daughter, who was barely twelve years old, had gone out with them, unknown to the elders. When news came of their capture, the aunt was utterly distraught. For the first time after the death of Nihal Shah, she went into his sanctuary and started to read a vazifa that Nihal Shah had taught her to be used in case of an emergency. The aim was to summon Abu-Hassan. When the jinn came into her presence (*hazri lagai*), she started crying and said, "Abu-Hassan, what kind of friend are you? Have you not seen what misfortunes have befallen on Nihal Shah's family, and you have not once cared to inquire about us?" Abu-Hassan gently explained that had to obey the order of the jinns, and he was not free to come into anyone's presence to give aid unless the person was an accomplished amil. Unfortunately, he said, Nihal Shah's son has abandoned the ways of his father. Abu-Hassan consoled her by giving her news about her daughter—all three girls, he said, had killed themselves to save the honor of their families. Strangely, this news, instead if adding to her agitation, calmed her, and she asked Abu-Hassan what she could do to save her family.[20] He urged her to abandon the village where, he said, Muslims were no longer safe. He regretted that he would not be able to visit them any longer, but he hoped that these adverse circumstances would teach Nihal Shah's son (whose name, I learned, was Gulshan) that the inheritance of an amil is not be squandered away. Then he left.

That night, under the cover of darkness, the family left their traditional haveli. They split into two teams. One team consisted of Hafiz Mian's father, two of his uncles (one father's brother and one mother's brother), his elder aunt, and a few other women and children. They left for Pakistan hoping to catch up with other Muslims on the way there. Hafiz Mian compared this to the *hijra*, the Prophet's migration to Medina. The second team consisted of Hafiz Mian, his mother (with whom he was left behind in India), another uncle, and some other relatives. They began a journey to a small town in Himachal that was to remain in India where some of his matrilineal relatives had a

19. The term *jatha* implies an organized and often mobile band of young men on the move, usually in warfare or in guerrilla-type resistance. The implication here is of organized violence by the Sikhs against the Muslims during the Partition.

20. The strangeness that I register here was pointed out to me by Hafiz Mian. It does not reflect any astonishment on my part, since this was the standard narrative of heroic sacrifice by girls and women that I had heard many times in the course of my earlier work (V. Das 2007).

summer residence. His mother's family was from Delhi. "Before I tell you what happened to me," continued Hafiz Mian, "let me tell you about what happened when the *kafila* [caravan] of my relatives reached Lahore, for, unknown to them, Padmini had now attached herself to my father. My aunt was the only one among them who knew about the pact made by Nihal Shah with Padmini; so what happened then put my father into complete confusion."

Although Hafiz Mian glossed over what he had heard about the travails faced by the group as they traveled through the nights toward Lahore, he mentioned that due to the rains, some women and children caught fevers and died and that the men had to fight marauding bands of Sikhs. His descriptions were vague. This vagueness stands in contrast to the specificity of events he described pertaining to the inheritance of *amiliyat*—figures of the occult or the *nadeeda duniya* were semiotically dressed with names and attributes of personas, place names as well as dates—a point I will elaborate in the concluding reflections.[21]

In this storied past, the topography of Lahore in these turbulent years was defined not just by the overt political events of independence for India and Pakistan and the mass movement of populations across the borders but also by vast changes taking place in the occult world. The most significant aspect of this turbulence was the ominous fact that the dead had been disturbed.

Hafiz Mian's aunt subsequently returned to India after a fight with her brother (Hafiz Mian's father). Hafiz Mian told me, almost shamefacedly, that his father had promised to come and take mother and son with him later, but he never returned. They learned from various relatives that his father had met and married another woman, a *muhajir* (a term referring historically to those Muslims who performed the hijra with the Prophet but here referring to migrants who went from India to Pakistan). For Hafiz Mian the father is the cause of his mother's sorrows and also the one who abandoned the obligation

---

21. For the moment le me just flag the fact that anthroponyms, toponyms, and chrononyms are more in evidence for the occult beings than for the people in Hafiz Mian's life. Thus, for instance, his mother throughout remains *ammi* and aunt remains *phuphi*, whereas subjects of collective travails are referred to as "women and children of the house." Men are given proper names more often than women in his narrative, but the greatest elaboration of personal traits is reserved for the occult beings. This dressing of semiotic figures exhaustively by names, dates, and locations might be compared to the iconization of figures geared toward creating a referential illusion or a facticity.

to carry on Nihal Shah's legacy, leaving his young son to carry on this burden-some task. Let us go back to the occult events in Pakistan in its early years.

Hafiz Mian said that there were two kinds of places in Lahore at that time that were full of dangers for Muslims—one consisted of the temples (mainly Kali temples, but he also mentioned Bansidhar temple,[22] which used to house an image of Lord Krishna) and the second consisted of the cremation grounds. Hafiz Mian's father, Gulshan, and the rest of the family, including his two uncles, had found a house in an area inhabited by the ironsmiths near the Ravi River. It is here that his father discovered that an abandoned temple on the edge of the cremation ground by the river was inhabited by the worshippers of the dark knowledge dominated by a priest by the name of Ramdev. These worshippers consisted of both Muslim and Hindu amils, and their activities were spurred by the fact that riots had left many dead without any proper cremation rituals or proper burial. As I noted earlier, dead bodies, the exhumed dead, as well as ashes from hastily cremated bodies, are considered to be potent resources for the practitioners of black knowledge.

A further set of events led Hafiz Mian's father to realize that as the descen-dants of Nihal Shah, his family and he were in great danger from the amils of dark knowledge, who would take revenge for the humiliations inflicted on them by Baba ji in his lifetime. The black amils had managed to lure his two uncles (the ones who had accompanied his father to Lahore) to become amils of the dark knowledge—a complete betrayal of Nihal Shah's legacy. His father would thus have to force his way into abandoned temples to free the two men, follow them to the cremation grounds where they were meeting up with amils of all kinds and summoning the jalali (fierce) maukil, who were guard-ians of other scriptures, in an attempt to bring them back home. Hafiz Mian's aunt was certain that somehow Padmini was aiding and abetting these events, so she told her brother (Hafiz Mian's father) about the pact that Nihal Shah

22. I have been unable to find references to this temple in the literature on Lahore. However, a survey of temples and cremation grounds in Lahore in 2005 found a temple on the banks of the Ravi near an earlier cremation ground that is called the Krishna temple and is supposed to be maintained by the Pakistan Balmiki Sabha. The survey, however, notes that the secretary of the Balmiki Sabha contended that this temple was a Kali temple at the time of the Partition and that followers of Ram and Krishna do not want of offer worship there. In the story that follows, I think the reference to a temple near the cremation ground might refer to this Kali temple.

had made with Padmini. "In telling my father about this pact, my aunt dug a deep abyss in which the whole family would fall," said Hafiz Mian.

Hafiz Mian's father, never one for restraint and patience, called on the soul of Padmini and reminded her that she had pledged that she would ensure that Nihal Shah's knowledge would be protected and transmitted to his descendants. Now, he said, his brother and brother-in-law were in danger of betraying that very knowledge that was precious to Nihal Shah, and he was summoning her to help. What he did not realize, said Hafiz Mian, was that calling out to Padmini released her as a force into the world.

Once Padmini was released and the constraining hand of Nihal Shah was removed, Padmini became the full embodiment of every imaginable evil impulse. She made the children suffer by igniting magical fires so that they felt they were burning, but the fire was not visible to anyone. She caused children to die, blinded one, and was in general a figure of fury and revenge.

It was at this stage that Hafiz Mian's aunt returned to India and pleaded with him to take on the mantle of his grandfather. Hafiz Mian was completely untrained in the arts of the amil's practice, but she recalled the close relation that Nihal Shah had maintained with the royal court of Nepal. She sent him there in search of a powerful guru who was a very old man now but who would still be able to give him some of the knowledge that Nihal Shah had shared with him. From this guru who was also the royal astrologer, Hafiz Mian learned the basics of what it was to draw the protective circle, how to recite appropriate vazifas, what duas (individual prayers) to read when in doubt so that Allah could send him the right message in the form of a dream. Although all of this seemed to Hafiz Mian to be legitimate knowledge (*nuri ilm*), the guru told him that Nihal Shah had been able to summon the help of jinns who had saved him from the priests of darkness as was the case in his encounters in the Kali temple. But now, if Hafiz Mian had to deal with the wild and satanic forces let loose by Padmini, he would have to take a decision to trust himself completely to a companion that the guru could direct him toward but who could only be conjured by work that Hafiz Mian had to perform himself.

It turns out that this "work" was a meditation he had to perform in the cremation ground with the help of a mantra for forty consecutive days (*chilla*). Hafiz Mian was not able or willing to give details of this apprenticeship, but at the end of this period, he was befriended by a very ordinary-looking man who told him about a secret destination to which they would have to head. Hafiz Mian described to me his apprehension that he was being led into non-Islamic practices, but the fear that Padmini would devour his whole family over-whelmed him though he also felt that he was risking his own destiny now and in the hereafter (*akhiriyat*) for the sake of a father who had abandoned them. He even feared that this companion was no other than the one-eyed liar (Masish ad-Dajjal), the false Prophet who is said to appear at the end of the world to lead the pious astray and against whom the Prophet warns in one of the hadiths.

Guru Maharaj and the Scene of Darshan

I had fully expected Hafiz Mian to say that the secret destination was some cave in the Himalayas, because some of the Hindu diviners or healers I have worked with always have a segment of the story in which meditation in a secret cave in the Himalayas figures in some way. I was surprised, then, when Hafiz Mian told me that the secret destination turned out to be Sindh in Pakistan. His companion and he had gone there without having obtained official visas, traveling through the deserts of Rajasthan. In Sindh they headed to the shrine of Hazrat Lala Shahbaz Qalandar, the well-known Sufi saint of the Suharwardi silsila. And it is from here that a miraculous journey ensued.

Hafiz Mian and his companion were given a direction and a piece of paper on which were written some words in red ink. Walking through the night, they reached a deserted village with an old abandoned Kali temple. There was a thick darkness that enveloped everything. There in front of the temple they recited the words, and as if by a magical key, the scene shifted, and they found themselves entering a golden gate. Inside a woman in white ushered them into the presence of a luminous person, but Hafiz Mian could see that there were signs of the dark magical practices having been performed—black pearls, a vessel full of red liquid that looked like blood, skulls of animals. Hafiz Mian was repelled, but, to his surprise, his companion bowed reverentially before this figure and said, "Guru Maharaj, we have come to your sanctuary. We do not have recourse to any other person against the terror [*atank*] of Padmini."[23]

23. It is again part of the semiotic dressing of these occult beings that the companion spoke in a sanskritized Hindi whereas Nihal Shah, the jinns, and even Padmini spoke more in Urdu.

Guru Maharaj spoke with a voice that resembled rumbling clouds and he said, "Do not speak of any terrors. We know this is the grandson of Nihal Shah—that is why we have permitted you to come here because Nihal Shah's grandson cannot be denied."

Guru Maharaj then invited his two visitors to take their seats in the presence of the image of Kali. Hafiz Mian said that he had always been scared of the image of Kali, but that day when he learned that all the amils of India and Pakistan, whether of the nuri ilm or the kala ilm, whether on the side of light or the side of darkness, were gathered there, he saw that the darkness of Kali was like the blueness of the clouds that signified the Prophet. He saw that her tongue that was sticking out was not that of a blood-demanding demoness but of a shy girl who has inadvertently done something wrong. He participated in some ceremonies that he did not understand, but at the end of them Guru Maharaj conjured the image of a woman he learned was Padmini. Guru Maharaj said, "Should the last rites be performed for you, Padmini? You have suffered enough over the centuries, now leave Nihal Shah's family alone. They are not the ones who made you suffer. Do not torment yourself, and do not torment them." But Padmini just laughed and said, "I have brought the grandson of Nihal Shah into your presence. I have fulfilled my promise to him. But even you, Guru Maharaj, are not capable of releasing me."

Hafiz Mian said, "Guru Maharaj told me, 'Go, my son, and learn that you have to fight evil. This is not evil that *you* have put into the world—maybe this Padmini is a young princess over whom the powerful kings fought—Muslim kings, Rajput Kings. Maybe she is just a girl whose corpse was insulted like in the satanic madness [*vahshiyat*] during the Partition, but the hurts that have been caused cannot be just taken away. If you want to pursue nuri ilm, you will have to first know what is darkness, what is the black ilm that Nihal Shah's own act in forming a pact with Padmini let loose in the world, gave her *wajud* [reality, being].'"

Hafiz Mian concluded suddenly and almost as an anticlimax, "This is how I came to be an amil. But no one understands how difficult the world of the amil is—he is always scared of early death, of mistaking the evil for the good—but this is the life that was intended for me." And then as I was ready to leave, he said, "Truthfully speaking, I cannot vouch that all this happened—these were stories I heard from my aunt—were they true? Was Padmini the legendary princess of Padmavat?[24] Can we ever be free from the imagination of the past [*mazi ka tassavur*]? That is why I said to you, maybe that revolutionary terrorist hiding in the train that you are trying to protect in your dream, may be he has *wajud*—find out what kind of *wajud*, just as I try to find out what stories I am destined to hear here as an amil. This anthropology that you do, maybe it is like amiliyat."

The Wajud of Illness, of Misfortune, and of Healing

I have asked myself often, do Hafiz Mian and I inhabit the same world? The philosopher Nelson Goodman (1978) famously argued that there are not many different versions of one real world but that there are different actual (as distinct from possible) worlds. In one reading of Goodman, one could say that he is pointing to the fact that any description of the world needs a frame of reference. For instance, within one frame of reference the sun never moves, while within another, the sun moves from the east to the west. But do the terms *sun* and *moves* mean the same thing in the two sentences? Goodman is not proposing a complete representational relativism but arguing that there is no neutral world with reference to which these claims can be adjudicated. Thus there is no way of aggregating pictures of the world described under different frames of reference to provide one composite picture. But neither is one entitled to say that no pressure is exerted among these different descriptions. But then, as he says, one never just stands outside as a judge would, and asks, Which world is genuine and which is spurious? These questions arise because we are always thrown in the middle of worlds that are being made (see Das, Jackson, Kleinman, and Singh 2014).

24. Hafiz Mian is referring to a legend depicted in Jayasi's poem "Padmavat" (1540), about the historic siege of Chittor by Alauddin Khilji, the Delhi emperor, in 1303 in order to seize Padmini, the legendary beauty and the queen of Chittor, for himself. According to the story, when Alauddin Khilji captures her husband by stealth, she, along with other queens and women of the palace, consign themselves to the fire. Alauddin enters Padmini's palace triumphantly but is only able to find her ashes. Although the medieval language of Hindawi in which Jayasi wrote is not widely understood, the story circulates in school textbooks as well as in popular literature. Hafiz Mian is not familiar with the poet, but he knows the legend. The historical accuracy of this legend is much debated.

It is interesting for me that Hafiz Mian and I both made a deep connection with each other (I think) because a certain skepticism regarding our experiences—mine with anthropology, his with amiliyat—haunts our lives. This is not simply an opposition between theoretical formulations that are systematic and implicit ways of living, but a struggle over what gives reality to the stories we have heard and the experiences of suffering that have deeply moved us. As Webb Keane (2013) notes, the ontological commitments we make carry ethical implications. For Hafiz Mian, his mode of caring for the world involves deep doubts about the status of the knowledge that he is compelled to use. He is well aware of the Islamic ideas of *kufr* (not accepting Islam or concealing that acceptance) and *shirk* (idolatry) and ever watchful of his own practice in terms of the sins of idolatry or of denial of the truths of Islam. He is acutely aware of the fine line between nuri ilm (the knowledge on the side of light) and kala ilm (knowledge on the side of darkness). Yet he has received his amiliyat from Guru Maharaj, and he has been taught that there is evil in the world and that in order to cure people, he will have to experience the darkness of evil that has been put into the world. He experiences amilyat as a burden. In the next chapter we will see that this is a common theme among the practitioners of the occult, whether Hindu or Muslim, whether belonging to upper castes or lower castes. Though less forcefully articulated, the theme also resonates with the way other practitioners expressed the weariness of having to deal with so much illness, suffering, and death. Similar to the way Hafiz Mian feels burdened by his knowledge, I too feel burdened by the fact that I cannot quite grasp what constitutes the wajud of the illness experiences I have documented. I try to grasp their reality through surveys, through elaboration of singular cases, through the impact that illness has both on the body of the person suffering and on the relations that are implicated in determining the course and severity of an illness experience. As an anthropologist deeply committed to an understanding of radical diversity, I respect the way people will run to an exorcist, a trained physician, a laboratory, or a hospital in an attempt to get to the bottom of the question, What ails me? For Hafiz Mian such questions cannot be answered without taking into account the history of the country, the proximity of Hindus and Muslims, the deep ambiguity of kinship, the presence of evil spirits, and the whisperings of the devil. For many other practitioners in the area, illness is purely the point at which a quick commercial transaction occurs between patient and healer. In order to treat illness they must subtract it from all the things that Hafiz Mian and others like him think belong to the illness itself. How does that affect the reality of illness?

In the next chapter, I take these questions to the diversity of practitioners who populate the neighborhoods I studied and ask what defines their technical and moral stance toward illness? As I indicated in the introduction, I move to a different scale in the next two chapters, asking how still other worlds are created around the prevalence and threats of illness. So what happens to ethics when we move to the markets and to global health policies? My hope is that, although we cannot think of a neutral world that would provide the perspective (the God's eye-view) and that would make these questions commensurable to each other, we can perhaps offer a critique of the technical bureaucratic apparatuses through which extremely rarefied discourses on poverty and illness circulate in the world of experts, on the one hand, and of the practices adopted by practitioners who function in low-income neighborhoods, such as frequent use of injections or quick transactions that end up in dispensing medications, on the other. Each of these worlds then might be seen as capable of providing a critique of the other as well as developing some disquiet about itself.

SIX

Medicines, Markets, and Healing

Although much public health discussion on India has focused on access to medical care, studies show that in both urban and rural areas (despite some exceptions pertaining to remote areas) quality of medical care poses a more pressing problem than access to medical care. For instance, based on a systematic survey of a random sample of households in one district in every state in India, authors of a recent study find that an average household in rural India can access 3.2 private and 2.3 public paramedical staff within their village (see MAQARI, Medical Advice Quality and Availability in Rural India, cited in J. Das 2011). In Delhi there are seventy practitioners (most of whom are private practitioners) within a fifteen-minutes walk of every household. The extent of medical training varies in all these sites. In rural Madhya Pradesh 65 percent of practitioners accessed had no formal training whereas in Delhi only 10–15 percent had no formal training, although what formal training consisted of showed wide variation (see J. Das, Holla, et al. 2012). A majority of visits by patients in this study were to providers who functioned in the private sector. In another study based in rural Udaipur, Abhijit Banerjee,

Angus Deaton, and Esther Duflo (2004) reported that out of 0.51 visits to a practitioner in a month that a person made on average, only a quarter were to a public facility and, further, that the rich used public facilities more often than the poor. In the urban cases we discussed in chapter 1, the opposite was true. In the next chapter, I discuss the implications of these findings for the broader issue of quality of medical care in urban and rural India. There is little doubt, though, that measured in terms of the competence of practitioners to recognize and diagnose a disease or assess the appropriateness of medicines they dispense or prescribe, the quality of care received by patients within this milieu is very poor indeed.

How do the practitioners in the private sector who have set up shop in these neighborhoods see their own practices? Are they indifferent to such questions as the quality of care that the patients in these neighborhoods receive? Why is there what the literature calls a know-do gap, in the sense that even when doctors in both the private and public sector in poor neighborhoods know what is to be done, they do not apply that knowledge to patient care? Was the story of Hafiz Mian and the complex terrain it covered regarding the existential burden of attending to misfortunes applicable only to the healers in occult traditions? Do those who attend to physical illnesses treat their patients as nothing more than sources of income? Do they see their transactions as distant arm's-length transactions appropriate to the impersonality and anonymity of the market? Or are there multiple perspectives with which we can see the practices that various healers engage in?

My aim in this chapter is to simply relate the multiple ways in which practitioners described their craft, their understanding of what kind of work they do, their relation to money and to sundry other practices. As in chapter 1 where we saw that there were no strict boundaries between symptom and diagnosis, and that words, objects, techniques and narratives carried histories of actual interactions between patients and healers rather than being bound by one system of medicine or another, here too we will see how the same practitioner who dispenses an antibiotic might also wave a trident of Lord Shiva on a patient to let divine energy flow into the patient, or another might define himself as practicing "scientific medicine" as he freely administers injections and intravenous drips. My aim is to try to see if we can understand these practices as part and parcel of the forms of life that grow them while also showing how the different practitioners in the same markets provide implicit critiques of their social milieus.

The data I present is based on surveys conducted for the ISERDD–World Bank study (see the various references to the work of Jishnu Das and Jeffrey Hammer in the References at the back of the book),various casual discussions with practitioners during cups of tea and snacks as I was invited into their shops or clinics, and twenty detailed interviews with practitioners who hold various kinds of degrees in alternate medicine conducted by ISERDD staff.

Who Are the Practitioners in Low-Income Neighborhoods?

I begin with a straightforward account of the distribution of various kinds of practitioners in the seven localities in the study, comparing the kind of practi-

Table 6. Distribution of practitioners according to qualifications

Code	Type of practitioners	All localities	Four low-income localities	Three middle-income and higher-income localities
1	No formal qualifications[a]	16	11	5
2	RMP[b]	37	29	8
3	BAMS/BUMS/BIMS[c]	120	102	18
4	MBBS and higher degrees[d]	189	47	142
5	BHMS/DHMS[e]	47	14	33
6	Others[f]	82	60	22
Total		491	263	228

Source: Survey conducted by ISERDD and World Bank, 2002.

[a] Practitioners who have no formal education but may have acted as apprentices to a practitioner or may have simply set up shop.
[b] Registered Medical Practitioner. Those who use this appellation might have a degree or diploma but are primarily recognized on the basis of their experience. The term "experience-based practitioner" is also in common use.
[c] Holders of degrees (BAMS or BUMS) in alternative medicine (Ayurveda and Unani) given by state-certified medical institutions.
[d] Degrees in biomedicine (MBBS/MD) that follow a standard curriculum in a recognized medical institution.
[e] Degrees in homeopathy (BHMS/DHMS) similar to BAMS or BUMS
[f] A mixed bag of practitioners, including holders of degrees in correspondence courses offered by private institutions without state certification or with a general degree such as a high school certificate or a graduate degree in a nonmedical subject.

tioners one finds in low-income localities with those in the middle-income and high-income localities.

In order to understand this particular distribution of practitioners between low-income, middle-income, and high-income neighborhoods, I briefly visit the debates on the role played by different kind of practitioners in the context of the health of the poor. The wide variation in the training of practitioners reflects a struggle between the state and organized groups of practitioners over the pedagogy and practice of medicine (see Jefferey 1982).

The state's attempt to control medical practice and training in India can be traced back to the Medical Registration Act of Bombay, enacted by the British colonial government in 1912, which legislated strict fines on anyone pretending to be a registered medical practitioner (RMP). Similarly, the Indigenous Medical Inquiry Committee (Punjab) set up in 1938 by the colonial government stated that it was "imperatively necessary" that the practitioners of indigenous systems of medicine should be controlled. The colonial state also had to contend, however, with the fact that such control was not easy to implement and that any draconian measures to regulate medical practice could potentially destabilize existing economic arrangements and thus create resentment against the government. Thus the 1938 report went on to add the following qualification: "We have also taken in view the economic aspects of the matter, the present day need of the public and the profession, and are of the opinion that an embargo on practice on persons who hold no diploma and degree but have been in practice for a number of years now will throw out of employment a large number of practitioners who will find it too late in the day to embark on a new career. We, therefore, recommend that there should be three classes of Registered Practitioners" (cited in Government of India 1948, 50–51). Scholars of health policy in India have argued that despite the ambivalence toward indigenous healers expressed in almost every official report, the Government of India (GOI) continued the colonial government's policies on health care (Jefferey 1982 Bala 1992; however, Banerji 1981 holds that enough support was not given to traditional practitioners as resources were shifted to support modern biomedicine).

There have been renewed attempts by the government to systematize the practices of alternative medicines since the 1990s. Thus a Department of

Indian Systems of Medicine and Homeopathy was created in 1995 under the Ministry of Health and Family Welfare to give greater attention and support to indigenous medicine. This department was renamed AYUSH (Department of Ayurveda, Yoga and Naturopathy and Unani, Siddha and Homeopathy) in 2003. According to the policy statements made by the Ministry of Health and Family Welfare, the newly constituted department would focus attention on education and research in these fields. According to the ministry handouts, there would be serous attempts to "upgrade AYUSH educational standards, quality control and standardization of drugs, improving the availability of medicinal plant material, research and development and awareness generation about the efficacy of the systems domestically and internationally" (www.indianmedicine.nic.in). The policy discussions need sustained analysis, but this is outside the scope of the present book.

My main concern in this chapter is to understand how practitioners who have received training through a wide variety of methods—ranging from apprenticeship to training for the degrees of BAMS (Bachelor of Ayurvedic Medicine and Surgery) and BUMS (Bachelor of Unani Medicine and Surgery)—understand and practice their craft. Given that we found no pronounced difference in the way practitioners with different kinds of qualifications use biomedical products such as injections and pills, the weight of the discussion needs to shift from traditional versus modern medicine, as if these were two fully constituted separate systems of knowledge and practice, to the way practitioners gather information and skills that they employ in their techniques of healing.

As we can see from table 6 there was a concentration of practitioners with degrees in BAMS and BUMS in low-income localities. Some practitioners in this category received training in state-recognized institutions whereas others took correspondence courses that did not require any practical training with patients. However, as we shall see, most people in these categories (as also in categories that I classify as containing untrained practitioners) had acquired skills through apprenticeship with a father or an uncle or by working in formal institutions as guards or as helpers of one sort or another. As an aid to understanding the proliferation of degrees and qualifications we encountered in the field, see the accompanying figure.

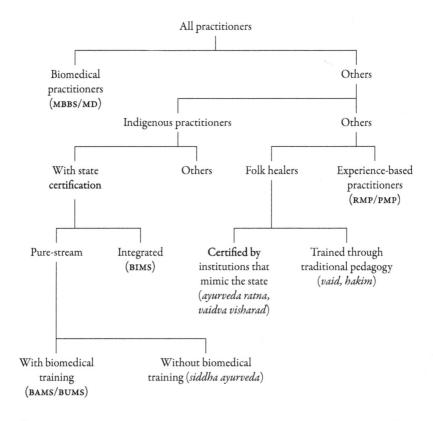

Key:

Ayurveda ratna: degree by correspondence given by various literary societies—literally, "jewel of ayurveda."

BAMS: bachelor in ayurvedic medicine and surgery.

BHMS: bachelor in homeopathic medicine and surgery.

BIMS: bachelor in integrated medicine.

BUMS: bachelor in unani medicine and surgery.

MBBS: bachelor of medicine and bachelor of surgery .

PMP: private medical practitioner or practitioner in experience-based medicine (title assumed by those without formal training).

RMP: registered medical practitioner; most lack a formal degree but do have a state license to practice.

Siddha: a form of ayurveda found primarily in Tamilnadu.

Vaidya visharad: degree offered in ayurveda from various organizations.

Deciphering the Signs in the Market

The different categories, therapies, and techniques at play strike one forcefully as one walks through the bustling markets in which the clinics and shops of the practitioners and pharmacists are located. Billboards and signboards announce what services one can get at this or that doctor's clinic or shop, what kind of degree a practitioner has, and in which institution the practitioner trained. Yet unless one has spent considerable time in these markets, it is easy to be misled by these signs. In some cases the name of one practitioner on the signboard nestles with that of another, who might have the same kind of degree but from a government-certified institution. One might never actually find the second practitioner in the clinic, and it may well turn out that this is the name of a son or a son-in-law who is also a practitioner in a different clinic: The father or father-in-law simply feels entitled to use the son's or son-in-law's name to give a better impression of his own clinic and to augment the clientele.

The following account based on direct observation for a day in a clinic in one of the neighborhoods might give some flesh to this picture.

Ms. Sundar is a typical patient who lives in urban Delhi. There are over 70 private-sector medical care providers within a 15-minute walk from her house (and virtually any household in her city). She chooses the private clinic run by Dr. SM and his wife. Above the clinic a prominent sign says *"Ms. MM, Gold Medalist, MBBS"* suggesting that the clinic is staffed by a highly proficient doctor. . . . As it turns out Ms. MM is rarely at the clinic. . . . We later learnt that she has "franchised" her name to a number of different clinics.

Therefore, Ms. Sundar sees Dr. SM and his wife, both of whom were trained in traditional Ayurvedic medicine through a six-month long-distance course. The doctor and his wife sit at a small table surrounded on one side by bottles full of pills, and on the other, by patients who sit on a bench that extends into the street. Ms. Sundar sits at the end of this bench. Dr. SM and his wife are the most popular medical care providers in the neighborhood, with more than 200 patients everyday. The doctor spends an average of 3.5 minutes with each patient, asks 3.2 questions, and performs an average of 2.5 examinations. Following the diagnosis the doctor takes two or three different pills, crushes them using a mortar and a pestle, and makes small paper packets from the resulting powder, gives it to

Ms. Sundar and asks her to take it for two or three days. (J. Das, Hammer, and Leonard 2008, 94)

Although many of the observations in this account would hold for other clinics in the area—such as bottles full of pills, the mortar and pestle, perhaps a thermometer and a blood pressure monitor (sphygmomanometer)—not all clinics attract two hundred patients a day; some get as few as nine or ten patients in the whole day. Nevertheless, the point that you cannot infer from what you see advertised as to what or whom you will find in the clinic is very well taken. Further, although the organization of space and of the objects in the clinic described above clearly indicate an exclusively medical setting, there are some other clinics in which various ritual objects such as a trident or black knotted threads hanging from a peg indicate that relief from the oppressive forces of the occult or remedies for spiritual malaise might also be found there.

Consider Dr. Saraswati, the owner of Poonam Clinic. We learn from the signboard on his clinic that Dr. Saraswati has a BAMS degree from some unspecified institution. The name of another practitioner, also with a BAMS degree, is inscribed on the board, though we usually find only Dr. Saraswati in the clinic. There is a large image of the goddess Kali and a trident resting against a wall. One day when Purshottam and I were passing by, Dr. Saraswati beckoned us to come in, ordered hot cups of sugary tea and began to ask us about our work. A woman came in to consult him, and we rose to leave but he gestured for us to stay,

The woman did not wait for him to ask what troubled her and instead poured out a story of an indifferent husband and a dominating mother-in-law. She said that his mother unduly influenced her husband, and she wanted a remedy for this situation. "Do something that he begins to listen to me." Saraswati asked her to get some sugar from the nearby market. When she returned with a packet of sugar, he recited some silent mantra over it and then blew over this treated sugar. He also gave her a black thread tied with thirteen knots placed at equal distances and said that she was to wear that on her wrist. Every morning she was to feed her husband tea with that sugar, undo one of the knots, and in thirteen days her husband would be completely under her influence. The use of this class of mantras, known as *vashikaran mantras*, is commonly understood in the popular imagination to exert a force that would make the person to whom it is directed completely under the spell of someone on whose behalf it is executed.

As we resumed our conversation, other patients came for consultation and medicine. One woman brought her young daughter who had a fever, and Dr. Saraswati gave her a syrup and a tablet. He did not check the child's temperature but looked at her eyes and her tongue. The woman kept up a lot of chatter. "See that she is properly treated—she is the only girl in this large joint family—she is the goddess Lakshmi of our house—if she does not get well her seven brothers and her uncles will come to beat you up." Dr .Saraswati smiled; clearly he knew the woman from previous encounters. As she was leaving with her medications tucked in her purse, she said "at least do a little more"—looking meaningfully at the trident. Dr Saraswati picked up the trident and briefly touched the girl's head with it, muttering a mantra under his breath. The woman left happily with the child.

A lot of local knowledge is packed into the encounters between Dr. Saraswati and his patients. I would be inclined to call them clients but prefer to use the terms that he employed to refer to them. There is nothing on his signboard to indicate that he might be able to give relief in such matters as that of an indifferent husband. However, he has a reputation in the neighborhood as a *tantric* (a learned practitioner of the left-handed, or clandestine, sacred) among those who respect him and also fear him; as a *bhut pret wala doctor* (doctor of ghosts and spirits) among those who seem to hold him in some contempt for taking advantage of people's naivety; and finally, as a "doctor"—the holder of a BAMS degree and part owner of an adjoining pharmacy from whom you can always pick up a medicine or two. This is what accounts for the wide range of maladies (physical, spiritual, and kinship related) for which people come to consult him, though compared to the first clinic he has overall few patients.

In the course of the morning we spent chatting with Dr. Saraswati we learned many things about his sense of himself as a practitioner, especially what he considered to be his qualifications to undertake the work he performed. Saraswati's own story of how he came to become a practitioner of the kind he is emphasizes his quest for the goddess. He was not searching to become a healer, as was the case in some other instances. He told us that as a young man he used to have repeated dreams about a beautiful woman who was beckoning him, though he could never discern who she was and what the meaning of the gesture was. Someone advised him that he should go to the holy town of Rishikesh, at the foot of the Himalayas, where he might find a guru or anther learned person who would be able to tell him what was required of him. After wandering around in the Himalayas, he found a guru, from whom he learned that the beautiful woman of his dreams was the goddess Kali. The guru instructed him to meditate on the goddess to achieve *sidhi* (perfection or completion). That, he learned, was the meaning of the dream.

Dr. Saraswati undertook what is known as *ghor tapasya*, a kind of fierce penance, during which he stayed in a cave in the Himalayas, survived exclusively on meat and liquor—foods dear to the goddess—and meditated exclusively on her form, expelling every other thought that came unbidden during the meditation. At the end of this period, the goddess was pleased, appeared before him,[1] and gave him a mantra with the injunction that he was to use it to alleviate the suffering of others. "But then," he continued, "something else happened. What happened was that the mantra that the goddess blessed me with gave so much power to my ordinary words that anything that I uttered would turn out to be true. If one wants to return to ordinary life, then carrying this kind of power is not possible." He explained that he might say something carelessly, or he might get angry with a child and in that momentary anger mutter some angry words, and what if they turned out to be true? "So, I decided to pursue a form of worship [*upasana*] that was more imbued with the *sattvik*, calmer qualities.[2] I stayed in a cave for another six months, meditating upon the god Hanuman and subsisting on milk and fruits till Hanuman gave me his blessings, and my powers were tempered with some quality [*bhava*] of peace and tranquility."[3]

I was curious as to why someone who had undertaken such severe penance and received the injunction to use his mantra to alleviate suffering was inter-

1. Did you actually see her, I had asked, and he had replied, I had seen her as one sees a goddess.

2. The term *sattvik* refers to the *guna*, or quality, of peace, purity, and a sense of calm. It is the first *guna* among the triad of *rajas* and *tamas*. For an exposition of the triadic structure of *gunas*, see V. Das (1985). It might be tempting to think that Saraswati's caste status as a Brahmin is consonant with his return to a sattvik power. Such an explanation, however, would be somewhat hasty, as the form of *ghor sadhna* associated with various Tantric practices such as illicit sex and eating of impure foods does not correspond with caste hierarchy.

3. The elaboration of both these deities, Kali and Hanuman, in the various Tantric texts is extremely complex. It is interesting that, at the local level, the division between the two types of meditation has been mapped onto the difference between *rajasik* and *sattvik gunas*. Whereas Kali, along with the nine other female deities known as *vidyas*, is associated with Tantric practices primarily in Bengal, Frederick Smith (2006) observes that Hanuman has emerged as one of the primary deities for possession in India, especially in his five-faced form.

ested in getting a degree in Ayurveda. Dr. Saraswati explained that having a degree of any kind in hand was necessary to save oneself from police harassment. Why would he not use his extraordinary powers to protect himself, I asked. "I do not want to use my powers for minor things," he replied. "For instance," he continued, "the woman who wanted me to say the mantra over her daughter who had fever—I could not do so because that would have been a waste of the great occult powers that have to be used sparingly. Her daughter had a simple fever—one or two antibiotics would have sufficed. One has to use ordinary [*sadharan*] remedies for ordinary illnesses. But I cannot give medicines unless I have a degree to show. So that is why I got this degree through a college in Rohtak, and I also put my son's name on the signboard. It wards off the lower-level officials who are always after a bribe."

Dr. Saraswati was not the only one in the area who had acquired a degree through distant learning, committing test lessons to memory but with no experience of working with actual patients during the training. These degrees, I remind the reader, are different from the BAMS degree offered by state-certified institutions where residency and clinical rounds in a hospital are required as part of the curriculum (see Langford 2002). So how do such practitioners with degrees through distant education actually get to learn how to give injections (which they frequently do) or what medicines to dispense or prescribe?

Medical Knowledge as Craft

An ubiquitous category of doctors who practice in Delhi are known as "Bangali Doctors"—the term is a composite of several predicates—their hailing from West Bengal, their training in indigenous medicine with degrees in BAMS (Bachelor of Ayurvedic Medicine and Surgery) or sometimes BHMS (Bachelor in Homeopathic Medicine and Surgery), and for their practice among both rural and urban poor. Although in other places, such as in Uttar Pradesh and Bihar, this category of practitioners overlaps with that of *jhola chaap* doctor—lit., doctors marked by the medicine bags they carry—here, in Delhi, it is Bangali doctor that dominates the landscape. One such doctor is Nandan Ghosh, about twenty-eight years old, who has a small shop in one of the shanty clusters in NOIDA, where he sells his services.

Dr. Ghosh had been practicing in this locale for the preceding five or six years when we met him in 2012, but he planned to go back to his village in

West Bengal. He studied through the eighth grade, and then he obtained a "degree" in RMP (Registered Medical Practitioner). He informed us that there are private institutions located in Kolkata that offer such courses leading to their eligibility to practice medicine. There is indeed a smattering of institutions in Kolkata (and perhaps in other places) that define themselves as "service providers" to those who have some experience as practitioners in alternative medicine. An example of one such institution is the Institute of Alternative Medicine located in Shyam Bazaar in the old part of the city, which offers to admit those who have a degree or a diploma in any subject along with an "experience certificate" that they have been practicing alternative medicine for at least three years. The institute aids the practitioner in the process of legally acquiring the status of Registered Medical Practitioner on payment of a fee and also offers courses in plant medicine, veterinary medicine, dental and oral hygiene, and electrohomeopathy to augment their qualifications. Although RMP is not a degree but a process of registration, in local parlance practitioners refer to it as a degree, as did Dr, Ghosh.[4]

From Dr. Ghosh's description of his practice, it became clear that the sources from which he picked up what fragments of knowledge and techniques he applies to his practice are varied. He said that after the short course in Kolkata he initially joined an uncle whose practice was located in a small rural market. There he learned how to administer glucose drips and to give injections. His uncle did not have any degree in medicine but was a very experienced practitioner. So it was by listening to how he advised patients, which medicines he gave, and what the diseases were that he treated that Dr. Ghosh first mastered the techniques that he employs now. He moved to NOIDA because another uncle who had a BIMS (Bachelor of Integrated Medicine and Surgery) degree practiced here. Dr. Ghosh said that in NOIDA he had learned about medicines from a salesman who visited the shanty settlements and the markets there to sell medicines to doctors like himself. Basically he learned that if the patient had a fever, then you could give a paracetamol with an antibiotic. He could recite the names of some well-known brands. In addition some laboratories had started sending rep-

---

4. Gillian Lê (2013) describes what she calls "everyday corruption" around renting and trading of certificates for traditional healers of Chinese medicine in Southern Vietnam and argues that it was not the certificate that a healer earned but the reputation for efficacy that was seen as essential to establish his or her practice.

resentatives to the markets and even to the shanty settlements who advised doctors that for any fever that lasted more than a few days they should get the patient tested for typhoid. So in those cases Dr. Ghosh now calls a technician from the laboratory who draws blood from the patient and lets him know the results of the WIDAL test (a presumptive serological test for enteric fever) by the evening. He prescribes "heavier" antibiotics for the treatment of typhoid.

Dr. Ghosh's sense of himself was that he could deal with ordinary diseases—fever, cough, cold, mild diarrhea—but that he immediately referred patients to another facility if he sensed that the case was beyond his competence. He classified such diseases that he could treat as "normal" diseases. "It is also the case," he said, "that the environment in NOIDA was so fraught with danger that if he were to treat a serious case and the patient were to take an adverse turn, then people would attack his shanty, break up his clinic, or even beat him up." He had witnessed such events and was therefore very cautious about how he treated his patients, how he talked to them, and how he treaded between diseases that are "normal" and those that can become "critical" (serious in his terminology). Dr. Ghosh planned to go back to his village after gathering more experience and is hopeful that his practice will flourish there because of his kinship connections. He was also optimistic that with his degree and experience he might be able to get a job in a government health setting as an assistant to physicians who have a proper MBBS degree (Bachelor of Medicine and Bachelor of Surgery equivalent to the MD in the United States) and permanent jobs in the health sector.

The Private and the Public

Although most practitioners in the category of alternative medicine followed the kind of trajectory Dr. Ghosh described, making use of kinship connections and networks to move between village and town, others had taken advantage of opportunities coming their way through experience in government-sponsored health-related programs, where they picked up enough expertise to set up their own practice. Dr. Manishekar Yadav's case, whose small clinic is located in Patel Nagar in West Delhi, illuminates this route.

Dr. Yadav was employed as a health educator on contract basis in the public health sector and was posted in a PHC (primary health center) in Madhubani

District in Bihar.[5] Each health educator, according to Dr. Yadav, was in charge of one block (a subdivision of a district), and his work was to spread awareness on family planning and immunization. In 2005 when the Rural Health Mission of India was established, these jobs were redefined and several health workers lost their jobs (see Mavalankar, Vora, and Sharma 2010). According to Dr. Yadav, there is a Supreme Court case that is pending on this issue, but he was not able to give any details on the case.

After he lost his job, Dr. Yadav earned both a bachelor of science degree and a BAMS degree. Initially, he earned some money by dispensing medicine to people in areas in which he had established contacts through his work as a health educator, hoping to be reinstated in his job. He explained, "There too in the PHC it was health-related work—multipurpose work. When you are a health worker, you have to do everything, whether it is the work of a peon or of a technician. So in those six or seven years in Madhubani when I was without a job, I did the same kind of work privately. During that time I also gathered these degrees." Asked how he managed to secure admission to the educational institutions and about the kind of training they gave, he said he knew someone with whose help he "managed" it: "I managed everything sitting at home [*ghar bathe*], and once I got my degree I moved back to Delhi." It is possible that Dr. Yadav was referring to the markets in certificates and degrees, which flourish in many towns, but it was not possible to pursue this line of inquiry further. Like Dr. Ghosh, this practitioner too was modest in his self-assessment. He too used the term "normal diseases" to refer to the kinds of complaints for which patients sought his advice and was categorical that if the patient did not get better in three or four days, then he would consider that the case was "beyond his understanding." In the course of discussion he did mention, however, that he knew the names of several antibiotics but only administered "lighter ones"—*halke phulke* antibiotic. He had also experienced pressure from patients occasionally that he must "do something." For instance, he recalled that a patient came to him with terrible back pain and insisted that he wanted treatment right there because he was tired of going to various hospitals. "I gave him an injection called 'penidual,' which is a 'high' antibiotic—I had to give him four injections before he became better." It is quite possible that Dr. Ghosh was referring to Penidure, a brand name for a generic benza-

---

5. See Government of India (2006) for a description of the public facilities and health infrastructure in a typical Indian district.

thine penicillin, often used for treatment of bacterial infections such as syph-ilis and rheumatic fever. However, in his classification the basic difference was between "light antibiotics" and "high antibiotics," not broad-spectrum antibi-otics or disease-specific ones. Like Dr. Ghosh, his main source of information and supply of medications was a local salesman.

There were other cases of low-level employees in government hospitals or paramedics in mobile health units who used the information they had picked up through observation to set up their own practice. In all these cases, the techniques were learned through an apprenticeship, and the medicines to be dispensed or prescribed were learned through networks of salesmen and phar-maceutical company representatives who operated in the market. Although some practitioners remained at the level of applying biomedicine as pure tech-nique, others seemed to have added greater depth to their understanding of medicines, injections, and drips through aligning them with other concepts such as those of poisons, and of a more complex idea of action itself.

Medicines and Poisons

It was a woman in Jahangirpuri who first drew my attention to the way that the idea of medicine also evokes the idea of poison. She gave me examples of an immunization that she said was nothing other than injecting a bit of poison in the body so that it could fight the poison in the disease. She made a distinction between home remedies and the medicine one got from a doc-tor by saying that the reason home remedies did not have side effects whereas antibiotics and medicines for depression that she had been taking had side effects was that the latter contained poisons. A good doctor is one, she said, who can balance the power of the medicine with the power of the disease.

This issue became a recurring theme in the discussion ISERDD members had with practitioners in their interviews. In ordinary everyday talk on medi-cines and injections, though, the theme was not frequent. Quite interestingly when I was growing up in a low-income locality in Delhi in the fifties, I remember the talk used to be all about how "hot" allopathic medicines were as compared to the home-brewed *kadhas* (bitter syrups) and pastes of various plants, which we were given as prophylactics to counter the ill effects of dif-ferent seasons. I did not encounter the hot-cold distinction any more in the context of medicines, but the idea of certain inherent dangers in the use of medicine has reappeared with the help of a new vocabulary.

Dr. Sarkar, another Bangali doctor in the main market of Jahangirpuri with a very successful practice, explained to me that earlier, diseases were gentle whereas the diseases we confront now have become "stronger" (*tagadi bimari*). "Who had heard of all these new diseases then? Now there is AIDS, TB, asthma, and everyone seems to be suffering from something or the other. This is because people do not get nourishing food. All the chemicals that are put in the ground take away the nutritional properties of food. So the medicines are now much stronger and harsher on the body."[6] He explained that the skill of the practitioner lay in being able to match what innate strength the patient had to fight the disease, how virulent the disease was, and how to use the medicine so that its poison could be turned into a healing potion. Dr. Sarkar had completed a four-year degree course in BAMS in Patna, which included clinical experience under the supervision of his teachers. He seemed far more confident than the other Bangali doctors I described earlier and also had elaborate ideas of the drama of disease and healing in the human body.

"If one wants to learn about the craft of the doctor, one can only learn it by observing those who are sitting in the market, not from those who practice in government dispensaries. I am not talking about the big doctors in big government hospitals like AIIMS (All India Institute of Medical Sciences)." I asked, what was so specific to the craft of those who practiced in the market? Dr. Sarkar in response to this formulation of the specificity of his craft explained that in the government-run dispensaries, the medicine that patients received depended completely on what "supplies" were received by the dispensary. The dispensaries, he explained, did not have any autonomy over which medicines they could order. "The government contracted with pharmaceutical companies or with government-run production centers for supply of medicines—in some months they might have Tetracycline in stock—so all patients coming to the dispensary that day regardless of what ailment they have will be given Tetracycline—another day the stock of medicine is exhausted—so everyone will be made to buzz off with just aspirin." (Incidentally, my own experience of the government dispensaries and outpatient departments of government hospitals in the vicinity of low-income localities shows that the description was not far off the mark.)

6. For similar ideas on nutrition expressed by farmers in rural Uttar Pradesh, see Gupta (1998).

Dr. Sarkar then went on to describe his own techniques of matching medicine to not only the disease but also the patient. He said that pharmaceutical representatives from several companies visited his clinic, as they did other doctors in the area. These representatives (known as medical representatives, or MR) are different from the salesmen described by Dr. Yadav and Dr. Ghosh in the sense that they are employees of pharmaceutical companies, whereas the salesmen are private small entrepreneurs. However, like the salesmen, medical representatives too are major sources of information for practitioners in these areas.[7] Dr. Sarkar then elaborated on how he used the information that he got from medical representatives. "You see, there are many doctors who just buy the medicines and then give them to patients in a very indiscriminate way. But one must ask why do some patients get better if they take an antibiotic of one company but not another? You must have seen that some medicines 'take' on some patients but not on others [*kisi ko dawa lag jati hai, kisi ko nahin*]. It is only with experience that a good doctor learns how to match medicine with the patient and not just with the disease. This is what is meant by balancing the 'poison' in the medicine with the body of the patient and the nature of the disease. Otherwise anyone could pick up names of medicines and give them to patients. That might work for colds and coughs and headaches but not for diseases that are difficult to treat."

Healing as a Gift and a Curse

On probing further the question of how a doctor really knew which medicines and which brands would suit one patient but not another, Dr. Sarkar was hes-

---

7. For a perceptive analysis of how global production and distribution of pharmaceuticals defy the processes of standardization see Petryna and Kleinman (2006). For a scathing analysis of how pharmaceutical companies influence medical decisions in Argentina, see Lakoff (2005). Stefan Ecks and Soumita Basu (2009) argue that the use of antidepressants has moved from psychiatrists to general physicians to rural medical practitioners in West Bengal. Unfortunately, their paper takes a rather simplistic and accusatory view of rural medical practitioners as simply unlicensed practitioners. Thus they show little curiosity about how these drugs are actually used by either practitioners or patients in different clinical settings. These authors concentrate much more on showing that it is not global capital that is influencing drug use in India but unregulated local practices that lead to increasing use of these products. Their models of agency and understanding of what constitutes a market retains a charming innocence about the ethnography of global capital.

itant to answer at first, but then he reluctantly admitted that this was an issue of "*haath ka hunar*." The term *hunar* (an Urdu word) could be translated as a composite of art, attainment, and skill, and the possessive term *haath ka* is equivalent to "of the hand." Indeed, many patients when comparing one doctor with another use such terms as "*unki dawa lag jaati hai*—his medicine takes on me," or "*unke haath mein hunar hai*—his hands have art/skill." "However," Dr. Sarkar continued, "it is not through the cultivation of skills or apprenticeship with a great physician that gives one *hunar*—rather it is through applying yourself to your work as you know best that you become aware of another healing force that flows into your hands through some mysterious divine process. This is why no doctor would ever claim that his hands have hunar. It is, they will say, for others to say so about them." In other words, the statement suggests that the healing that occurs in a case is only partly through the effort of the doctor; the other part is to let your hands be the recipients of a gift over which you do not have any control.

Not all practitioners gave much thought to this aspect of healing. In fact, some, like Dr. Ghosh and Dr. Yadav, were quite explicit that their profession was like any other profession or skill; it was the means of earning a livelihood. Even Dr. Sarkar will administer injections primarily because he says that this is the era of science and speed, and most people want the doctor to look "scientific" and in tune with a world that is moving fast. Despite all this, the theme of gift and service (*seva*) surfaced in discussions often enough for me to think that there is a model of action here that is quite distinct, in that agency is the composite of a remote actor and an actor present at the scene of action. Moreover, it is not simply that the subject (the healer) projects his knowledge outward to the object (the patient), but he receives something back from the patient—namely, the endorsement that he has *hunar*, which allows the medicines to work. I take up this issue later in the Conclusion, but one cannot but be reminded of Claude Lévi-Strauss's (1967) classic essay on the sorcerer and his magic or the question of the symbolic efficacy of healing.

In the essay Lévi-Strauss analyzed a ritual performed by the Kuna of Panama to assist a woman in the case of a difficult childbirth. He based his analysis on a text compiled by Henry Wassen and Nils Homer in 1947. The ritual consists of a recitation of a long and difficult journey undertaken by the shaman to the dangerous land of spirits where after some bloody battles, he rescues the soul of the woman abducted by Muu, a malicious spirit who targets the womb of women. Weaving a complex series of metaphors as the recitation proceeds, the shaman presents the woman's body as a theater of a mythical battle in which the task is to free the woman from the clutches of the malignant spirit and thus allow the child to be born. Through the use of a web of metaphors the ritual transposes the present event onto a symbolic plane and thus into a larger collective story. Lévi-Strauss's claim was that through this psychological manipulation the shaman was able to elicit a physiological response from the woman. The shared symbolic space created by the shaman allowed the suffering woman to gain control over a previously intractable situation, converting difficult labor into a normal one.[8]

Many scholars have criticized Lévi-Strauss's analysis: Most significantly, Carlos Severi (2007) has argued that the shaman performs his ritual among the Kuna in a highly esoteric language, so what the woman hears is a long and monotonous sequence of unintelligible words. Severi contends that what the ritual does is not so much to transpose the suffering of the woman into a larger story of a mythic battle by semantic means but rather that by providing an acoustic mask—sounds that create the right environment through performative acts—the woman is enabled to take distance from her pain and thus gain control over the event (see also Severi 2002).

Anthropologists have questioned the thesis of symbolic efficacy on several grounds. Many have pointed out that rituals fail (Laderman 1997); sometimes performances of possession are seen as staged and thus treated as suspect by participants (Gold 1988); and in any case, even a genuine diviner or shaman might face skepticism in his early career (B. Singh 2014). Yet anthropologists have contended that a first order of healing in which problems are addressed at a social level is necessary before physical cure can happen (Daniel 1996; Davis 2000; Turner 1967). As Adrianna Petryna and Arthur Kleinman (2006) note, however, with the fetishization of pharmaceuticals the social principle of healing can be completely short-circuited or ignored altogether. Initially, in the grip of the results from the first surveys on morbidity for this study, I too thought that a desire for pharmaceutical efficacy had completely eclipsed the symbolic and narrative aspects of health and illness, and indeed, in many cases this seems to be the case. Nevertheless, a more sustained attention to some of the ways that doctors in the markets talk about their healing practices seems to suggest that some fragments of the social principle coexist with other concepts

---

8. See also Janice Boddy's (1989) classic work on the Zar cult in Sudan, which similarly deals with miscarriages and the targeting of women by the Zar spirits.

that seem to privilege a mechanical relation between the body and the pharmaceutical product. I hope to return in future work to the question of how we might frame such healing through models of action derived from Hindu theories of ritual (e.g., in the *mimamsa* school of Indian philosophy) and how healing is expected to be achieved by the collaborative acts of several kinds of agents. For now I am content to suggest that underlying the almost mechanical way in which medicines and injections are used, we might glimpse some deeper layers of a cosmology carried in the most humble of circumstances.[9]

Finally, some healers see the gift of healing as simultaneously a curse. I found the most elaborate expression of this theme in Nathu Ram's story, a Dalit who works as a gardener at a government dispensary but must act as a medium for a spirit every Thursday evening and offer divination and healing to those who seek him. The story goes as follows: When Nathu Ram was a young boy he became fatally ill. No one could understand or diagnose his illness. His father, who worked as an unskilled laborer, went to various healers, but to no avail. Then, one day, when Nathu Ram was at death's door, a person whom his father knew and who also worked in a government dispensary offered to cure him, on condition that he would apprentice himself to this person and learn the art of healing. Under the ministrations of this person, whom he simply calls Babaji (a generic term for an elderly holy wanderer), Nathu Ram was cured and also learned that the deity that had cured him was Bhairava—a fierce form related to Shiva.[10] After that, his body became a vessel for this deity, who began to possess him. Because the deity now resides in him, he has to allow it to find expression in healing every Thursday.

People who came to consult Nathu Ram usually brought a series of familial conflicts and misfortunes for which they sought divination and remedies. Nathu

9. I do not dispute the fact that at the level of cognitive systems there are fundamental differences in the principles of Ayurveda and the principles on which modern biomedicine functions or that traditional healers such as well-trained vaidyas and hakims employ healing practices that are very different than the ones described here. But my concern is with the actual practices of those who serve in the low-income areas. The larger question of how modernization and commoditization have influenced the new ways in which Ayurvedic products are packaged and sold is a fascinating one, but I do not engage it here. See Bode (2006, 2011) for a passionate critique of the dominance of biomedicine.

10. The characterization of Bhairav as a fierce form of Shiva is Nathu Ram's characterization of what possesses him. The story of Bhairav is more complex, for as in the case of many other deities, Bhairavas are a class of deities and not a single deity. They relate both to Shiva and the goddesses in complex ways in the manner of other "demon devotees" (see Hiltebeitel 1989).

Ram insisted that it was not he who provided the diagnosis of what ails them but the spirit who possessed him. Several people in the neighborhood, including his elder brother's wife thought he was possessed by a bad, unholy spirit—*un par gandi cheez aati ha*i—lit., a dirty thing comes upon him. Nathu Ram did not reflect so much on the nature of the spirit that came to possess him in his discussion with me but said that his body was now tiring of becoming the host of such powerful forces. Yet if he were to stop his Thursday sessions, he would simply die, for that was the condition on which he had been given life. "This ability to divine and to give remedies is a curse I have to bear," he lamented.

In a more muted form I found others giving expression to this theme. For instance, Dr. Singh, a successful practitioner in Bhagwanpur Kheda, said that a doctor cannot turn away a patient, however dangerous his illness might be. "Always the risk of infection is there,"[11] he said, and then went on to add that the infection was not only of the body, but the soul became infected with the stories of human failings that illness brought forth. Since Dr. Singh had used the English term "infection," it seemed that he had made this biomedical term absorb the ideas of social failings and betrayals, which the illness experience often brings forth. I do not want to give the impression that doctors were always submerged in these melancholic thoughts. Mostly they went about their business in a pretty straightforward manner, dispensing medications, giving injections, receiving their fees, but off and on, one would find expressions that hinted at shadows of some deeper reflections on what the art of healing demanded of them. My contention is not that their moral lives were most clearly visible in the moments when they stood apart from their practices and reflected on them but, rather, that it was in the way ordinary words such as *infection, diagnosis,* and *service* were projected to absorb more than the biomedical or bureaucratic meanings that one found that outside of their official meanings, words led lives that stitched together the processes of social healing with those of medical healing.

Appendix

Medicines prescribed or dispensed for suspected angina in Delhi and Madhya Pradesh in Standardized Patient Study (J. Das, Holla, et al. 2012). Word picture provided courtesy of Jishnu Das.

11. I keep to the Hindi syntax in my translation of his comments.

Note: The only recommended medicines for angina are aspirin or Sorbitrate. The sample size and methods were described in the introduction, but to remind the reader there were 926 visits that were made to a sample of 305 practitioners.

SEVEN

Global Health Discourse and the View from Planet Earth

A new consensus on health as a global public good has emerged since the 1990s with international organizations taking a major role in redefining health. Thus a programmatic statement from the World Health Organization states the following:

> As globalization progresses, it is becoming clear in many areas that matters which were once confined to national policy are now issues of global impact and concern. For example, carbon emissions and global warming not only affect the nation involved in their production, but also impact significantly on other nations; yet no one nation necessarily has the ability, or the incentive, to address the problem. Recognition of this led to the development of the concept of Global Public Goods. Health too is an ever more international phenomenon. The most obvious example of this is in communicable disease, which is often a problem against which no single country can orchestrate a response sufficient to protect the health of its population. With health moving up the global agenda, it is therefore an opportune

time to consider the application of the Global Public Good concept to health and health care. (Woodward and Smith 2003)

The emphasis in defining global health goods settles mostly on control of communicable diseases, and much discussion has been generated on such issues as how to secure national cooperation to enact laws or administrative actions and how to decide who would fund initiatives to control spread of these diseases. Of course, international cooperation in the control of infectious diseases such as smallpox, plague, and cholera is already more than a century old (Arnold 1993; Cooper and Packard 1997; Harrison 1994). Moreover, the global spread of the human immunodeficiency virus that began in the early 1980s brought home to the international community the importance of controlling the new bacterial or viral pathogens that are capable of global spread (CISET 1995; Morens, Folkers, and Fauci 2004). A greater urgency was felt for putting into place surveillance mechanisms because new infectious diseases or resistant strains of old pathogens made it obvious to many that these threats not only affected local populations but also constituted a serious danger to international health. In addition, the inappropriate use of antibiotics in many parts of the world among both human and animal populations is likely to have contributed to the emergence of resistant strains of pathogens, causing such diseases as tuberculosis, cholera, and typhoid to take more virulent forms (Levy and Marshall 2004).

In the light of these developments, there is a broad agreement in the global health community that control of infectious diseases, including mechanisms for disease surveillance, should be treated as a global public good defined by the criteria of "nondivisibility" and "nonexcludability." But on reviewing the preceding chapters, one is entitled to ask: Is there something else at stake? Traditionally, the division between what is private and what is public in disease was considered clear-cut: The control of communicable diseases was regarded as a public good because of the presence of externalities, traditionally defined as an indirect consequence of production or consumption that affects not the producer or the consumer but a third party, which could be society as a whole or a subpopulation within it. Conversely, since noncommunicable diseases were regarded as lifestyle diseases, it was assumed that the burden for these should be borne by individuals whose private choices with regard to diet or exercise increased the risk and severity of these diseases. Lincoln Chen, Tim Evans, and Richard Cash interrogated this assumption in a powerful paper and argued that globalization is blurring the distinction between what is public and what is private in health (Chen, Evans, and Cash 1999). For instance, although tobacco or other drug consumption is regarded as a matter of private decisions, the use of advertising, the manipulation of international networks, and the dumping of pharmaceuticals in low-income countries, the authors argued, created conditions for the consumption of the drugs as a direct consequence of globalization. Hence, diseases resulting from such abuses cannot be regarded as only of private concern. In what manner might this complicated scenario that looks at responsibility for individual decisions as located in structural conditions rather than in individual choices alone alter the questions of the responsibility of the state for providing health provisions for so-called lifestyle diseases? And what form should state intervention or support take?

The deeper question is what happens to equity in health care? If the emphasis in the discussion on global public goods is on the biosecurity of advanced nations, how does it affect which diseases are prioritized to receive resources from international organizations and national programs? It seems that the global consensus on the eradication or elimination of certain diseases, such as smallpox or polio, which represent global threats under this conception of global public goods, may well have been reached at the cost of other diseases that are of greater local importance. Though technical feasibility may have led certain diseases to be prioritized for international attention, such dividing practices in global programming are hardly conducive to equity in health-delivery systems.[1] As Chen, Evans, and Cash state:

> A recurring issue in building international cooperation for surveillance is the comparative importance of various threats to different population groups. The public in rich countries fears the importation of a devastating new virus, while ordinary people in poor countries suffer from common infections such as diarrhea and respiratory diseases. These different health concerns present divergent

1. Though I concede that the question of which diseases are given priority in global programming is determined by what is technically and administratively feasible, one often forgets that the determination of feasibility is also a function of the imagination of a particular kind of future. If, for example, the emphasis is on eradication of a particular disease, then not many diseases can be candidates for prioritization. However, if the concern is with reduction of case loads or the case fatality ratio of a particular disease, then the policy implications and the technological requirements are quite different.

surveillance priorities, generated by the ready access of rich populations to effective vaccines and antibiotics that are financially or logistically inaccessible to many poor populations. Similarly, a global goods perspective does not by itself resolve the dilemma of which disease should receive priority in global surveillance or how limited global resources should be prioritized. (Chen, Evans, and Cash 1999, 292)

Is there an even more fundamental contradiction that marks global discourses on health now? Didier Fassin (forthcoming) points out that a contradiction between the abstract principle that the life of each individual is sacred and of equal value and the actual circumstances in which individual lives are evaluated very differently runs through modern practices whether of international humanitarianism, national policies of asylum, or the actual distribution of resources. In the preceding chapters I tried to show that suffering that is ordinary and cruddy asks for a detailed investigation of how the "letting die" among those living with severe resource constraints happens, especially as the letting die is the symmetrical opposite of killing through the act of a sovereign. Like Fassin's acute discomfort with the mismatch between the rhetoric of life being sacred and the actual distribution of life chances in the world today, I too am struck by the mismatch between the rhetoric of global health and the way that the actual circumstances of the lives of the poor continue to be shaped through neglect. It is not because global or national policies have become more attentive to the actual needs of the poor but because the poor are able to marshal resources for offering care through ties of kinship or locality that the lives of the poor may be thought of in terms of plenitude rather than purely in terms of lack. Even in the case of the practitioners I described in the preceding chapter, I feel that it is their entrepreneurship that has enabled health care to be reached, in whatever form it takes, by the poor. As we shall see, the quality of this health care leaves much to be desired; but, instead of creative solutions to the problems faced by these practitioners and creating better opportunities for improving their qualifications, all we get from those who dominate policy discussions is blanket condemnation or complete neglect.

Numbers, Narratives, and Standardization in Global Health

Since disease surveillance has appeared as a major concern in global health, the impetus toward generation of data on global disease prevalence through statistical models has gained considerable prominence. The hope is for rational decision making through which global interventions can be made in setting priorities for different countries. It is to this literature that I turn in order to learn how health is imagined in the context of ambitions for standardized ways of tackling the health problems of low-income countries through global programming. Though I acknowledge the need for further qualifications and a more nuanced analysis in my argument, I think it is useful to start by asking: Have the expert discourses created a self-sufficient universe in which there is a near disappearance of the actual data that are needed while the projections that substitute for that data circulate widely?

An explicit aim of global institutions now is to gather health intelligence and use standardized protocols for recording of data on disease prevalence and incidence. Although the attempt to classify diseases systematically goes back to the eighteenth century along with the invention of population as an object of study and intervention, until 1900 the classification of disease was primarily of interest in relation to cause of death statistics. The French government convened the first International Conference for the Revision of the International List of Causes of Death in Paris in 1900, at which a detailed classification of causes of death, consisting of 179 groups and an abridged classification of 35 groups, was adopted. Succeeding conferences were held in 1920, 1929, and 1938. The revised *Manual of International Statistical Classification of Diseases, Injuries, and Causes of Death* was adopted by the WHO in 1948. Presently the tenth revision of the *ICDC (International Consensus for Diagnostic Criteria)* has been adopted internationally as providing the standard of classification of causes of death for all official purposes. There is a large literature that reviews the conditions under which disease classification and standardization became implicated in the emergence of the biopolitical state, though, we should note that there were several variations in local histories in relation to the adoption of this standard classification. What I am interested in here is less the story of population surveillance and more the disconnect between the sophistication of the statistical models through which precise calculations on how to maximize investments in health are being advocated in global health initiatives now and what is happening on the ground in relation to the health of the poor.

The World Development Report, 1993, was crucial in bringing the importance of morbidity (and not only mortality) to the forefront for assessing the health status of different populations. The emphasis in this report was on the invention of a measure that would combine mortality and morbidity into a single index; the report argued that comparing populations by mortality rates alone obscured the impact of illness on the quality of life and especially on the loss of economic productivity. Since the impact of different diseases on the ability of a person or on the economic productivity of a population could differ, an attempt was made to assign relative weights to different diseases through which the differential impact of particular diseases on productivity could be measured. Many in the global health community adopted the composite index, Disability-Adjusted Life Years (DALY) in the *World Development Report*, with enthusiasm. Following this development, the WHO's *Global Burden of Disease*, 2004 (revised 2008) study provided detailed global and regional estimates of premature mortality, disability and loss of health by age and sex for 135 causes, drawing on "extensive WHO databases and on information provided by Member States" (WHO 2004). Further development of new methods for calculating DALYs led to a 2010 study, which provided revisions of estimates as well as region-specific estimates of the global burden of disease.

Important criticisms of DALYs have been offered on both philosophical and methodological grounds (Anand and Hanson 1997, 1998). Philosophically, it is feared that the emphasis on loss of economic productivity devalues the claims of those who are not economically productive members of society, such as older people or women who are not in the labor force. Methodologically, one of the difficulties arises from the fact that the magnitude of a parameter estimated on a global basis does not provide a valid estimate of a parameter in any one region. Thus, for instance, if one were calculating the disability weight assigned to blindness, one would have to take into account the facilities for the blind in public spaces or in work environments. From that point of view blindness in Sweden might not mean the same thing as blindness in rural Rajashtan (see Reidpath, Allotey, et al. 2003). In fact, ignoring regional environments within which disease is experienced might lead to the impression of objectivity to facilitate comparison but violates a fundamental premise of how diseases are experienced in everyday life. Such comparisons would be valid only if the social milieu within which disease is experienced was the same across different regions. We are faced with formidable problems, then, on how to assess the impact of a disease across poor neighborhoods versus rich neighborhoods even in the same city, as we saw in the earlier chapters of this book, let alone the comparisons of whole regions of the world.

Even more fundamental is the question of what exactly is being measured. Christopher Murray and Julio Frenk declare:

> As the importance of health in the global agenda grows, so does the responsibility to measure accurately its complex dimensions and access the effects of increasing investments. The present burst of political and financial will to improve global health has to be matched by an adequate response from the community of experts to assure that the challenges are well understood and resources are applied in the best possible ways. (Murray and Frenk 2008, 1191)

Yet paper after paper that I have read on the subject reiterates that the reporting on cause of death is very poor in countries such as India. Thus Prabhat Jha and his colleagues who have been trying to prospectively determine cause of death through the method of verbal autopsy in their Million Death Study[2] have this to say on the state of the existing data on India:

> About 46 million of the estimated 60 million deaths per year worldwide occur in developing countries. However, there is a dearth of reliable and accurate information on the causes and distribution of mortality in these countries. India has about 9.5 million deaths a year, or about one in six of all deaths worldwide. Over three-quarters of deaths in India occur in the home; more than half of these do not have a certified cause. (Jha, Gajalakshmi, et al. 2005)

I appreciate the fact that the method of verbal autopsy has been validated by Jha and his colleagues in a systematic way and that in the absence of good data for the prevalence of particular diseases and cause of death in India (and other low-income countries) such estimations can prove important for planning. However, it seems to me that the real problem is surely not that the cause of death is not being recorded properly, especially for the majority of deaths that

---

2. The Million Death Study (MDS) is described by its authors as one of the largest studies of premature mortality in the world. The MDS is an ongoing study that is conducted in India, where, like most low- and middle-income countries, the majority of deaths occur at home and without medical attention. As a result, the majority of global deaths do not have a certified cause. Verbal autopsy refers to a method of determining cause of death by interviewing relatives or caregivers after a death has occurred to elicit symptoms of the disease that caused the death and then getting a team of trained physicians to assign cause of death on the basis of these reported symptoms.

occur at home, but rather, what this lack of consistency in identifying causes of death says about the medical system as it operates for the poor. In an attempt to ascertain the actual practices at cremation and burial grounds in Delhi, ISERDD researchers Rajan Singh and Purshottam visited 50 of the 216 cremation grounds in Delhi and found that although most maintained registers for recording the demographic information of the dead person, there were only two places at which medical certificates were systematically demanded and produced, and these were mostly for hospital deaths. Legally, the production of such a certificate is compulsory for cremation or burial to take place, but most attendants, especially in small cremation grounds, enter "cause of death" in the register on the basis of oral information provided by relatives, and they would think it heartless to ask for a medical certificate at such a moment of grief.

In a CPR-ISERDD survey of 1,600 households conducted in 2012 in four low-income localities in Delhi,[3] only 35 percent of families where a death had occurred in the last five years reported having a death certificate for any deceased member of the family, although 98 percent reported having ration cards. What is, then, the process by which the cause of death as reported at funeral grounds is converted into ICDC categories? As we saw in the chapter 1, most patients do not receive any diagnosis when they visit practitioners in the poorer localities in Delhi. Recent work tends to show further that in rural areas in poorly administered states such as Uttar Pradesh and Madhya Pradesh, as well as in the poorer localities in Delhi, the quality of practitioners in terms of knowledge and effort is poor (see especially J. Das 2011; J. Das, Hammer and Leonard 2008). So the categories of diagnosis they use, such as low blood pressure, asthma, pneumonia, and so on, are often incorrect, and serious diseases are not diagnosed until an emergency causes the patient to seek medical intervention in a better medical facility.[4]

3. This survey was conducted for a larger study titled Citizenship and the State in Urban India, funded by ESRC as project RES-167-25-0520, and located at the Center for Policy Research (CPR) and ISERDD, Delhi.

4. In an effort to formulate a pilot project that would compare how the cause of death was reported in the cremation ground register and in the final *ICDC* (*International Consensus Diagnostic Criteria*) classification, Ranendra Das and I explored the possibility of getting such data on 1 percent of the sample of deaths reported in the three municipalities in Delhi for one year. Despite meeting several high-level officials, we could not get permission that would have allowed us to pursue this project.

So the solution to the problem of poor reporting of cause of death or disease incidence and prevalence is not to simply increase registration through punitive regulations but to improve the actual quality of care that the poor receive. Here we face a new set of issues, some of which have emerged from the description in the earlier chapters and some come from further reflection on the understanding of health as a conceptual category as well as an experiential category.

Health as a Credence Good, a Norm, and an Aspiration

A recent review based on a large database of published papers on the quality of medical care in low-income and middle-income countries (Berendes, Heywood, Oliver, and Garner 2011) tried to identify field-based studies that compared quality of ambulatory care in private and public medical health services. Quality of care was defined through several dimensions—structural quality, delivery mechanisms, and quality of professional care. Although most traditional measures of quality of care have looked at structural features such as quality of buildings, availability of diagnostic tools, medications, running water, and so on, it is equally important to ask: How competent are the practitioners who serve the patients? Are patients treated with courtesy? Do they get the right medications? The authors noted that while there is considerable ideological debate on the private versus public health care in many countries, there is not much work done that compares the actual quality of care offered in these clinical settings. Yet such comparisons would have important policy implications. As the authors say: "If the private sector is generally poorer quality of care than the public sector, then there is an imperative to improve the quality and outcomes; on the other hand, if the quality of the private-sector care is good, the priority for policy is to influence the market somehow to further improve access for low income groups." Yet out of the 8,812 titles and abstracts that the authors identified as likely pertaining to these issues, they could find only 80 studies that included direct qualitative comparisons of formal public and private providers and only two studies that compared public providers with informal private providers. These two studies had to be excluded for methodological reasons. It is obvious that much discussion on private versus public health care providers is based on very slim data; thus any conclusion on their relative measure would have to treated with caution. But the studies that do exist show that in terms of quality there was not much difference between the two sectors in terms of structural components such as buildings, equipment, materials, and supplies; in terms of competence there was not much difference again, but in general, competence was poor in both public and private sectors. The private sector practitioner scored better for responsiveness—a point that people repeatedly made in the low-income neighborhoods in Delhi too.

What are the facts then on the basis of which we can deduce something about the health care facilities available to the poor in India? Although much public health discussion on India has been focused on access, recent studies show, and my own work confirms this fact, that in both urban and rural areas (despite some exceptions pertaining to remote areas) access is not a problem. As we saw in the last chapter there are seventy practitioners (most of whom are private practitioners) within a fifteen-minute walk of every household in the localities we studied. Systematic work by Jishnu Das and Jeffrey Hammer (2004, 2005, 2007) and Jishnu Das, Alaka Holla, and colleagues (2012) that used two different methods for ascertaining quality of care has shown that, in general, medical competence of practitioners located in rural areas and in poor neighborhoods in Delhi was poor. Das and Hammer (2005) first defined competence of practitioners in terms of the knowledge of a disease: What kind of history questions did a practitioner ask if a patient presented with particular symptoms? What were the necessary diagnostic tests? Could the practitioner arrive at a differential diagnosis? What treatment was appropriate for that disease?

Each of the practitioners in a sample of 250 practitioners recruited for this study, was presented with five case scenarios and asked about diagnosis and treatment plans. The answers were then evaluated by a set of physicians. Using an item-response methodology, the authors gave each practitioner a single summary score that captured his or her competence. The average competence of practitioners as measured by the vignettes was very low. In the top quintile of the competence index, practitioners asked only 48 percent of history questions that they were supposed to ask, and in the bottom quintile it went down to 15 percent. Although in general practitioners with a medical degree (MBBS) showed a better grasp over diagnosis and medicines, there was considerable variation in the competence of those located in richer neighborhoods as compared to those in the poor neighborhoods. The vignette methodology was accompanied with observation for one full day in the clinic of the participating practitioners during which surveyors recorded the actual inter-action between patients and practitioners.

The second component of this methodology was very important for show-ing what the authors subsequently came to call the "know-do gap." What this means is that even when the better-trained practitioners knew what should be done, they did not apply this knowledge in actual clinical conditions, espe-cially in the poor neighborhoods. Recently Das, Holla, et al. (2012) have made innovative use of standardized simulated-patient methodology in both urban (Delhi) and rural (Madhya Pradesh) areas to show that in terms of actual diag-nosis and treatment offered there was no significant difference between prac-titioners with degrees in biomedicine and those with no formal training when they are located in poor neighborhoods. What this means is that despite the fact that the practitioners trained in biomedicine know more, the actual treat-ment a patient in a poor neighborhood receives is not very different regard-less of the qualifications of the practitioner.

As we saw in chapter 1, our weekly morbidity surveys showed that the medications patients were given were a combination of analgesics and anti-biotics, regardless of the disease and its severity. The treatment was often inappropriate in the sense that either the patient was undermedicated or over-medicated with very little attention given to whether the course of medication was followed or whether there was follow-up with appropriate diagnostic tests. A diagnosis was very rarely offered, and pills were handed over, as many doctors themselves stated, entirely on the basis of symptoms. Surprisingly, the work of Das, Hammer, and others shows that even when there are better doc-tors, in terms of their criteria of competence, available in the area, patients do not always choose to go to them. We saw in the last chapter that although many practitioners with degrees in BAMS or BUMS had very complex ideas of what healing entailed, they were completely dependent on salesmen or medical representatives from pharmaceutical companies to garner knowledge about medicines. Nevertheless, notions such as that of hunar (skill) could be employed to make sense of these practices by both practitioners and patients, creating a milieu to which they could both feel they belonged. In contrast, the vignettes I provided in chapter 1, of the kinds of experiences of humiliation that patients reported for government hospitals marked these spaces as hostile and distant even when they were nearby.

How might we view the complexity of the lurking presence of social models of healing even when not explicitly articulated, which I noted in the preceding chapter, under what looked like a purely mechanical application of techniques? Might one speculate that this is important for understanding why patients seem to get along with practitioners whose competence when measured through biomedical definitions of disease and care is poor? This takes us once again to the idea that, conceptualized in broader terms, what constitutes cure or efficacy from one point of view might look different from another point of view.

When thinking of health, one obvious point is that there are some goods (health being one of them) in which an expert is expected to know more about the good than the consumer. Michael Darby and Edi Karni (1973) named such goods "credence goods" and added them to Philip Nelson's (1970) basic classification of ordinary goods, search goods, and experiential goods. Much of the economic literature has been concerned with asking what mechanisms might exist to prevent fraud when knowledge is differentially distributed. But unlike, say, a car owner asking a mechanic to repair her car, where she does not have experiential knowledge of how the car feels—in the context of patients accessing practitioners for care, there are not only preexisting ideas about what the disease might be and what treatment is expected, but also the patient might try to judge how good or bad the doctor is by judging how well or poorly she feels. Such a mix of ideas and emotions, however, exists along with the notion that the practitioner is better placed to diagnose the matter and suggest therapy. Otherwise, why would the patient go to the practitioner in the first place? This fact complicates the issue, since there are no clear-cut criteria that patients can apply to judge the competence of a practitioner. For instance, in the case of self-limiting diseases (viral flu, viral diarrhea) a patient cannot know if the disease got cured due to medications or if it was self-limiting. Similarly, several scholars have shown that although we might judge if unnecessary surgical procedures were performed at the level of a population. it is not easy to make that judgment for an individual, given the asymmetry of information between the physician and the patient. Add to that the fact that patients will often demand injections or pills or a glucose drip because they feel that a visit to the practitioner is not so much about getting a diagnosis as getting medicine. The notion of health as a credence good, then, would have to include more than simply an asymmetry of information.

The second way we might look at health is in terms of Georges Canguilhem's (1991) notions of the normal and the pathological. For Canguilhem, the interaction with the medical practitioner is always located in the consciousness of the patient. Thus medical diagnosis begins with the initiative of lay-people who seek expert knowledge to either confirm or rule out a disease. Pathology does not, however, simply lie in the knowledge that the physician might bring to bear on the symptoms reported by the patient or the diagnostic categories generated through laboratory examinations. Rather, pathology is a lived reality for Canguilhem, generated by the relation between an organism and its environment. Thus as he famously noted, a state of being that might be considered healthy in one environment if it does not interfere with the ability to carry on with one's ordinary life might begin to be seen as deficient if the same person is placed in a different environment, as when a city dweller has to negotiate a difficult climb on the hills. But if health and disease are continuous experiments with life, then how do we take account of the dazzling plurality of configurations, mixtures and expressions of multiple normalities? (Mol 1998, 2002). Canguilhem's distinction between vital norms and social norms is helpful here, and as Annemarie Mol and John Law demonstrate in their own work with diabetic patients (Mol and Law 2004) the striving for keeping blood sugar within a normal range as measured by diagnostic instruments that define "normality" are in continuous interaction with sustaining one's life in the form that is normal in terms of, say, work and family obligations. In the case studies presented in this book, we saw how varied the forms are in which the pathology of disease is sought to be contained. Yet much discussion in global health has been to generate numbers or indexes as substitutes for any understanding of the multiplicity of ways in which vital norms and social norms intersect in the lives of the poor.

How does our understanding of the complexities inherent in the very definition of health—its character as a credence good or the notion of health as a moving norm that cannot be understood independent of the environment in which people live and function—relate to the fact that from certain objective viewpoints we can see that the poor are frequently sick and that the competence of practitioners in low-income neighborhoods is poor. resulting in inappropriate treatments that sometimes prolong illness and even lead to death? I believe that this kind of dilemma mirrors the contradictions that the poor themselves experience as they try to negotiate this treacherous territory. It also mirrors the way that practitioners deal with disease and disorder. As we saw in the last chapter, the range of attitudes that practitioners displayed varied from the feeling that the vocation of healing was simultaneously a blessing and a curse to thinking of the clinical transaction as nothing more than a transaction over a commodity—that is, that the patient needs a service and the practitioner provides it. Ahead, in the next chapter, I show how this affects the ontology of disease or its wajud, as Hafiz Mian (chapter 5) was prone to put matters.

Are Piecemeal Interventions the Answer?

I turn now to a different trend coming from behavioral economics that emphasizes the importance of piecemeal interventions undertaken within a local context to nudge people toward a desired outcome. Thus the economists Abhijit Banerjee and Esther Duflo make a strong case for evidence-based interventions that will nudge the poor toward desirable ends as defined by various public health measures, such as vaccinating the children, using bed nets in malaria-infested areas, sending their children to school, and so on (Banerjee, Deaton, and Duflo 2004; Banerjee and Duflo 2011; Banerjee, Duflo, et al. 2010). The question for these scholars, one that has intrigued many others, is that even when various low-cost public health programs and facilities exist (low-hanging fruit, as the public health community calls them), such as free vaccinations for children or the availability of free government clinics or schools, why do the poor not use them in larger numbers? What kind of incentives might make the poor better consumers of these programs and facilities? However, if the obstacle to the use of various facilities is that of the high rates of absenteeism of, say, doctors, nurses, and teachers, what methods of surveillance to increase attendance will work?

In order to answer these questions in a systematic way, Banerjee and Duflo (2011) advocate the use of randomized trials to determine the efficacy of particular interventions. If, for example, there is a small subsidy of lentils, will it make mothers in poverty-ridden rural areas in Rajasthan take their children for free vaccinations (Banerjee, Duflo, et al. 2010); or, as in another study by Edward Miguel and Michael Kremer (2004), would dispensing cheap medications to eradicate intestinal worms improve school attendance? The method essentially involves a comparison between an experimental group and a control group. The claim of the authors is that the results of such trials give reliable data on which to base limited interventions, which can, nevertheless, have huge positive results for the poor. We shall see in a moment the underlying theory behind such a justification for interventions on a piecemeal basis, and we will inquire into the robustness of the claims that the results of these trials are generalizable.[5]

Let us take a concrete case study described by Banerjee, Duflo, et al. (2010) regarding the attempts to increase vaccination in rural Rajasthan. The aim of the study was to assess the efficacy of modest nonfinancial incentives on immunization rates in children aged one to three and to compare it with the effect of only improving the reliability of the supply of services. The main outcome measures were the proportion of children ages one to three who were partially or fully immunized at the end point. It was found that rates of full immunization after the intervention were 39 percent for families to whom reliable immunization was offered along with a small nonfinancial incentive; 18 percent for the intervention in which reliable immunization was offered, but there were no incentives; and only 6 percent families in which there was no intervention or availability of reliable immunization camps.

Thus the study shows that there was a modest increase in the immunization when along with reliable dates on which immunization camps were held, families were offered a small nonfinancial incentive. However, the authors also found that even with a more substantial reward, such as a set of steel plates, mothers could not be nudged into completing the immunization process for their children.

In order to explain these outcomes, Banerjee and Duflo (2011) draw from the research in psychology, concluding that people's preferences are not consistent or unchanging. Thus they argue, "Beliefs that are held for convenience and comfort may well be more flexible than beliefs that are held out of true conviction" (62). What comes in the way of investing in action that incurs small costs now but will lead to huge benefits later is not belief against vaccination in these cases but what Giles Saint-Paul (2011) called "time consistency"—namely, the fact that our present self prefers to postpone the small costs if the benefits are not immediately obvious rather than incur these small costs for benefits that will accrue to a future self. One policy conclusion that would follow would be that as many public goods as possible should be

5. Banerjee and Duflo do not deny that their proposals for interventions in health and education seem paternalistic, but they defend paternalism as ubiquitous in our lives. In their words, "All this sounds paternalistic, and in a way, it certainly is. But then it is easy, too easy, to sermonize about the danger of paternalism and the need to take responsibility for our own lives, from the comfort of our couch in our safe and sanitary home" (Banerjee and Duflo 2011, 69).

provided as "default options." This makes sense given that what appear as a small cost from the perspective of middle-class families, such as investment of some time, might be much more difficult for a poor family.

Banerjee and Duflo state:

> We should recognize that no one is wise, patient, or knowledgeable enough to be fully responsible for making the right decisions for his or her own health. For the same reason that those who live in rich countries live a life surrounded by invisible nudges, the primary goal for health care policies in poor countries should make it as easy as possible for the poor to obtain preventive care, while at the same time regulating the quality of treatment that people can get. An obvious place to start, given the high sensitivity to prices, is delivering preventive services for free or even rewarding households for getting them, and making getting them the natural default option when possible. (2011, 69)

If we unpack this policy prescription, one important recommendation that emerges is that in many cases it is not important to concentrate on changing the beliefs of people but rather making it easier for them to do what is good for their health. However, the authors seem to pay somewhat less attention to the fact that getting clean drinking water as a default option is quite different from getting children fully immunized or regulating the supply of antibiotics—all of which they lump together as action that one can "nudge" the poor to perform. Even in the case of the immunization study they describe, one wonders what impact the context had on the outcomes. For instance, they could assume a reliable supply of immunization since it was managed by a trusted NGO that had worked in that area for a long time over several issues. However, in most cases, delivery of immunization is in the hands of the government—so in those states in which there is rampant absenteeism, for instance, the results of their experiment might turn out to be very different.

In a finely tuned analysis of Banerjee and Duflo's findings, J. Das (2010) offers a more pessimistic reading of the results. In his words, "The best implemented camp and incentives model, held in a region with low population resistance to vaccination; an established relationship with the implementing organisation; and enormous mobilisation, with health workers visiting households to educate them about vaccinations and inform them about camps, only increased the proportion of children immunized with a basic package to 39 percent—far short of what is needed to achieve herd immunity." J. Das also points out that it would be hard for the government, even with the best of intentions, to replicate the gold standard conditions under which this study was implemented. How would such food incentives work in the poorly administered states like Uttar Pradesh and Madhya Pradesh, where doctors and nurses are regularly absent from government run clinics? (See also Ravallion 2012 for a similar critique.)

The second issue in this behavioral approach with RCT is the question of method. Since the authors have conducted a rigorous behavioral experiment within the limits they set themselves, one cannot expect them to incorporate other methods in their study as a matter of course. I wonder, though, if it might not have been helpful to ask some people why they did not bring their children for immunization despite the subsidy or why they did not complete the recommended immunizations. It is true that one does not expect consistent answers from people about their motives, but we might consider how our understanding might have been enhanced by combining the randomized control trial with methods that yield less certainty but more depth. Banerjee and Duflo infer certain psychological mechanisms from a general picture of psychological processes but do not trust the idea that people might have had explanations of what was happening with the intervention.

To sum up the discussion up to this point: Once it is accepted that for certain outcomes, the preferences of the people (but especially the poor) are not the crucial variables that the policy maker needs to take into account for designing policy, then we end up at a point at which it becomes acceptable that people can be nudged into doing some things that someone else deems to be good for them (e.g., getting vaccinations for their children, sending the children to school). I am entirely in sympathy with the idea that piecemeal interventions might achieve results in certain areas of social life, but I am not at all certain that this solution is even desirable in many other cases. Thus to provide the poor with certain default options such as the provision of clean drinking water so that they do not have to make enormous efforts to get water or to provide schools that are near the house so that a child can negotiate the distance easily is one thing, but to assume that we can nudge them to act in ways that we feel we know is good for them in all matters is another. In the first case private and public institutions cannot avoid a form of paternalism so long as they establish default rules and starting points for themselves. In the second case, one needs much more societal agreement on setting the goals, and I feel that Banerjee and Duflo as well as others of the same persuasion do not devote sufficient attention to the matter of distinguishing means and ends.

Take another example about immunization. In the eighties and early nineties, when UNICEF was aggressively promoting childhood immunization, there was a period when it was considered justified to withhold certain provisions to the poor (such as provision of birth certificates) if their children were not vaccinated (see V. Das 1999). In another kind of scenario, missionaries have considered it right to offer incentives for conversion when they felt strongly that people's souls were in peril. Under what conditions paternalism slips into benevolent authoritarianism is a tricky question. I hope that the case studies in this book give sufficient evidence that the urgent task is to reform the institutions within which the poor function, a goal that requires a much larger concentration on the behavior of state actors as well as the functioning of markets such as the practices of pharmaceutical companies. In that sphere the theory of nudging might not work so well. Banerjee and Duflo (2006, 2011) themselves admit that they have had less success in interventions to improve attendance by nurses in primary health clinics (PHCs) as was evident when cameras installed to monitor their presence or absence were broken by them.

From the theoretical impulse in Banerjee and Duflo, I would infer that the findings of behavioral psychology (and neurology) are increasingly being used to argue that people need to be protected from themselves (see Conly 2013 for a defense of this position—one not shared by Banerjee and Duflo)— but that, in effect, the research showing that people's preferences are not consistent and are subject to errors of several kinds ends up in a distrust of the poor and their ability to take responsibility for themselves. Thus, on the one hand, I agree with Banerjee and Duflo's impulse that instead of opting for punitive measures to make the poor comply with policy requirements even if they are for their own good, it is better to give them incentives to act in ways that will lead them to take decisions that are proven to prevent disease or promote health or lead to removal of inequities in the family. On the other hand, I am not sure that enough discussion is taking place about policies that might be based on trust in the poor to be able to expand their own understanding of institutions and how these affect them (see V. Das and Walton forthcoming). The arena for discussion on these issues is more open and invites (at least for me) more public discussion on the grounds for policy and intervention.

Emergent Issues in the Criteria for Determining State Interventions

Dominant notions of utility that provided the backbone for determining what the conditions are under which an intelligent policy maker might intervene to change social conditions worked with the picture of the rational unitary individual who evaluates all his or her available choices and selects that which would maximize utility. This notion of the atomistic individual in economic theory has been the object of repeated criticism from anthropologists and sociologists who argued that individuals belong to social groups (Nyamnjoh and Englund 2004) and that this fact has profound implications for how they might view their own utility in relation to the utility of the others with whom they are connected. In response to the criticism of the isolated utility maximizing individual of economic theory, economists had generated important models to capture the ways in which an individual might take someone else's utility into account through notions of empathy, sympathy, or altruism (Becker 1981; Sen 1977). Despite the attempts to develop economic theory in these directions the dual notions of markets that could work as efficient mechanisms for allocation of resources and welfare models that were premised on aggregation of revealed preferences of individuals provided the framework that had important influence on policy discussions.

These two assumptions about the efficiency of markets and the sanctity of revealed preferences led to a model of social policy in which, in theory at least, a policy maker could intervene legitimately only under three specific conditions. The first was intervention in cases of market failure or missing markets. For example, supply of drinking water is typically in the hands of the state or of a single supplier, since for technical reasons it would be inefficient for competitive markets in water to emerge.[6] The second condition in which interventions were considered legitimate was in the case of powerful negative externalities when a person's actions could indirectly affect someone else's well-being adversely. This was, for instance, the rationale for intervention in such cases as that of restricting an individual's freedom to move about freely during epidemics. The third case was that of redistributive concerns that might lead the state to intervene to increase access to health for vulnerable

6. This does not mean that water markets do not emerge, but they are often in the nature of informal arrangements when the state fails to supply drinking water or powerful landlords manage to corner irrigation channels, for instance (Anand 2011; Dubash 2002).

populations. A complex literature on the conditions under which a planner might intervene to address redistributive concerns has emerged that covers the question of what the state owes those who are not in a position to compete in the market or who lose out through such exigencies as illness, disability, or historical injustices that are barriers to acquiring the capabilities to compete.

My point is not that this model for understanding the rationale for state intervention in the interests of the social good was applied in any straightforward way earlier or that political and other considerations did not intervene, but there was some consensus on what constituted the parameters within which debate between the state's obligation to the poor or the disadvantaged could be expressed and debated. I believe that a subtle shift is under way on the underlying consensus on what grounds can be adduced for intervention in the theoretical literature, though policy discourse on health in India is still dominated by a statist approach and allegiance to high modernist planning in the health sector with little attention to where the poor are actually getting their health care from (see Reddy et al. 2011 for an example) or any attention to the pathways through which the suggested reforms could be enacted.

The field then is not yet a settled one, and I do not think that we can yet speak of a new consensus or philosophical agreement on the grounds on which programs of intervention might be ethically justified. Yet I find it interesting that there is a recognition that the model of unitary individuals is not empirically valid; hence policy interventions based on the aggregation of revealed preferences cannot be sustained, since preferences are neither consistent nor stable. Further, the inconsistency and instability of individual preferences might approximate something like "irrational" behavior since the inconsistency has been demonstrated in psychological research as independent of the flow of new information or a shift of circumstances. It is there simply because individuals may turn out to have multiple selves. This understanding of multiple selves opens up a space for paternalistic arguments to enter the discussion, which have an impact on the way that the poor are conceptualized as objects of policy.

As we saw in Banerjee and Duflo, a limited case has been made for justifying certain kinds of paternalism and the question is, When would the kind of paternalism that defines such default conditions as provision of clean drinking water slip into authoritarian control over individual rights in the name of protecting their best interests? Given that public health has historically been in close alliance with police and military operations and that even now the most spectacular success stories of public health have emerged from strongly authoritarian regimes (China, Rwanda), what place can we make to discuss cases in which individuals may prefer certain other goods, such as liberty or dignity, over health narrowly or even broadly defined?

What about curtailment of individual liberties under democracies? The basic tenets of paternalistic interventions imply, first of all, that it has become increasingly acceptable to assume that since people cannot make choices that are rational and consistent, experts can legitimately play a greater role in determining how behavior might be modified according to goals set not by an aggregation of revealed preferences but by some other criterion that determines what would be good for people as individuals and as members of the social body. As Saint-Paul (2011) puts the matter, "To date, there is no equivalent of the fundamental welfare theorems that would provide a scientific basis for defining the scope of government intervention if one no longer assumes the validity of revealed preferences" (65). I agree with Saint-Paul in his diagnosis of what has happened to the scaffolding concepts on which policy was earlier (theoretically) based, though I think he overlooks the fact that paternalism becomes either punitive with regard to the poor (Han 2012) or remains at the level of discourse without being translated into state action, thereby abandoning the poor altogether.

The questions that we have touched on in this chapter take us into regions of ethics and morality that are far removed from simple notions of bioethics as it is conceived now (see V. Das 1999). For one, the issues pertain not only to what happens at the bedside of the patient but also what happens when disease becomes reconstructed as a discursive entity that makes facts on the ground disappear. In his influential book, *The Taming of Chance* (1990), Ian Hacking argued that the processes of statistical compilations "make people up." Categories and counting, for him, are not merely technical procedures, they define new categories of people and normalize certain ways of being in the world. But as João Biehl argues in relation to his own fieldwork, "I am concerned with how technical and political interventions make people invisible . . . bureaucratic procedures, informational difficulties, sheer medical neglect, moral contempt and unresolved disputes over diagnostic criteria mediate the process by which these people are turned into absent things" (2006, 230–31). I have tried to argue that indeed the people I describe are invisible to some regions of public health discourse but they are also objects of intervention for others—sometimes for the better and other times for the worse. What concerns me most is that the spaces are shrinking within which one could argue for robust discussions on what kind of data counts as evidence, how the preferences of the poor are to be taken into account, what the multiple normalities are that might be put into relations of agreement or contest with the toll that disease takes on the poor, or the forms of care that have evolved in these worlds and how these are to be sustained. The accountability cultures that dominate discussion might end up devouring the very lives that they are supposed to be monitoring, as much more energy is spent on the mechanisms of accountability and less on understanding how the poor sustain their lives. From those of us who live on planet earth it might be necessary to put up a notice to the effect "Mind the Gap" to guard against the lure of moon talk.

Conclusion: Thoughts for the Day after Tomorrow

In this concluding chapter I reflect on the themes that stitch the different parts of this book together. To recapitulate the movement of the text—chapters 1 through 4 started with the clinical encounters between patients and practitioners and then moved to the biography of different illnesses in terms of their dispersal over networks of institutions and relationships. Although three of the chapters on illness are individual case studies, as we saw, the focus is not so much on individual protagonists as is common in the literary genre of illness narratives often written in the first person. Rather, it is on the reconfiguration of relations that are brought into view as an illness unfolds. The larger institutional complexes such as the state and the market are, from this perspective, folded into the biography of an illness rather than made to stand out as commanding entities that regulate policy, set prices, and monitor the quality of medical care, thus determining the outcomes of diseases for both individuals and populations.

Chapters 5 and 6 looked at healers who range from practitioners of the occult to those who are certified as licensed practitioners and work in the local medical markets. Here, the story is told not through the illness but through the delineation of the complex cosmologies as well as the market within which healers come to depict their own relation to illness and cure. Even when practitioners seemed to be applying the techniques of biomedicine, such as administering injections, dispensing drugs, and checking vital signs—usually in a mechanistic manner without much understanding of what diagnosis or cure entailed from a biomedical perspective—their understanding of what was at stake for the patient and for themselves was embedded in complex issues of what is normal and what is critical; what is medicine and what is poison; what is gift and what is commodity; what is the work of human hands and what is the grace of the divine. I hope the text makes it sufficiently clear that these criteria constitute the kind of judgments that are grown within forms of life and not from abstract principles of moral philosophy or bioethics.

Finally, chapter 7 took us to a different scale of phenomena at which we entered the world of experts, however obliquely—experts who define overarching categories like global health, construct statistical models of disease prevalence, work with measures like DALYs and QALYs,[1] and in general try to find ways to standardize the range of locally variable phenomena in what Arthur Kleinman (1999) calls local moral worlds. Although I have constructed the expert languages employed in these exercises through the discursive forms in which they circulate without having participated in the complex controversies, crises, and negotiations that must lie hidden behind the agreements presented to the world, I have tried to see if the fieldwork itself might be displaced to the places from which presumably the data for aggregation are generated. Thus the visits to the cremation grounds were conducted simply to make a surface assessment of what kind of practices could be seen on the ground for collecting information on causes of death that are simply obscured when we look at the statistics on mortality and morbidity. These places were not fieldwork sites in the manner in which the urban neighborhoods where I worked were, yet they were crucial for my own distrust in the numbers that now appeared in alienated majesty in government reports and WHO figures. I do not think of the world of policy making on health as a single monolith, and

1. As explained in the previous chapter, DALY refers to Disability Adjusted Life Year. QALY is a modification of DALY that refers to Quality Adjusted Life Year. Both measures relate to time, but in the former case the reference is to the years lost due to illness or disability whereas in the latter case the reference is to health gain (see Gold et al. 2002).

the last chapter tried to show the two opposite moves: one of building models of disease prevalence and morbidity burden at global levels and the other of advocating piecemeal interventions based on behavioral models. It is not that the latter models are more modest and the former more grandiose, but rather that the underlying principles through which human action is conceived under the two models is different. At stake is the question of how much uncertainty we can tolerate and how willing the experts are to acknowledge the areas of ignorance that we confront in our understanding of health, disease, and poverty. How does the pressure to speak with absolute certainty create conditions under which other forms of knowing, such as through ethnography or literature, are made to disappear?

I have tried to ask myself: What is the imagination of the whole text here? Clearly, the chapters are not constructed to reflect a movement from a smaller scale (e.g., that of the individual disease) to larger scales (e.g., those of markets, states, and global institutions). I do not think of the individuals who appear in this book as units that can be aggregated to form higher units of family or community or market. First, individuals themselves have fractal qualities, and as we saw in the preceding chapters, there are different aspects of individual lives that emerge or get eclipsed in the thick of relationships.[2] The boundaries of the human body are not the boundaries of the subject. So the subject of illness or madness is not simply the individual but the web of relations. This was clear in all its starkness in the case of Swapan, whose madness can be read as an expression of the fragility of the agreements through which his life was defined. His action of speaking in English through the accord he found with his companion, the mad professor, might be then read as the impossibility of agreement between his words and his world—so that he could recover his voice only in words that he barely understood. The pathology struggles here to find an environment in which it can become a new norm.[3]

Second, any suggestion that the movement between different chapters is one of smaller scale to a larger scale would entail a spatial imaginary—each

2. Roy Wagner's delineation of a fractal person is felicitous: "A fractal person is never a unit standing in relation to an aggregate [read individual to society or group] or an aggregate standing in relation to a unit, but always an entity with a relationship integrally implied" (Wagner 1991, 163).

3. For an extraordinary reading of this particular turn in Swapan's story and its philosophical implications, see Laugier (2013).

larger scale containing the objects at the smaller scale within it; further, it would imply that these different phenomena can be added together—smaller units added together to constitute larger units. However, although space has the characteristic that would lend itself to aggregation of this sort, in the case of other kinds of entities, the whole cannot be arrived at through simple aggregation. To take the simplest example, one can gather together all the parts of a car but unless assembled in a particular order, they will not become a car. Organic entities or chemical compositions too would provide good examples of this kind of part-whole relation, but I have other possibilities in mind.

Parts and Wholes

The problem of how to connect parts and wholes is, of course, not new, but it has received renewed attention in anthropology, in part because of the tendency of constructing the history of the discipline as a series of ruptures and partly because of the misconception of what the relation between the single ethnographer and the particular society that he or she is studying actually entails. It is a commonplace now to state that globalization has put into question earlier models of fieldwork, in which one anthropologist was supposed to represent one society; further, comparison between societies does not serve as a good analytical tool because different societies are much more connected now than ever before. George Marcus (1989, 2010), for instance, claims that the anxiety about parts and wholes is symptomatic of the difficulties of imagining what a whole society might look like when the parts themselves do not function as discrete units any more.[4] But what does the claim to represent one society actually mean? Marilyn Strathern's (2004) description of this process is helpful here:

4. It is difficult to fully endorse Marcus's claim that when he was coming of age in the 1970s there was not a single work on holism, thus implying that some kind of representational crisis had brought this whole issue into focus. Finding my own anthropological feet in the profession around the same time in Delhi, my colleagues and I were passionately involved in debates centered on issues of holism versus individualism through the analysis of Louis Dumont's (1980) work and his claim (widely contested in India) that hierarchy was the dominant mode through which the whole was constituted in Indian society whereas the locus of value in the West was the individual (see V. Das 1977, 1995).

But that lone figure from the past was quite a complex character. Cooperative ventures and teamwork aside, the fieldworker was typically one person. Yet her head, or his head, became the locus for gathering together of diverse materials. . . . The single scholar did not replicate the diverse experiences of another single person, then, but encompassed within his or her person what went on between diverse peoples—*their* interrelation—as an object of reflection (*their* society/culture). . . . The observer's vision was a holistic, unifying assumption about the integration of meaning. (Strathern 2004, 9)

Strathern is surely right that the single fieldworker's knowledge or under-standing was more than that of any single person, but, of course, as any field-worker knows, it is also *less* than that of any single person in the social world being studied; and, this is true regardless of whether the individual belongs to a so-called simple society or to a complex society. At first impression it might seem that Strathern thinks of holism as more appropriate to small island soci-eties of the Pacific but not to modern so-called complex societies such as the English: "Home is a place where anthropologists never imagined it was possi-ble for the fieldworker to act as 'one person' or claim a single object of study" (2004, 21). Yet this contrast between integration and fragmentation is perhaps grounded more in the preconceived ideas about which societies can be treated as already given totalities and for which others might one only speak of parts, as Strathern suggests (22). To take but one example, the ideology of holism attributed to caste society by Louis Dumont (1980) was not a matter of small versus large or simple versus complex, but a matter of how parts and wholes were imagined to hold together either through the ideology of holism or indi-vidualism.

Taking these themes in a somewhat different direction, Thornton (1992) makes the claim that holism of ethnographic descriptions is the result of a rhetoric trope—a fiction created by the form of the ethnographic text. An image of coherence and closure is created by the very fact that the text is orga-nized to make references to something larger like social structure or society as a whole. But surely one can ask if such rhetorical tropes are not themselves premised on the idea that a division of chapters in the anthropological text cor-responded in some way to the notion that different domains of life—economic, political, religious, familial—are like parts of jigsaw puzzle that can be added up to make up something called "society." But what if the pieces do not fit with each other so neatly?

Although Strathern sometimes writes as if the fragment and the part are interchangeable, I have suggested in my earlier work that whereas the sketch has the imagination of the whole built into it, the fragment, always partial and torn from its original context, is that in which the imagination of the whole is lost (V. Das 2007). What happens when such a fragment is incorporated into a whole? I argue that such a fragment even if momentarily contained within the whole carries a lethal potential that could unravel the whole. Examples from architecture come readily to mind. For instance, in his masterly analysis of mosque architecture associated with the eastward expansion of the Ghurid imperium, Finbarr Flood (2009) shows the complicated relation between fragments taken from destroyed Hindu temples and the newly built mosques in which they were incorporated, symbolizing the power of the new, conquering sultans in some cases and representing a new domain for the older architectural traditions of incorporating the "foreign" into existing architecture in other cases. The point is that such a possibility of the fragment allows a double vision—seeing it as part of the whole at some moments and reopening the potential for disruption at other moments.

It is in some such spirit that I have conceived of the sets of chapters in this book. Although the chapters on the biography of illness complement the two chapters on healing to some extent, they also stand as fragments that are in tension with each other, for the worlds of patients and healers never fully meet. Patients can move from regarding healers as "gods" to assigning the most sinister attributes to them. Practitioners sometimes think they are being pushed into certain practices to satisfy patients but fear that those practices might ultimately bounce back on them and hurt them. Yet neither is free from the other, since whether for good or ill their practices are made out of the same kinds of local worlds and in interaction with each other.

I have struggled to see how to align the kinds of judgments patients make about the efficacy of treatments they receive with the judgments my colleagues and I arrived at when we took illness to be purely a biomedical entity and found most practitioners to be extremely ill-equipped to deal with illness in these terms or simply unwilling to apply the knowledge (biomedically defined) that they possessed to actual cases of patients. Fully recognizing that illness is much more than its symptoms and the cure, I think that it is at the heart of illness entailed in the very ontology of disease that one suffering from illness desires treatment and cure, or at least a relief from the suffering that illness brings. I realize that there are complex questions of how one comes to translate something like discomfort or pain into a category of illness or disease. Further on, I take up these issues again, but for now I ask that we concede that one is propelled toward some form of address to the other (human or nonhuman) when one experiences pain or discomfort. This is what Sandra Laugier (2013) calls "ordinary realism" to emphasize that our touch with reality is more a matter of accepting the flesh-and-blood character of the others with whom we share a life, and particularly a life in language, than of solving the intellectual puzzle of the existence of the other. Thus she states that "ordinary realism" is the simple fact that it calls us to be "realists" with the life that we live—a vision, she says, that the grand theories of social and moral life are simply not able to incorporate in their thinking.

In the preceding chapter my distrust of reified policy discourses, including those on global public goods, is evident. But I do not give up the hope that such literature can teach us, anthropologists, something new. The problem in this discourse, it seems to me, is that the connection to the ground is lost. In no way does this mean that I mistrust experts in general or feel that informed policy on training of medical practitioners, availability and pricing of drugs, or regulation of medical practice have no place in thinking about health, disease, and poverty. However, the earlier chapters on illness and on healing ended up showing the emptiness of the powerful discourses on global health as the field in which abstract principles are applied to decisions. Yet in a world in which these realities touch each other in many contingent ways, even if the global public health discourses do not define the realities of illness and of practitioner markets at local levels, they do constitute the kind of strong languages, in Talal Asad's words (1986, 2002), that seep into local worlds (see also Clifford 1990). At the very least, they constitute worlds in which discourses and practices become completely disconnected. Utopias are woven in the form of slogans like "health for all," but these become translated purely as opening up markets for more pharmaceutical products. Meanwhile, the poor live and die as best as they can.

Narrative Form and That Which Exceeds Its Frame

In her short, insightful book on the narrative form of illness, Ann Jurecic (2012) reflects on Virginia Woolf's ([1930] 2002) lament that the commonness of illness had prevented it from taking its place with love, battle, and jealousy among the prime themes of literature. Jurecic points out that whereas certain diseases such as tuberculosis had a definite place in the romantic imagination, and the plague appeared as the protagonist in great works of literature and cinema, less romantic but no less lethal illnesses such as the influenza epidemic of 1918 did not capture the imagination or provide occasion for critical commentary. She suggests that the lack of a narrative form might be tied to the absence of great literature on these kinds of illnesses. I would add that in the case of such majestic depictions of tuberculosis as in Thomas Mann's *The Magic Mountain,* and its profound reflections on life and death through the texture of the ordinary in a sanitarium, it is the way that time slows down that is so haunting. In the case of many ordinary illnesses we still do not yet grasp the full implications of the small changes and shifts that take place—afflictions that come to inhabit the body like parasites (Weil 1951).

Jurecic argues that it was the experience of the havoc that HIV/AIDS caused in the 1980s in the literary and artistic communities that opened up the literary field to illness experience, but she cautions that this was not a direct, unmediated result of the epidemic. Rather, this trend followed the development of a narrative form that was not available for the 1918 flu epidemic. Simultaneously, the attempt to wrest the experience of patients from the overbearing biomedical power to define illness and therapy led to such notions as illness narrative, explanatory models of illness held by patients, and to patient rights movements within the field of biomedicine through the pioneering efforts of anthropologists such as Arthur Kleinman (1989) among others. Patient rights movements and the juridical interventions to empower patients also coincided with the redefinition of the patients as consumers and opening up markets for aggressive marketing of drugs to patients. Thus, it is no one's position that the development of the genre of illness narrative automatically led to improvement in patient care but rather that the appearance of the genre is symptomatic of the recognition that biomedical power was indeed becoming ubiquitous and needed to be contested even by medical experts and caregivers within the space of the clinic. Yet an interesting split is evident in both anthropology and literature on how to assess this particular genre and its application in medical education and clinical care.

On the side of literature, we find that some of the most compelling stories have emerged through autobiographical modes of writing, and as can be imagined, such stories display a deep ambivalence toward one's deteriorating body and the burden placed on one's intimate relationships as the requirements of care become overwhelming (Esposito 1987.) The emergence of the whole field of medical humanities gestures toward the importance of giving some place to patient experiences in the training of physicians as the work of Kleinman (1989), Mattingly (1998), and Charon (2006), among others, shows. Yet both in literature and medicine there is also disquiet about the extent to which we as readers can trust the genre of illness narratives.

Lauren Berlant (1998, 2007) argues that in a globalized world, the similarity of motifs and styles in which stories of individual misfortune are told, for instance by NGOs or organizations asking for aid or charity, is striking. She warns against the sentimental, compassionate, or empathetic reading practices that can create a false sense of connection to the protagonist or the author of the narration. For Berlant the politics of sentimental reading practices blunts the capacity to recognize and criticize the objective conditions under which illness is produced in the world of global capital. There is no doubt that that the circulation of certain motifs and the standardization of such templates as "phases of the illness or of dying trajectory," in which the patient is seen to move in an orderly way from denial to acceptance of a difficult diagnosis, almost begs for a hermeneutic of suspicion toward illness narratives, but one might ask why is this not the beginning of the story rather than its end? As Eve K. Sedgwick (2003) wrote, allowing her own experience with cancer to find expression, the cultivation of suspicion has become coterminous with criticism itself. Yet those writing about their own illness experiences are themselves cautious that their experience cannot be so simply assimilated to the templates others have of what it is to suffer—as for instance, in the extraordinary memoir by Reynolds Price (2000) on his descent into chronic pain, in which he wants the reader to be able to imagine his experience and yet to retain a distance from him so as to preserve the idea that one cannot fully understand the pain of the other. The issue is not empathy but the capacity to pay attention, to be able to hear the words of pain in a way that calls for tact and delicacy and an understanding of one's own finitude.[5] I can do no better here than cite Stanley Cavell's (1994) masterly understatement about what it means to be silenced in the face of suffering—for not all silences are the same.

5. I draw from Jurecic's excellent discussion on this issue (see especially Jurecic 2012, 56–60).

That there is something between language and the world that is not captured in the idea of representation is the minimum that Wittgenstein's *Tractatus* captures in its idea of propositions as *showing* the logical form of reality. The implication here of silence, of, I sometimes like to say, unassertiveness, is equally fundamental in the *Investigations*. But there silence is not to be found once and for all at, or as, the limit of philosophy but philosophy ever and again is to refind its silence at the limit of the human. (Cavell 1994, 119)

As I read this paragraph, it is the signature theme of refinding "its" silence "again and again" that strikes me as the best response one can offer to those who propose a hermeneutic of suspicion in the reading and hearing of illness narratives. In Cavell's modesty and hesitancy in the face of suffering, one is tempted to recall Kant's ([1791] 1973) discussion of Job, who rejects doctrinal explanations of his suffering, opting instead for the more modest notion that the "ultimate purpose" of his inexplicable suffering must remain inscrutable to him. This does not, of course, mean that people do nothing in the face of suffering but that one refrains from offering grand theories in favor of or against the idea of suffering—opting instead to respond in the best way one can. Such burdens can make one's voice tremble or make for a certain incoherence in how one responds, but I think the ability to sustain an openness and tolerance toward the uncertainties that mark, for example, my own text is necessary for me to allow the different dimensions of disease to be maintained in some kind of balance, to keep the various pathways to our conceptual and ethical responses open.

Disease and the Claims over the Real

Although I have tracked the trajectories of various diseases as these were experienced, narrated, treated, neglected, cured, or became chronic, I have not found it necessary to offer a definition of disease. The time has come to ask: Is it necessary to define the terms—illness, disease, diagnosis, health— that provide the scaffolding concepts through which we intuitively come to know the disturbances in our world but which defy any neat characterization? The question turns out to be much more difficult than one might imagine at first glance.

In chapter 1, "How the Body Speaks," I tried to calculate how often people were sick. This was partly to counter the tendency to find the most dramatic instances of illness around which one can tell a compelling story and neglect the other more mundane kinds of illnesses that Elizabeth Povinelli repeatedly calls the "ordinary, chronic and cruddy" (Povinelli 2011, 132) and partly because I wanted to get at the way words of illness were used and projected to cover new situations. The primary instrument for getting at this phenomenon was the use of weekly morbidity surveys. The first question a surveyor asked a member of a household, the reader may recall, was "In the last week was anyone in the household sick [*koi beemar hua*]?" Respondents were free to interpret the question as they wished. When answering this question, people varied from reporting acne, common colds, vague aches and pains to serious, life-threatening diseases or accidents. One could gather a whole lot of information about how diagnosis was arrived at. Was it household knowledge, advice of neighbors, or the turn to an expert, such as a local doctor or a hospital, that defined what steps households would take to deal with what they identified as illness? It was, however, not easy to find any single criterion for determining what constituted disease itself. Thus the questions I have asked skirt around issues about categorical clarity to arrive at issues about the practices described: How were therapeutic strategies crafted? How did people know if a treatment had been successful? How did they see repetition of symptoms—as evidence that they had not been cured or as evidence of a bad environment or as indicative of their being prone to illnesses because they were poor? A skeptical reader might intervene here and say that this is surely true for all language, for did Wittgenstein not remind us that the meaning of a word lies in its use? Yet the issue is not only that of meaning but of trying to understand what the *being* of this entity (illness, disease) is that seems to have such a restless relation to one's own experience and such a need to find authorization of "its" reality.

As I have described in the latter part of the book, I did not define myself exclusively as an ethnographer. I also participated in multidisciplinary teams where some of my expertise as an anthropologist was aligned to other investigations, those of devising standard measures for ascertaining the quality of care that patients received through an assessment of practitioner competence and effort. For this project to succeed, it was imperative for our team of researchers to arrive at an agreed-on definition of a particular disease, on which the practitioner was to be evaluated. If the use of standardized patients was to serve as the gold standard for measuring quality of care, the training of these "fake" patients had to be very carefully calibrated. However many different ways there might be for people to describe the symptoms of TB among families and in the neighborhoods, in the context of case presentation to a practitioner, standardized patients had to be taught to present symptoms for TB that were specific to this disease, and not to confuse these with, say, symptoms of asthma or bronchitis. Yet the patients had to sound as if they were like any other patients from the local community and hence use expressions that were both appropriate in biomedical terms and also within the prevalent vocabularies used within local communities where the poor reside. I try to show later how the simulated standardized patient[6] scenario provided a window into the world of actual patients, but for the moment let me note some other features of the issues that came up in the training.

The field manual for the training of standardized patients (SPs) that our team prepared (see Mohanan et al. 2011 described an important challenge we faced in the training, particularly because these simulated patients were being used in an epidemiological study different from the way SPs are used in routine medical school examinations in which their status as simulated patients is known to all.

> The most important issue is that unlike the vignettes presented, where the scene
> of interaction is one in which the provider knows that the case being discussed is
> hypothetical, the SPs must bring the case to life and be prepared to give convincing answers, whether relating to the clinical details of the condition they
> portray or their personal history. Further this prepared improvisation must be
> done in a manner that takes account of the cultural and social milieu of the
> patient—hence only patients drawn from low-income or middle-income neighborhoods would have the cultural knowledge to spontaneously come up with
> good answers. A disease, after all, is more than the sum of clinical symptoms. A
> patient is not only a body on which different symptoms appear, he or she is a
> social-cultural being. Thus, the patient's experience of disease is mediated by his
> or her social setting, the attitudes of others, and the languages (including words,
> tones, and gestures) that circulate in a given community. This requires an intui-

---

6. The simulated standardized patients are often referred to simply as standardized patients, mystery patients, or fake patients in the literature.

tive grasp over community norms that determine our sense of the "rightness" of ways of representing a disease in a particular local setting and an ability to answer questions posed by providers about one's medical as well as social history. (Mohanan et al. 2011)

Although our team did not need to define disease in any generic sense during the training or to distinguish biomedical notions from folk ones, since both had to be incorporated in the case design, a consequence of the training was that diseases were presented to standardized patients as discrete entities with distinct therapies. What impact did this new way of presenting with disease have on them? Recall that all our standardized patients were recruited from low-income neighborhoods in Delhi or small towns and villages in Madhya Pradesh. Hence their own illness experiences and interactions with practitioners had been of the kind described in the preceding chapters. For most illnesses the practitioner might see the patient for a few minutes, ask one or two questions, do a perfunctory examination, and either administer an injection or dispense some medicine from a jar. I became intrigued as to how their training might alter their understanding of illness or treatment in every-day life although this question was not central to the aims of measurement of quality of care.

Let me illustrate the issues that came up with an example related to the training of standardized patients for presenting with symptoms of asthma. One of the trainees, Pushpa, had volunteered to go around her neighbor-hood and talk to asthma patients in order to elicit the varied expressions used by them to talk about their illness since she had never herself experi-enced the disease. She found that the descriptions people used sometimes related to the imagery of an "attack" from outside that affected breathing (e.g., *saans ka attack aaya tha*—lit., an attack of breathing came) or as a description of the difficulties in breathing (*saans lene mein takleef hoti hai*—lit., in taking breath I feel difficulty) or as a chronic condition (*saans ki bimari hai*—lit., I have the disease of breathing). These expressions seemed to be a retrospective rendering of asthma, so we asked the standardized patients to ask asthma patients in their locality to describe how they felt when they were in the middle of a severe asthma episode. Now we found other expres-sions such as *mujhe lagaa ke meri upar ki saans upar reh gai hai aur neeche ki saans neeche*—lit., I felt that my "top breath" remained on top and "bottom breath" remained on bottom. This is not how a person fluent in English might have described the symptoms, but it seemed to precisely convey the experience of a breathing spasm. Yet some of the trainees persisted that they could not understand what such a description could mean. What are these two "breaths"—one "top" and one "bottom"?—a young man with some experience as a college student asked with obvious irony.

At this point it was thought best to devote some of the teaching sessions to explaining what asthma did to the body and what it was to experience the kind of breathlessness that occurred in the case of asthma. Toward this end the physician in our team, Brian Chan, and the standardized patient expert, Diana Tabak, showed videos of lungs and small airways and what happens when these small airways get obstructed. The concept of triggers was explained in response to why asthma was more common in some environments than in others. The trainees were also given exercises such as breathing through a straw with their noses pinched so that they could get a bodily feeling close to that of the asthma patients. Now thoroughly engrossed in the mysteries of the body as seen from a biomedical lens, some trainees asked, What kind of treatment would a good practitioner give for these symptoms? Dr. Chan explained that if the disease were due to airways obstruction, then the medicine must be related to opening up the airways and not prescriptions for painkillers and antibiotics that were indicated for other conditions that superficially resembled asthma, but not for this condition.

Another aspect of the training of standardized patients was to make a global assessment of the practitioner, which they then recorded in exit interviews. To garner the SPs' subjective impressions of the nature of the interaction, we began with simple yes/no questions: Did you like the doctor? Would you go to this doctor again? The SPs were asked to give reasons for their answers. These questions were then followed by somewhat more difficult questions.

> Did the doctor create an environment in which you could convey your symptoms and concerns easily?
> Did the doctor address your worries seriously?
> Did the doctor explain anything about your illness?
> Did the doctor appear to be knowledgeable about your illness?

The standardized patients had no difficulty in arriving at judgments on the first three questions, but as they began to reflect more on the last question (did the doctor appear knowledgeable about your illness?), they began to stumble. Pushpa asked, should she respond to it as Radha (the name assigned to her as the standardized patient) or should she respond as Pushpa, her own pretraining self? When asked to explain the difference she said, Pushpa would have been satisfied if she got some medicine or even an injection, and if she felt better she would have kept going back to the same practitioner; if not, she would have switched to another practitioner on the ground that the medicine was not "taking" (*dawa lagti nahin*). Radha, however, would be more questioning in her attitude. Why is she being given "antibiotics" or told that a "course" needed to be completed (as I made clear in chapters 1 and 6, practitioners and patients use these terms in everyday clinical interactions even though they might not be clear what exactly *antibiotic* or *course* actually means in biomedical terms) when asthma could be eased with inhalation of steam or a medicine that would open airways?

I asked during discussion if these issues now arose for Pushpa and others because of the training they had received. Did these issues appear important to them earlier? Did they entertain doubts about the efficacy of a treatment given by a practitioner? Some standardized patients replied that one received so many different kinds of advice from relatives, neighbors, and family members about how to treat a medical condition, that doubts about the "correctness" of the treatment were always lurking in the background, as my earlier discussion on the biography of illnesses also made clear. They felt that their own understanding of why a treatment "worked" was something that we (the trainers) were not able to comprehend because our thinking was different (*soch alag hai*). For them it was some mysterious harmony between a doctor, a medicine, and a patient that made a medicine "work." They thought it intriguing that for doctors in our team, the correct medicine would work regardless of who was administering it. Let us recall that a common response to the question why a person went to a particular doctor was *unki dawa mujhe lag jaati hai*—his medicine "takes" on me. The SPs would often say words to the effect that "yes, they understood all the objective points that they had learned about disease and treatment, and though they may not be able to explain why, yet the fact remained that for them, when they fell ill even during the course of the training and the fieldwork, they searched for a doctor whose medicines would 'take.'" I pressed on and asked, Why then did people go to a specialist? It then emerged that there were "normal " illnesses for which such remedies as indicated by the idea of the necessary harmony between doctors and patients worked, and then there were critical turning points in an illness—when, for instance, it became incomprehensible to their normal practitioners and then the "big" doctors had to be accessed. The distinction between the normal and the critical that has run through all the chapters in one way or another retained a tenuous hold on the standardized patients, and for a while at least they were content to speak in a double register—should I judge this as Radha or as Pushpa? I realize that some behavioral experiments tend to show that people consider price to be the best indicator of the quality of a practitioner in a market. But I do not understand how to reconcile this idea with the detailed and elaborate narratives about the layering of one conception over another that I found in people's views about what it was to be ill and what it was to be cured. I believe each discipline reaches its limit here.

At this point it becomes interesting to see how the concept of disease is articulated in discussions in theoretical medicine and medical informatics, where too the ontological status of disease is hotly debated. It is important to underscore, though, that the notion of ontology here is that of formal ontology, which concerns itself with questions around arrangements of concepts. The kinds of debates around ontology that are taking place in anthropology now are much more on the relation between ontology and cosmology or the relation between ontology and naturalism, but that is only one way one might define questions of ontology. Discussion in medical informatics sciences, for instance, has ranged from asking if there is any objective reality to disease or whether the concept of disease simply corresponds to constructions of conceptual worlds of arbitrary complexity involving entities and phenomena that have no direct counterpart in our current experience—such as predictions of the future, dreams, and stories.[7] Clearly, no one is denying that people suffer from illness, disabilities, and several negative conditions; what is being contested is whether the notion of disease has any objective reality as opposed to that of discrete diseases. Germund Hesslow (1993, 1) strongly asserts that "the health/disease distinction is irrelevant." It is not of much use in clinical work and the patient does not want to know if he or she has disease but, rather, which disease? Hesslow's formulation becomes clearer when he explains that we use the notion of disease to meet specific contextual requirements. These contexts often entail determining responsibility in law or entitlements within

---

7. This is a complicated question since such entities, even if in the realm of fiction, are part of one's everyday reality, but in this view they do not have an objective reality in the same way that chairs and tables do.

the context of insurance or getting medical leave and so on within a bureaucratic organization. None of these contexts requires that we know what the
meaning of disease is in a deep sense. In these discussions questions of ontology cannot be separated from questions of alternate epistemologies.

Perhaps the issue can be restated as follows. How do we think of knowledge in relation to the diagnosis and treatment of a disease in a clinical setting? What role does knowledge play in treating patients? Is the patient's
knowledge of what is affecting him or her of relevance in defining medical
knowledge? In an uncanny way the questions resonate with the questions I
had asked about pain in my previous work when I took Cavell's insight that
overall our relationship to the world is defined not so much by the modality
of knowing as of acknowledgment (V. Das 2007). But does the arena of
health and disease lend itself to similar formulations? After all, we do seek
expert opinions for diagnosis and treatment. The understanding of health as
credence good and an experience good (see chapter 7) raises an interesting
challenge for the conceptions we have of what the doctor knows and how that
relates to what the patient knows.

Knowing as/or Acknowledging?

The notion that doctors apply a set of concepts they have learned through
classroom training and textbooks has been questioned in anthropological literature no less than in Michel Foucault's (1973) account of the birth of the clinic.
Many anthropologists have pointed out the difficulties of applying Western
epistemological categories to the practices of doctors in other medical systems
(e.g., Chinese and Indian) but with the underlying assumption that these categories work for understanding Western medicine. Thus in her classical paper
on this theme Judith Farquhar (1987) contrasts the Western epistemological
tradition that approaches knowledge from the point of view of an isolated
observer with that of her Chinese interlocutors who told her that for them
knowing was a personal experience tied to learning from those with whom
they were in a close relation. Knowledge for them, she says, is not as radically
cognitive as it is in the Western epistemological traditions. She concludes that
"experienced Chinese doctors sense that any radical abstraction of theory from
practice is profoundly inconsistent with the entire canonical corpus that has
guided their way of knowing and doing medicine" (Farquhar 1987, 1020).

It is, however, the case that this dichotomy between the Western epistemological tradition and Chinese medicine is too sharply drawn. A closer look at the issues under consideration shows that if the notion of experience as a teacher is important for Chinese doctors, it is equally important for physicians practicing Western medicine. Annemarie Mol (2002) in her work on the forms that medical knowledge takes in a university hospital in a middle-level town in the Netherlands emphasizes the importance of "enactment" on the part of both patients and doctors. The empirical scenes in her book presented alongside a kind of multichannel engagement with literature are designed to show that it is only in the context of listening to the presentation of symptoms by the patients that doctors can activate such epistemic categories as related to diagnosis and treatment protocols. Of course, other ways of accessing what is happening to the patient's body through laboratory-constructed knowledge such as pathology reports or body scans also contribute to this process, but Mol shows that they never replace the collaborative aspects of doctor-patient relations in the construction of the actual case-by-case construction of medical knowledge.

There are two important caveats I would add to Mol's claims about medical knowledge. First, I agree that it is a bold epistemic move to treat the patient's experience about his or her discomfort and symptoms as central to the making of medical knowledge as against the other inputs in the form of laboratory reports, pathology reports, images, and numbers. Yet by confining herself to the hospital setting, Mol is able to create a picture of the therapeutically naïve patient who has the pure experience of, say, pain or difficulty in walking but has not been privy to any previous knowledge of medical vocabularies, possible diagnostic tests, likely surgical procedures, or names of medicine that might be prescribed. This is what allows her to construct the patient and the doctor as two relatively independent sources of knowledge who meet together in the clinical encounter. As I showed in chapter 1, vocabularies for representing disease circulate in local worlds. Patients will learn about diagnostic tests, even when walking in a bazaar and seeing images of medicines, doctors, and public health messages displayed on signs or billboards, just as doctors get their knowledge not only from textbooks and the clinical encounter but also from visits from pharmaceutical representatives, advertisements, and even by talking to patients. To that extent, the making of medical knowledge cannot be isolated from the social knowledge about disease, medical technologies, market strategies for sale of medicines, advertisements, and hundreds of other ways in which knowledge is secreted in the social world. It is true that once a diagnosis is put on the symptoms after the act of translation from discomfort to symptom and therapy have been accomplished, new ways of understanding the disease will be generated, as Livingston (2012) too shows in her marvelous work in an oncology ward in Botswana. This means, though, that the central place accorded to the clinical encounter in deciphering the nature of medical knowledge might need to be modified to take care of other modes of circulation. That is a task I attempted through the morbidity surveys and the detailed illness biographies in which people were encouraged to share stories about the various sources of information that were used in arriving at a diagnosis or trying out a therapy.

The second point, which is perhaps less salient for my ethnography but extremely important in its own right, is the issue of how statistical knowledge of the epidemiology of a disease and genetic and other forms of screening introduce new ways of experiencing disease. Jeremy Greene (2007) argues perceptively that there is shift in understanding certain diseases (e.g., diabetes and hypertension) where "prescription by numbers," referring to the exclusive reliance on laboratory reports, has replaced the diagnosis and prescription by attentiveness to the symptoms reported by patients. This shift is caused by and related to multiple shifts in, for instance, the marketing strategies used by pharmaceutical companies, training of physicians as well as patient perceptions of what kind of preventive steps they need to take in order to constitute themselves as responsible and compliant patients. Robert Aronowitz's (2007) work on the proliferation of what he calls "risk rhetoric" surrounding breast cancer in North America leads to heightened fears among women that are disproportionate to the actual risk of breast cancer. Bernadette Wegenstein's (forthcoming) work on the formation of the medical technology and beauty industry complex shows that prophylactic mastectomy is often bundled with reconstruction of the breast and represented (both by the experts and the women) as the opportunity for a better breast. Clearly, we are far from the scene in which a symptom awaits the transformation into diagnosis by the application of expert knowledge.

In my own field sites the notions of risk management were quite different. The kinds of issues patients and practitioners worried about were the efficacy of medicines and the relation between money and the adequacy of treatments they received. In the introduction of this book I described several scenes in which when patients were propelled outside their known local worlds they experienced bafflement about documents, OPD (outpatient department) cards, and the inability of the doctors in the settings of hospitals and expensive clinics to "hear" them. I suggest that a lot of the time "risk management" here is not about translating statistical data into personal trajectories of care but rather working out a therapeutic geography that can be consistent with the need to find a cure despite the tremendous constraints that lack of resources entails.

It would have been evident to the astute reader that my discussion about the experience of illness, the quest for getting at the reality of a disease, and the nature of medical knowledge assumes that these questions reveal something about health and disease that is both embedded in social and economic conditions but also transcends these conditions; I touch on matters that pertain to existential conditions of human life. One of the burdens of this book has been to keep the play between these two registers and not expel either one from the framework of description and analysis. I draw here from Wittgenstein's profound thoughts on the relation between life and forms or the absorption of the natural and the social into each other (V. Das 2007). At a minimum, I hope that this double register of description will prevent us from assuming that the poor are a category apart and that we have the right to impose preferences derived from other forms of authoritative knowledge on them, although this does not mean that their knowledge of their own conditions has to remain static and imprisoned in something called "folk beliefs."

I want this book to be haunted by the stories of suffering and loss but also by the courage and the stupendous efforts to affirm life made by so many of my interlocutors. And in yet another contradictory impulse I wish not to put a burden of heroic forms of self-formation on the people I encountered and lived alongside. In the end I think that if some of the poor do spend money on alcohol rather than schooling and others manage in the terrible conditions of dirt and squalor to keep their houses neat and tidy, then this diversity should be normalized as it is for those who are not poor (see V. Das 2014a and b). The phrase often used in the slums for explaining why electricity failed, or the fever returned, or the child did not feel like completing her homework is "*yeh to normal hai—this is normal.*" The lives of the poor are strongly defined by living this normal—yet remaining attentive to the critical—and I have tried to think of an anthropology that would be mindful of this tonality of their lives.

Taking a Measure of Things

Given my strong attachment to ethnography as a mode of inquiry, I have asked myself: Why am I still attracted to the projects that try to generate different kinds of evidence through measurement? For instance, there is my participation in projects that have been oriented to the objectives of finding out through surveys how practitioner markets function on the ground, or making an assessment of the quality of care by construction of vignettes that document what practitioners know about a particular disease in biomedical terms, or, above all, the work on standardized patients, which demonstrated how this instrument might be used as an epidemiological tool in the field in a way quite different from its use as a pedagogic tool for teaching institutions. The short answer to this question I posed to myself is that I am compelled to think about interventions just as much as those who are officially in the field of global health, and my participation on the multidisciplinary teams has taught me that there is considerable room for both experimentation and criticism in the broad field of health policy. Yet I am acutely aware of the dangers of using measurements without an underlying theory—something that is happening increasingly in the controlled laboratory-type experiments in the field, which define much of behavioral economics today. Are people just becoming data points? as Michael Fischer asks (2013). This is a question I am concerned with, but one that asks for a far greater tolerance for openness even toward those who treat people as data points. Just as the chapters in this book are not seen as the unfolding of a plot but rather stand in a relation of tension to each other, I think the different modes of apprehending disease also stand in that relation to each other.

Vincanne Adams (2013) offers a compelling critique of the new kinds of moral and political economies of knowledge in the health field based on her reading of the hierarchies of evidence that have become established in health sciences and economics that elevate evidence-based medicine (EBM) as the only way to provide trustworthy knowledge, while consigning ethnographic modes of research to the margins as merely "anecdotal" evidence. In her words: "Notably EBM has created a platform for the buying and selling of truth and reliability abstracting clinical caregiving from the social relationships on which they depend" (55). Evidence-based medicine is not only propelled by the desire to establish scientific foundations for clinical practice, says Adams, but also by mandated cost controls. As I discussed in the last chapter, the legitimacy accorded to double-blind trials as the gold standard through which an intervention is to be judged, scaled up, and implemented brackets such questions as the theory that explains why an intervention worked or whether the context is irrelevant in transporting an intervention from one site to another. As Adams argues persuasively, there are many health interventions that cannot be scaled up but that have clearly benefited local communities. It is only within the kind of accountability cultures that insist on measurable outcomes that we find that such successes, oriented to the local, are simply ignored as of no consequence.

I think Adams makes an important point, yet I find that I cannot dismiss some of the experimental results, and I will try to indicate what kinds of puzzles this double allegiance creates. I want to first acknowledge that the work of some economists has changed many of our taken-for-granted ideas about the way that the health care system functions for the poor even as others in the same disciplines of economics or health policy create a simulacrum of knowledge that is completely disconnected from facts on the ground. Let me for now concentrate on the first kind. For me the most counterintuitive finding from the new data generated by surveys, meta-analysis, and experiments conducted by this group of scholars is the finding that the poor access health care in larger numbers than the rich, yet because of the poor quality of health care that they receive this access does not translate into better health. In some cases practitioners may be even harming the poor by the rampant use of injections, antibiotics, or unnecessary tests and procedures. May Sudhinaraset and colleagues (2013) have documented the role of informal health care providers in low-income countries, reviewing 334 references between 2000 and 2011. Their review suggests, first, that the percentage of informal providers (i.e., those who receive money in exchange for advice or medicine but who have no medical qualifications) is consistently high across many countries, accounting, for instance, for 65 to 77 percent of care seeking in Bangladesh, 36 to 49 percent in Nigeria, 33 percent in Kenya, and 55 to 77 percent in Thailand. Second, they point to the very few studies that attempt to determine the size of the informal sector; in Bangladesh estimates range from 88 to 96 percent and Uganda 77 percent. The MAQARI (Medical Advice Quality and Availability in Rural India) study from India, referred to in the last chapter, suggests that close to 80 percent of all health care providers fall in this category in rural areas in India (J. Das and Hammer 2014). In all these cases the actual enumeration was very important to get a handle on the extent to which people resort to the market for health care. My own case studies make more sense to me when I understand the "normality" of many of the practices such as the switching between different kinds of practitioners in search of better diagnosis or different medicines. Such restless movements happened in all the cases—that of Meena, Swapan, and Billu—that I described.

Yet important puzzles remain. Let me illustrate one such puzzle. Michelle Brock, Andreas Lange, and Kenneth Leonard (2013) describe three kinds of interventions they made in Tanzania within an experimental framework to improve the efforts made by practitioners to apply more effort in treating patients. (This design is partly related to the know-do gap discussed in the last chapter.) In one intervention, peer monitors visited providers. In a second intervention, providers were given a motivational book that talked about the nobility of medical practice and the saving of human lives. In a third experimental group providers were encouraged to follow a set of clinical protocols or a checklist by a peer. Surprisingly all three kinds of incentives led to significant improvements in provider effort, and in fact, large gains were observed among clinicians by just participating in the experiment, which involved an encouragement visit by a peer followed by the presence of the research team at several points to collect data.

In a discussion of these remarkable results Jishnu Das and Jeffrey Hammer (2014) contend that these studies demonstrate the extent to which quality of care can be improved by increasing provider effort and demonstrate a range of possibilities that can be used to increase the efforts of providers. One caveat they add is that the experimental studies that look to improve the motivation of practitioners to spend time and effort on their patients are all public-sector oriented. Given the important role of private practitioner markets in determining health outcomes for the poor, will such incentives work for private health care providers? As they say, public providers can be studied within their very constrained work environments whereas in the private sector, all relevant variables (prices, effort exerted, patient choice, provider location) are endogenous and simultaneously determined. Lacking the theoretical framework to explain why such incentives worked and how market conditions would alter the outcomes, we descend, as Das and Hammer say, into uncharted waters. Nevertheless, it is clear from their discussion that given the nature of clinical transactions in terms of both proliferation and dispersion between various kinds of practitioners and locales, no government can oversee all transactions; hence, instead of punitive measures it would be better to think of incentives to improve performance of practitioners. But why some incentives work and why nonfinancial incentives work better than, say, financial ones is not apparent and will need more sustained work at both theoretical and empirical levels.

I do not know if such experiments to motivate practitioners in private markets would work and also if these can be replicated in the government dispensaries in the low-performing states in India. But here is what I would speculate. As I described in chapter 6, many practitioners in the markets in Delhi, even when engaged in what seem like mechanical applications of some medical techniques, had very complex ideas of what their work actually involved, making distinctions between medicine and poison or homing in on the appropriateness of some brands versus others for the treatment of their patients. Their frameworks also moved between showing themselves to be "scientific" and yet drawing on religious ideas such as the ability to somehow harness divine grace to flow through their hands. For others the practice of medicine was little more than handing over pills they had acquired from medical salesmen. The kinds of incentives described by Brock, Lange, and Leonard (2013) seem to consist of communicating an acknowledgment or recognition of the importance of the practitioners' work to them: What do these results then tell us about the relation between the practitioners' own ethical and moral dispositions that they bring to their clinical practice and the change in provider effort consequent upon these acts of recognition by peers or even by researchers? Since the design of these studies does not have an ethnographic component, we have no clue as to what the practitioners themselves thought of these interventions. The issue raises for me (perhaps traumatically) the question of whether the complex rendering of their own practices by practitioners were actual beliefs or just words at hand, which were spun to cover up the fact that the transactions between practitioners and patients are merely market transactions, with no deep significance for either. What does this tell us about the ontology of disease under market conditions? And could it then be that my critiques of the emptiness of the exercises conducted by the kinds of practices that Adams also effectively critiques are not that different from the web of words that practitioners use to explain their actions, but that their significance lies elsewhere? This elsewhere could be the market for truth and validation, as Adams contends, for the whole community of researchers in such projects as the projection of disease burdens through statistical models that lack any grounding in the actual social worlds for which data is projected; or it could be, as I suspect it was, for some practitioners in the local markets I came to know well, the place from which you could gather political leverage and influence. In other words the issue of skepticism attaches itself to the words of both the global health community and practitioners and patients in local worlds

It is not that the local is somehow innocent and the global actors always culpable but that there is a difference in the effects each has in shaping discourse. The local practitioners simply do not have the power that global health institutions have to exclude other forms of thinking. Further, relations sometimes succeed and sometimes fail, but in the family and neighborhood ties I participated in, the response that was offered was related to the minute shifts and particular events that disease gave rise to—what Laugier (2013) calls the *ethics of care* and I call *ordinary ethics* (V. Das 2012). Aditya Bharadwaj (2013) calls this *subaltern ethicality*, which, for him, privileges the experience of patients even when the therapies offered are not recognized within the formal protocols of medicine and research and which in time will either be incorporated under new names within science or will disappear, having done their work at this time and this place. Then I might simply say that I have tried to keep faith with my interlocutors but that I can proceed this far and no further. I hope that they would find that my voice and pitch for speaking about their lives shows the power of ethnography to disclose worlds that are ours too.

About a week before I finished the book (for now) and decided that the time to begin again on these questions will be a year or two later, I had a dream. In this dream I saw Vivan Sundaram, an artist whose work I love, Geeta Kapur, the astute art critic and art historian, and Kumar Shahani, the filmmaker of exquisite sensibility—three friends with whom I had once spent a week in Kasauli as I tried to fight a writer's panic. In the dream they had come for a visit to my house in Delhi. I said that there was some scotch and some wine, and as they became pleasantly high, I drifted off to sleep. I took this dream as a sign that I could step away from this book for now—I wonder, though, how would Hafiz Mian, the amil, have interpreted this dream and my telling of it?

REFERENCES

Abbas, Ackbar. n.d. "Poor Theory: Notes toward a Manifesto." http://www
.humanities.uci.edu/critical/poortheory.pdf.

Adams, Vincanne. 2013. "Evidence-Based Global Public Health: Subjects, Profits,
Erasures." In *When People Come First: Critical Studies in Global Health*, edited by João
Biehl and Adriana Petryna, 54–90. Princeton, N.J: Princeton University Press.

Adams, Vincanne, Thomas E. Novotony, and Hannah Leslie. 2008. "Global Health
Diplomacy." *Medical Anthropology* 27 (4): 315–23.

Addlakha, Renu. 2008. *Deconstructing Mental Illness: An Ethnography of Psychiatry,
Women and the Family.* New Delhi: Zubaan.

Addlakha, Renu, Jishnu Das, Saumya Das, Veena Das, Charu Kumar, and Carolina
Sanchez. 2000. "Weekly Morbidity Survey Documentation." Delhi: Institute for
Socio-Economic Research on Development and Democracy.

Alam, A. M., F. U. Ahmed, and M. E. Rahman. 1998. "Misuse of Drugs in Acute Diarrhea in Under-Five Children." *Bangladesh Medical Research Council Bulletin* 24 (2):
27–31.

Al-Bagdadi, Nadia. 2006. "The Other Eye: Sight and Insight in Arabic Classical
Dream Literature." *Medieval History Journal* 9 (15): 115–41.

Allison, Anne. 2013. "Indebted Intimacy." *HAU: Journal of Ethnographic Theory* 3 (1):
221–24.

Anand, Nikhil. 2011. "Pressure: The PoliTechnics of Water Supply in Mumbai." *Cultural Anthropology* 26 (4): 542–64.

Anand, Sudhir, and K. Hanson 1997. "Disability Adjusted Life Years: A Critical
Review." *Journal of Health Economics* 16 (6) :685–702.

———. 1998. "DALYs: Efficiency versus Equity." *World Development* 26 (2): 307–10.

Appadurai, Arjun. 2000. "Spectral Housing and Urban Cleansing: Notes on Millennial
Mumbai." *Public Culture* 12 (3): 627–51.

Arnold, David. 1993. *Colonizing the Body: State, Medicine and Epidemic Disease in
Nineteenth-Century India.* Berkeley: University of California Press.

Aronowitz, Robert. 2007. *Unnatural History: Breast Cancer and American Society*. Cambridge: Cambridge University Press.

Asad, Talal. 1986. "The Concept of Cultural Translation in British Social Anthropology." In *Writing Culture: The Poetics and Politics of Cultural Anthropology*, edited by James Clifford and George E. Marcus, 141–64. Berkeley: University of California Press.

————. 2002. "Ethnographic Representation, Statistics, and Modern Power." In *From the Margins: Historical Anthropology and Its Futures*, edited by Brian Keith Axel, 66–91. Durham, N.C.: Duke University Press.

Austin, J. L. [1962] 1975. *How to Do Things with Words*. Edited by J. O. Urmson and Marina Sbisà. Cambridge, Mass.: Harvard University Press.

Bala, Poonam. 1992. *Imperialism and Medicine in Bengal: A Socio-historical Perspective*. New Delhi: Sage Publications.

Banerjee, Abhijit, Angus Deaton, and Esther Duflo. 2004. "Health, Health Care, and Economic Development: Wealth, Health, and Health Services in Rural Rajasthan." *American Economic Review* 94 (2): 326–30.

Banerjee, Abhijit, and Esther Duflo. 2006. "Addressing Absence." *Journal of Economic Perspectives* 20 (1): 117–32.

————. 2011. *Poor Economics: A Radical Rethinking of the Way to Fight Global Poverty*. New York: Public Affairs.

Banerjee, Abhijit V., Esther Duflo, Rachel Glennerster, and Dhruva Kothari. 2010. "Improving Immunisation Coverage in Rural India: Clustered Randomised Controlled Evaluation of Immunisation Campaigns with and without Incentives." *British Medical Journal* 340 (7759): c2220.

Banerji, Debabar. 1981. "The Place of Indigenous and Western Systems of Medicine in the Health Services of India." *Social Science and Medicine*. 15 (2): 109–14.

Beauchamp, T. L., and R. R. Faden. 1995. "Informed Consent II: Meaning and Elements for Informed Consent." In *Encyclopedia of Bioethics*, edited by Warren T Reich, 3:1240. New York: Macmillan.

Becker, Gary S. 1981. "Altruism in the Family and Selfishness in the Marketplace." *Econometrica*, n.s., 48 (189): 1–15.

Benjamin, Walter. 1986. "Critique of Violence." In *Reflections: Essays, Aphorisms, Autobiographical Writings*, edited by Peter Demetz, 277–300. New York: Schocken Books.

Berendes Sima, Peter Heywood, Sandy Oliver, and Paul Garner. 2011. "Quality of Private and Public Ambulatory Health Care in Low and Middle Income Countries: Systematic Review of Comparative Studies." *PLoS Medicine* 8 (4): e1000433, doi:10.1371.

Berlant, Lauren. 1998. "Poor Eliza." *American Literature* 70 (3): 635–68.

————. 2007. "Slow Death (Sovereignty, Obesity, Lateral Agency)." *Critical Inquiry* 33 (4): 754–80.

Bharadwaj, Aditya. 2013. "Ethic of Consensibility, Subaltern Ethicality: The Clinical Application of Embryonic Stem Cells in India." *BioSocieties* 8 (1): 25–40.

Bhardwaj, Surinder M. 1975. "Attitude toward Different Systems of Medicine: A Survey of Four Villages in the Punjab—India." *Social Science and Medicine* 9 (11): 603–12.

Biehl, João. 2005. *Vita: Life in a Zone of Social Abandonment.* Berkeley: University of California Press.

————. 2006. "Pharmaceutical Governance." In *Global Pharmaceuticals: Ethics, Markets, Practices,* edited by Adriana Petryna, Andrew Lakoff, and Arhur Kleinman, 206–39. Durham, N.C.: Duke University Press.

Blad, N. 1856. "On the Muhammadan Science of Tâbir or Interpretation of Dreams." *Journal of the Royal Asiatic Society of Great Britain and Ireland* 16:118–72.

Blanchot, Maurice. 1982. *The Space of Literature.* Translated by Anne Smock. Lincoln: University of Nebraska Press.

Blower, S. M., and C. L. Daley. 2002. "Problems and Solutions for the Stop TB Partnership." *Lancet* 2 (6): 374–76.

Bluebond-Langner, Myra. 1978. *The Private World of Dying Children.* Princeton, N.J.: Princeton University Press.

Boddy, Janice. 1989. *Wombs and Alien Spirits: Women, Men, and the Zar Cult in Northern Sudan.* Madison: University of Wisconsin Press.

Bode, Maarten. 2006. "Taking Traditional Knowledge to the Market: The Commoditization of Indian Medicine." *Anthropology and Medicine* 13 (3): 225–36.

————. 2011. "The Transformation of Diseases in Expert and Lay Medical Cultures." *Journal of Ayurveda and Integrative Medicine* 2 (1): 14–20.

Boli-Bennett, John, and John W. Meyer. 1978. "The Ideology of Childhood and the State: Rules Distinguishing Children in National Constitutions, 1870–1970." *Annual Sociological Review* 43 (6): 797–812.

Bourdieu, Pierre. 1990. *The Logic of Practice.* London: Polity Press.

Bridge, Sir Robert Leth. 1900. *The Golden Book of India.* Simla: Government of India Press.

Brock, Michelle J., Andreas Lange, and Kenneth L. Leonard. 2013. "Generosity Norms and Intrinsic Motivation in Health Care Provision: Evidence from the Laboratory and Field." Working Paper #147. London: European Bank for Reconstruction and Development.

Butler, Judith. 2004. *Precarious Life: The Powers of Mourning and Violence.* London: Verso.

————. 2005. *Giving an Account of Oneself.* New York: Fordham University Press.

Cairns, Ed. 1995. *Children and Political Violence*. Oxford: Blackwell.

Canguilhem, Georges C. 1991. *The Normal and the Pathological*. Translated by C. R. Fawcett. Cambridge, Mass.: MIT Press.

———. 1994. "Knowledge and the Living." In *Georges Canguilhem: A Vital Rationalist*, edited by François Delaporte, 303–25. New York: Zone Books.

Cantlie, Audrey. 1993. "The Non-Lover: Desire and Discourse in the Psychoanalytic Session." *Free Associations* 4 (30, pt. 2): 210–40.

Caruth, Cathy. 1996. *Unclaimed Experience: Trauma, Narrative and History*. Baltimore: Johns Hopkins University Press.

Cavell, Stanley. 1979. *The Claim of Reason: Wittgenstein, Skepticism, Morality, and Tragedy*. New York: Oxford University Press.

———. 1989. *This New Yet Unapproachable America*. Albuquerque, N.M.: Living Batch Press.

———. 1994. *A Pitch of Philosophy: Autobiographical Exercises*. Cambridge, Mass.: Harvard University Press.

———. 2005. *Philosophy the Day after Tomorrow*. Cambridge, Mass.: Belknap Press of Harvard University Press.

———. 2010. *Little Did I Know: Excerpts from Memory*. Stanford: Stanford University Press.

Cavell, Stanley, Cora Diamond, John McDowell, et al. 2008. *Philosophy and Animal Life*. New York: Columbia University Press.

Charon, Rita. 2006. *Narrative Medicine: Honoring the Stories of Illness*. New York: Oxford University Press.

Charsley, Katharine, and Alison Shaw. 2006. "South Asian Transnational Marriages in Comparative Perspective." *Global Networks* 6 (4) : 331–44.

Chauviré, Christiane. 2003. *Voir le visible: Le seconde philosophie de Wittgenstein*. Paris: PUF.

Chen, Lincoln, Tim G. Evans, and Richard A. Cash. 1999. "Health as a Public Global Good." In *Global Public Goods: International Cooperation in the 21st Century*, edited by Inge Kaul, Isabelle Grunberg, and Marc A. Stern, 284–304. New York: Oxford University Press.

Christensen, P. H. 2004. "Children's Participation in Ethnographic Research: Issues of Power and Representation." *Children and Society* 18 (2): 165–76.

Chua, Jocelyn Lim. 2014. *In Pursuit of the Good Life: Aspiration and Suicide in Globalizing South India*. Berkeley: University of California Press.

CISET (Committee on International Science, Engineering and Technology). 1995. *Infectious Diseases: A Global Health Threat*. Washington, D.C.: Government Printing Office.

Clifford, James. 1990. "Notes on (Field)notes." In *Fieldnotes: The Making of Anthropology*, edited by Roger Sanjek, 47–70. Ithaca, N.Y.: Cornell University Press.

Coetzee, J. M. 2001. *The Lives of Animals*. Edited by Amy Gutmann. Princeton, N.J.: Princeton University Press.

———. 2003. *Elizabeth Costello*. New York: Viking Books.

Cohen, Lawrence. 2005. "Operability, Bioavailability, and Exception." In *Global Assemblages: Technology, Politics, and Ethics as Anthropological Problems*, edited by Aihwa Ong and Stephen J. Collier, 79–90. Malden, Mass.: Blackwell.

Collins, D., J. Morduch, S. Rutherford, and O. Ruthven. 2009. *How the World's Poor Live on $2 a Day*. Princeton, N.J.: Princeton University Press.

Conly, Sarah. 2013. *Against Autonomy: Justifying Coercive Paternalism*. Cambridge: Cambridge University Press.

Connolly, N., and P. Nunn. 1996. "Women and Tuberculosis." *World Health Statistics Quarterly* 49 (2): 115–19.

Cooper, Frederick, and Randall M. Packard, eds. 1997. *International Development and the Social Sciences: Essays on the History and Politics of Knowledge*. Berkeley: University of California Press.

Copeman, Jacob. 2009. *Veins of Devotion: Blood Donation and Religious Experience in North India*. New Brunswick, N.J.: Rutgers University Press.

Corin, Ellen. 2007. "The 'Other' of Culture in Psychosis: The Ex-Centricity of the Subject." In *Subjectivity: Ethnographic Investigations*, edited by João Biehl, Byron Good, and Arthur Kleinman, 273–314. Berkeley: University of California Press.

Crary, Alice. 2007. *Beyond Moral Judgment*. Cambridge, Mass.: Harvard University Press.

Critchley, Simon. 2005. "Cavell's 'Romanticism' and Cavell's Romanticism." In *Contending with Stanley Cavell*, edited by Russell B. Goodman, 37–54. New York: Oxford University Press.

Da Col, Giovanni, and Caroline Humphrey. 2012. "Introduction: Subjects of Luck—Contingency, Morality and the Anticipation of Everyday Life." *Social Analysis* 56 (2): 1–18.

Daniel, Valentine E. 1996. *Charred Lullabies: Chapters in an Anthropography of Violence*. Princeton, N.J.: Princeton University Press.

Darby, Michael R., and Edi Karni. 1973. "Free Competition and the Optimal Amount of Fraud." *Journal of Law and Economics* 16 (1): 67–88.

Das, Jishnu. 2010. "Improving Immunisation Coverage in Rural India." *BMJ* 340: c2553.

———. 2011. "The Quality of Medical Care in Low-Income Countries: From Providers to Markets." *PLoS Medicine* 8 (4), e1000432.

Das, Jishnu, Ranendra Kumar Das, and Veena Das. 2012. "The Mental Health Gender-Gap in Urban India: Patterns and Narratives." *Social Science and Medicine* 75 (9): 1660–72.

Das, Jishnu, and Saumya Das. 1999. "Health Seeking and the Poor: Evidence from India." Mimeo.

———. 2003. "Trust, Learning and Vaccination: A Case Study of a North Indian Village." *Social Science and Medicine* 5 (1): 97–112.

Das, Jishnu, Quy-Toan Do, Jed Friedman, David McKenzie, and Kinnon Scott. 2007. "Mental Health and Poverty in Developing Countries: Revisiting the Relationship." *Social Science and Medicine* 65 (3): 467–80.

Das, Jishnu, and Jeffrey Hammer. 2004. "Strained Mercy: Quality of Medical Care in Delhi." *Economic and Political Weekly.* 39 (9): 951–61.

———. 2005. "Which Doctor? Combining Vignettes and Item Response to Measure Clinical Competence." *Journal of Development Economics* 78 (2): 348–83.

———. 2007. "Money for Nothing: The Dire Straits of Medical Practice in Delhi, India." *Journal of Development Economics* 83 (1): 1–36.

———. 2014. "Quality of Primary Care in Low-Income Countries." *Annual Review of Economics.* DOI 10.1146/annurev-economics-080213_041350.

Das, Jishnu, Jeffrey Hammer, and Kenneth Leonard. 2008. "The Quality of Medical Advice in Low-Income Countries." *Journal of Economic Perspectives* 22 (2): 93–114.

Das, Jishnu, Jeffrey Hammer, and Carolina Sánchez-Paramo. 2012. "The Impact of Recall Periods on Reported Morbidity and Health-Seeking Behavior." *Journal of Development Economics* 98 (1): 76–88.

Das, Jishnu, Alaka Holla, Veena Das, Manoj Mohanan, Diana Tabak, and Brian Chan. 2012. "In Urban and Rural India: A Standardized Patient Study Showed Low Levels of Provider Training and Huge Quality Gaps." *Health Affairs* 31 (12): 2774–84.

Das, Jishnu, and Carolina Sánchez. 2002. "Short but Not Sweet: New Evidence on Short Duration Morbidity from India." Paper presented to All Bank Conference on Development Economics. March 11–17, Washington, D.C.

Das, Ranendra K., and Purnamita Dasgupta. 2000. "Childhood Immunisation in India: A Macro Perspective." *Economic and Political Weekly* 35 (8/9): 645–55.

Das, Veena. 1976. "Masks and Faces: An Essay on Punjabi Kinship." *Contributions to Indian Sociology,* n.s., 10 (1): 1–35.

———. 1977. *Structure and Cognition: Aspects of Hindu Caste and Ritual.* Delhi: Oxford University Press.

———. 1980. "The Mythological Film and Its Framework of Meaning: An Analysis of Jai Santoshi Ma." *India International Center Quarterly* 8 (1): 43–56.

———. 1985. "Paradigms of Body Symbolism: An Analysis of Selected Themes in Hindu Culture." In *Indian Religion,* edited by R. Burghart and A. Cantlie, 180–207.

———. 1991. "Voices of Children." Special issue on another India, *Daedalus* 118 (3): 41–56.

———. 1995. *Critical Events: An Anthropological Perspective on Contemporary India*. Delhi: Oxford University Press.

———. 1999. "Public Good, Ethics, and Everyday Life: Beyond the Boundaries of Bioethics." *Daedalus: Journal of the American Academy of Arts and Sciences* 128 (4): 99–133.

———. 2004. "The Signature of the State." In *Anthropology at the Margins of the State*, edited by V. Das and D. Poole, 225–52. Santa Fe, N.M.: SAR Press.

———. 2007. *Life and Words: Violence and the Descent into the Ordinary*. Berkeley: University of California Press.

———. 2008. "If This Be Magic . . . : Excursions into Contemporary Hindu Lives." In *Religion beyond a Concept*, edited by Hent de Vries, 259–83. New York: Fordham University Press.

———. 2010. "Moral and Spiritual Striving in the Everyday: To Be a Muslim in Contemporary India." In *Ethical Life in South Asia*, edited by Anand Pandian and Daud Ali, 232–53. Bloomington: Indiana University Press.

———. 2011. "State, Citizenship and the Urban Poor." *Citizenship Studies* 15 (3): 319–33.

———. 2012. "Ordinary Ethics." In *A Companion to Moral Anthropology*, edited by Didier Fassin, 113–49. Malden, Mass.: Wiley Blackwell.

———. 2013. "Neighbours and Acts of Silent Kindness." *HAU: Journal of Ethnographic Theory* 3 (1): 217–20.

———. 2014a. "Action and Expression: Recounting Household Events." In *The Ground Between: Anthropologists Engage Philosophy*, edited by Veena Das, Michael Jackson, Arthur Kleinman, and Bhrigupati Singh, 279–304. Durham, N.C.: Duke University Press.

———. 2014b. "Adjacent Thinking." In *Wording the World: Veena Das and the Scenes of Inheritance*, edited by Roma Chatterji, chap. 20. New York: Fordham University Press.

Das, Veena, and Renu Addlakha. 2007. "Disability and Domestic Citizenship." In *Disability in Local and Global Worlds*, edited by Benedicte Ingstad and Susan Reynolds Whyte, 128–48. Berkeley: University of California Press.

Das, Veena, and Ranendra K. Das. 2006. "Pharmaceuticals in Urban Ecologies: The Register of the Local." In *Global Pharmaceuticals*, edited by Adriana Petryna, Andrew Lakoff, and Arthur Kleinman, 171–205. Durham, N.C.: Duke University Press.

———. 2007. "How the Body Speaks: Illness and Lifeworld among the Urban Poor." In *Subjectivity: Ethnographic Investigations*, edited by João Biehl, Byron Good, and Arthur Kleinman, 66–97. Berkeley: University of California Press.

Das, Veena, Ranendra K. Das, and Lester Coutinho. 2000. "Disease Control and Immunisation: A Sociological Enquiry." *Economic and Political Weekly* 35 (8/9): 625–32.

Das, Veena, Michael Jackson, Arthur Kleinman, and Bhrigupati Singh. 2014. "Experiments between Anthropology and Philosophy: Affinities and Antagonisms." In *The Ground Between: Anthropologists Engage Philosophy*, edited by Veena, Das, Michael Jackson, Arthur Kleinman, and Bhrigupati Singh, 1–26. Durham, N.C: Duke University Press.

Das, Veena, and Arthur Kleinman. 2001. Introduction to *Remaking a World: Violence, Social Suffering and Recovery*, edited by Veena Das, Arthur Kleinman, Margaret Lock, Mamphela Ramphele and Pamela Reynolds, 1–30. Berkeley: University of California Press.

Das, Veena, and Deborah Poole. 2004. *Anthropology in the Margins of the State*. Santa Fe, N.M.: SAR Press.

Das, Veena, and Michael Walton. Forthcoming. "Political Leadership and the Urban Poor: Local Histories." *Current Anthropology*.

Davar, Bhargavi V. 1999. *Mental Health of Indian Women: A Feminist Agenda*. Delhi: Sage Publications.

Davis, Christopher. 2000. *Death in Abeyance*. Edinburgh: Edinburgh University Press.

De Alwis, Malathi. 1998. "Motherhood as a Space of Protest: Women's Political Participation in Contemporary Sri Lanka." In *Appropriating Gender: Women's Activism and Politicized Religion in South Asia*, edited by Patricia Jeffery and Amrita Basu, 185–202. New York: Routledge.

Desjarlais, Robert R. 2003. *Sensory Biographies: Lives and Deaths among Nepal's Yolmo Buddhists*. Berkeley: University of California Press.

Desjarlais, Robert, Leon Eisenberg, Byron J. Good, and Arthur Kleinman, eds. 1995. *World Mental Health: Problems and Priorities in Low-Income Countries*. New York: Oxford University Press.

Detienne, Marcel, ed. 1995. *La desse paroles: Quatre figures de la langue des dieux: Sierie d'entretriens entre Georges Charachidze, Marcle Detienne, Gilbert Harmone, Charles Malamoud, et Carlo Severi*. Paris: Flammarion.

Dhanda, Amita. 2000. *Legal Order and Mental Disorder*. London: Sage.

Diamond, Cora. 2008. "The Difficulty of Reality and the Difficulty of Philosophy." In *Philosophy and Animal Life*, edited by Stanley Cavell, Cora Diamond, John McDowell, et al., 43–89. New York: Oxford University Press.

Dua, V., C. V. Kunin, and L. V. White. 1994. "The Use of Antimicrobial Drugs in Nagpur, India: A Window on Medical Care in a Developing Country." *Social Science and Medicine* 38 (5): 717–24.

Dubash, Navroz K. 2002. *Tubewell Capitalism: Groundwater Development and Agrarian Change in Gujarat*. New York: Oxford University Press.

Dumont, Louis. 1980. *Homo Hierarchicus: The Caste System and Its Implications*. Chicago: University of Chicago Press.

Durkheim, Émile. [1912] 2001. *The Elementary Forms of Religious Life*. Translated by Carol Cosman. Edited by Mark S. Cladis. London: Oxford University Press.

Dwyer, Graham. 2003. *The Divine and the Demonic: Supernatural Affliction and Its Treatment in North India*. London: Routledge.

Eckert, Julia. 2004. "Urban Governance and Emergent Forms of Legal Pluralism in Mumbai." *Journal of Legal Pluralism* 36 (50): 29–60.

Ecks, Stefan, and Soumita Basu. 2009. "The Unlicensed Lives of Antidepressants in India: Generic Drugs, Unqualified Practitioners, and Floating Prescriptions." *Transcultural Psychiatry* 46 (1): 86–106.

Emerson, Ralph Waldo. 1844. "Experience." In *Essays: Second Series*. Boston: James Munroe.

Erb, Cynthia. 2006. "Have You Ever Seen the Inside of One of Those Places? *Psycho*, Foucault, and the Postwar Context of Madness." *Cinema* 45 (4): 44–63.

Esposito, Roberto. 1987. *The Obsolete Self: Philosophical Dimensions of Aging*. Berkeley: University of California Press.

———. 2008. *Bios: Biopolitics and Philosophy*. Minneapolis: University of Minnesota Press.

Evans-Pritchard, E. E. 1950 [1939]. *Witchcraft, Oracles and Magic among the Azande*. Oxford: Clarendon Press.

Ewing, Katherine P. 1997. *Arguing Sainthood: Modernity, Psychoanalysis, and Islam*. Durham, N.C.: Duke University Press.

Farbman, M. 2005. "Blanchot on Dreams and Writing." *SubStance* 34 (2): 118–40.

Farmer, Paul. 1999. *Infections and Inequalites: The Modern Plagues*. Berkeley: University of California Press.

———. 2003. *Pathologies of Power: Health, Human Rights, and the New War on the Poor*. Berkeley: University of California Press.

Farquhar, Judith. 1987. "Problems of Knowledge in Contemporary Chinese Medical Discourse." *Social Science & Medicine* 24 (12): 1013–21.

Fassin, Didier. 2007. *When Bodies Remember: Experiences and Politics of AIDS in South Africa*. Berkeley: University of California Press.

———. 2009. "Another Politics of Life Is Possible." *Theory, Culture and Society* 26 (44), doi: 10.1177/0263276409106349.

———. 2010. "Ethics of Survival: A Democratic Approach to the Politics of Life." *Humanity: An International Journal of Human Rights* 1 (1): 81–95.

———. Forthcoming. "The Value of Life and the Worth of Lives." In *A Companion to the Anthropology of Living and Dying*. Berkeley: University of California Press.

Fassin, Didier, Collective. 2004. *Afflictions: L'Afrique du sud, de l'apartheid au sida*. Paris: Karthala.

Favret-Saada, Jeanne. 1980. *Deadly Words: Witchcraft in the Bocage*. Translated by Catherine Cullen. Cambridge: Cambridge University Press .

Ferenczi, Sandor. 1949. "Confusion of the Tongues between the Adults and the Child: The Language of Tenderness and of Passion." *International Journal of Psychoanalysis* 30 (4): 225–30.

Fischer, Michael M. J. 2013. "The Peopling of Technologies." In *When People Come First: Critical Studies in Global Health*, edited by João Biehl and Adriana Petryna, 347–74. Princeton, N.J.: Princeton University Press.

Fisher, Michael H. 2010. *The Inordinately Strange Life of Doyce Sombre: Victorian Anglo-Indian MP and Chancery "Lunatic."* New York: Columbia University Press.

Flood, Finbarr Barry. 2009. *Objects of Translation: Material Culture and Medieval Hindu-Muslim Encounter*. Princeton, N.J.: Princeton University Press.

Flueckiger, Joyce B. 2006. *In Amma's Healing Room: Gender and Vernacular Islam in South India*. Bloomington: Indiana University Press.

Fortun, Kim. 2009. *Advocacy after Bhopal: Environmentalism, Disaster, New Global Orders*. Chicago: University of Chicago Press.

Foucault, Michel. 1972. *Histoire de la folie à l'âge classique*. Paris: Gallimard.

———. 1973. *The Birth of the Clinic*. Translated by Alan Sheridan. London: Tavistock.

———. 1977. *Discipline and Punish: The Birth of the Prison*. Translated by Alan Sheridan. New York: Vintage.

———. 1991. "Governmentality." In *The Foucault Effect: Studies in Governmentality*, edited by Graham Burchell, Colin Gordon, and Peter Miller, 87–104. Chicago: University of Chicago Press.

———. 1999. *Les Anormaux, cours au Collège de France, 1975–1976*. Paris: Seuil.

———. 2003. *Society Must Be Defended: Lectures at the College de France, 1975–1976*. London: Picador.

———. 2006. *History of Madness*. Edited by Jean Khalfa. Translated by Jonathan Murphy and Jean Khalfa. New York: Routledge.

Frank, Arthur W. 1995. *The Wounded Storyteller: Body, Illness and Ethics*. Chicago: University of Chicago Press.

Freud, Sigmund. 1913. *The Interpretation of Dreams*. New York: Macmillan.

Friedrich, M. J. 2013. "Gaps in India's Health Care." *JAMA* 309 (3): 223.

Glendinning, Simon. 1998. *On Being with Others*. New York: Routledge.

Godelier, Maurice, and Marilyn Strathern. 1991. *Big Men and Great Men: Personifications of Power in Melanesia*. Cambridge: Cambridge University Press.

Gold, A. G. 1988. "Spirit Possession Perceived and Performed in Rural Rajasthan." *Contributions to Indian Sociology* 22 (1): 35–63.

Gold, M. R., D. Stevenson, and D. G. Fryback. 2002. "HALYs and QALYs and DALYs, Oh My: Similarities and Differences in Summary Measures of Population Health." *Annual Review of Public Health* 23:115–34.

Good, Byron J. 1994. *Medicine, Rationality and Experience: An Anthropological Perspective*. Cambridge: Cambridge University Press.

———. 2012. "Theorizing the 'Subject' of Medical and Psychiatric Anthropology." *Journal of the Royal Anthropological Institute* 18 (3): 515–35.

Good, Byron J., and Mary-Jo DelVecchio Good. 1986. "The Cultural Context of Diagnosis and Therapy: A View from Medical Anthropology." In *Medical Health Research and Practice in Minority Communities: Development of Culturally Sensitive Programs*, edited by M. R. Miranda and H. H. L Kitano, 1–27. Rockville, Md.: National Institute of Mental Health.

Good, Mary-Jo DelVecchio, Sandra Teresa Hyde, Sarah Pinto, Byron J. Good, eds. 2008. *Postcolonial Disorders*. Berkeley: University of California Press,

Goodman, Nelson. 1978. *Ways of Worldmaking*. Indianapolis: Hackett.

Gouda, Yehia. 2006. *Dreams and Their Meanings in the Old Arab Tradition*. New York: Vintage Press.

Government of India. 1948. *The Report of the Committee on Indigenous Systems of Medicine*. Chopra Report. Delhi: Government of India Publications.

———. 2006. *Bulletin of Rural Health Statistics*. Delhi: Ministry of Health and Family Welfare, GOI Press.

Greene, Jeremy. 2007. *Prescribing by Numbers: Drugs and the Definition of Disease*. Baltimore: Johns Hopkins University Press.

Gupta, Akhil. 1995. "Blurred Boundaries: The Discourse of Corruption, the Culture of Politics, and the Imagined State." *American Ethnologist* 22 (2): 375–402.

———. 1998. *Postcolonial Developments: Agriculture in the Making of Modern India*. Durham, N.C.: Duke University Press.

———. 2012. *Red Tape: Bureaucracy, Structural Violence, and Poverty in India*. Durham, N.C.: Duke University Press.

Hacking, Ian. 1990. *The Taming of Chance*. Cambridge: Cambridge University Press.

———. 2002. *Mad Travelers: Reflections on the Reality of Transient Mental Illness*. Cambridge, Mass.: Harvard University Press.

Han, Clara. 2012. *Life in Debt: Times of Care and Violence in Neoliberal Chile*. Berkeley: University of California Press.

———. 2013."Suffering and Pictures of Anthropological Inquiry: A Response to Comments on Life in Debt." *HAU: Journal of Ethnographic Theory* 3 (1): 231–40.

Harrison, Mark. 1994. *Public Health in British India: Anglo-Indian Preventive Medicine, 1859–1914*. Cambridge: Cambridge University Press.

Hesslow, Germund. 1993. "Do We Need a Concept of Disease?" *Theoretical Medicine* 14 (1): 1–14.

Hiltebeitel, Alf, ed. 1989. *Criminal Gods and Demon Devotees: Essays on the Guardians of Popular Hinduism*. Albany: State University of New York Press.

Hull, Isabel. 1996. *Sexuality, State, and Civil Society in Germany, 1700–1815*. Ithaca, N.Y.: Cornell University Press.

Jackson, Michael. 2011. *Life within Limits: Well-Being in a World of Want*. Durham, N.C.: Duke University Press.

Jefferey, Roger. 1982. "Policies towards Indigenous Healers in Independent India." *Social Science and Medicine* 16 (21): 1835–41.

Jesani, Amar, P. C. Singhi, and Padma Prakash. 1997. "Market Medicine and Malpractice." Mumbai: Center for Enquiry into Health and Allied Themes and Society for Public Health Awareness and Action.

Jha, P., V. Gajalakshmi, P. C. Gupta, R. Kumar, P. Mony, N. Dhingra, and R. Peto. 2005. "Prospective Study of One Million Deaths in India: Rationale, Design, and Validation Results." *PLoS Medicine* 3 (2): e18.

Joas, Hans. 1997. *G. H. Mead: A Contemporary Re-examination of His Thought*. Cambridge, Mass.: MIT Press.

Johansson, S. Ryan. 1991. "The Health Transition: The Cultural Inflation of Morbidity during the Decline of Mortality." *Health Transition Review* 1 (1): 39–68.

Jurecic, Ann. 2012. *Illness as Narrative*. Pittsburgh: University of Pittsburgh Press.

Justice, Judith. 1989. *Policies, Plans, and People: Foreign Aid and Health Development*. Berkeley: University of California Press.

Kakar, Sudhir. 1982. *Shamans, Mystics, and Healers: A Psychological Inquiry into India and Its Healing Traditions*. Chicago: University of Chicago Press.

Kamat, Vinay R., and Mark Nichter. 1998. "Pharmacies, Self-Medication and Pharmaceutical Marketing in Bombay, India." *Social Science and Medicine* 47 (6): 779–94.

Kant, Immanuel. [1791] 1973. "On the Failure of All Possible Theologies." In *Kant on History and Religion (Appendix)*, by Michel Despland. Montreal: McGill-Queens University Press.

Kapoor, S. K., A. V. Raman, K. S. Sachdeva, and S. Satyanarayana. 2012. "How Did TB Patients Reach DOTS Services in Delhi? A Study of Patient Treatment-Seeking Behavior." *PLoS One* 7 (8): e42458.

Keane, Webb. 2007. *Christian Moderns: Freedom and Fetish in the Mission Encounter*. Berkeley: University of California Press.

———. 2013. "Ontologists, Anthropologists and Ethical Life." *HAU: Journal of Ethnographic Theory* 3 (1): 186–91.

Khan, Naveeda. 2006. "Of Children and Jinns: An Inquiry into an Unexpected Friendship during Uncertain Times." *Cultural Anthropology* 21 (6): 231–64.

———. 2011. "Images That Come Unbidden: Some Thoughts on the Danish Cartoons Controversy." *Borderlands* 9 (3). http://www.borderlands.net.au/vol9no3_2010/khan_images.pdf.

Kleinman, Arthur. 1980. *Patients and Healers in the Context of Culture: An Exploration of the Borderland between Anthropology, Medicine, and Psychiatry*. Berkeley: University of California Press.

———. 1989. *The Illness Narratives: Suffering, Healing, and the Human Condition*. New York: Basic Books.

————. 1999. "Experience and Its Moral Codes: Culture, Human Condition, and Disorder." In *The Tanner Lectures on Human Values*, 357–420. Salt Lake City: University of Uttah Press.

————. 2006. *What Really Matters: Living a Moral Life amidst Uncertainty and Danger.* New York: Oxford University Press.

————. 2009. "Caregiving: The Odyssey of Becoming More Human." *Lancet* 373 (9660): 292–93.

————. 2014. "The Search for Wisdom: Why William James Still Matters." In *The Ground Between: Anthropologists Engage Philosophy*, 119–37. Durham, N.C.: Duke University Press.

Korbin, Jill E. 2003. "Children, Childhoods and Violence." *Annual Review of Anthropology* 32:431–46.

Kurtz, Stanley N. 1992. *All the Mothers Are One: Hindu India and the Cultural Reshaping of Psychoanalysis.* New York: Columbia University Press.

Kwon, Heonik. 2008. *Ghosts of War in Vietnam.* Cambridge: Cambridge University Press.

————. 2012. "The Ghosts of War and the Ethics of Memory." In *Ordinary Ethics: Anthropology, Language and Action*, edited by Michael Lambek, 200–214. New York: Fordham University Press.

Laderman, Carol. 1997. "The Limits of Magic." *American Anthropologist* 99 (2): 333–41.

Lakoff, Andrew. 2005. *Pharmaceutical Reason: Knowledge and Value in Global Psychiatry.* Cambridge: Cambridge University Press.

Lall, John. 1997. *Begem Samru of Sardhana.* New Delhi: Roli Books.

Lambek, Michael. 2012. "Toward an Ethics of the Act." In *Ordinary Ethics: Anthropology, Language and Action*, edited by Michael Lambek, 36–63. New York: Fordham University Press.

Lambregts-van Weezenbeek, Catharina. 2004. "Multidrug-Resistant Tuberculosis: Prevention or Cure?" Presentation in Oslo, Norway, October 8, under the auspices of WHO HQ/STOP TB/THD.

Langer, Susanne K. 1957. *Philosophy in a New Key: A Study in the Symbolism of Reason, Rite, and Art.* Cambridge, Mass.: Harvard University Press.

Langford, Jean. 1995. "Ayurvedic Interiors: Person, Space, and Episteme in Three Medical Practices." *Cultural Anthropology* 10 (3): 330–66.

————. 2002. *Fluent Bodies: Ayurvedic Remedies for Postcolonial Imbalance.* Durham, N.C.: Duke University Press.

————. 2005. "Spirits of Dissent: Southeast Asian Memories and Disciplines of Death." *Comparative Studies of South Asia, Africa and the Middle East* 25 (1): 161–76.

Laugier, Sandra. 2005. "Rethinking the Ordinary." In *Contending with Stanley Cavell*, edited by Russell B. Goodman, 82–99. New York: Oxford University Press.

————. 2013. "Veena Das, Wittgenstein et Cavell: Le care, l'ordinaire et la folie." In *Face aux désastres: Une conversation à quatre voix sur la folie, le care, et les grandes détresses collectives*, edited by Anne Lovell, 161–92. Paris: Les Éditions d'Ithaque.

Lê, Gillian. 2013. "Trading Legitimacy: Everyday Corruption and Its Consequences for Medical Regulation in Southern Vietnam." *Medical Anthropological Quarterly* 27 (3): 457–70.

Leach, Edmund. [1961] 2004. "Rethinking Anthropology." in *Rethinking Anthropology*, 1–28. Oxford: Berg.

Lempert, Michael. 2013. "No Ordinary Ethics." *Anthropological Theory* 13 (4): 370–93.

Lévinas, Emmanuel. 1989. *The Lévinas Reader*. Edited by Seán Hand. Malden, Mass.: Blackwell.

Lévi-Strauss, Claude. 1967. *Structural Anthropology*. Translated by Claire Jacobson and Brooke Grundfest Schoepf. New York: Doubleday Anchor.

Levy, Stuart B., and Bonnie Marshall. 2004. "Antibacterial Resistance Worldwide: Causes, Challenges and Responses." *Nature Medicine* 10 (2004): S122–29.

Livingston, Julia. 2012. *Improvising Medicine: An African Oncology Ward in an Emerging Cancer Epidemic*. Durham, N.C.: Duke University Press.

Lock, Margaret. 2001. *Twice Dead: Organ Transplants and the Reinvention of Death*. Berkeley: University of California Press.

Locker, David. 1981. *Symptoms and Illness*. London: Tavistock.

Lopez, A. D., C. D. Mathers, M. Ezzati, D. T. Jamison, and Christopher J. L. Murray. 2008. *Global Burden of Disease and Risk Factors*. Washington, D.C.: World Bank and Oxford University Press.

Lutgendorf, Philip. 2002a. "Jai Santoshi Maa and Caste Hierarchy in Indian Films." *Manushi*, http://free.freeaccess.org/manushi/121/maa1.html.

————. 2002b. "A Made-to-Satisfaction 'Goddess': Jai Santoshi Maa Revisited." *Manushi*, http://free.freeaccess.org/manushi/121/maa2.html.

Marcus, George E. 1989. "Imagining the Whole: Ethnography's Contemporary Efforts to Situate Itself." *Critique of Anthropology* 9 (3): 7–30.

————. 2010. "Holism and the Expectations of Critique in Post-1980s Anthropology." In *Experiments in Holism: Theory and Practice in Contemporary Anthropology*, edited by T. Otto and N. Bubandt, 28–46. Oxford: Wiley-Blackwell.

Margree, Victoria. 2002. "Normal and Abnormal: Georges Canguilhem and the Question of Mental Pathology." *Philosophy, Psychiatry and Psychology* 9 (4): 299–312.

Martin, Emily. 2007. *Bipolar Expeditions: Mania and Depression in American Culture*. Princeton, N.J.: Princeton University Press.

Marx, Karl. 1887. *Capital*. Vol. 1. Edited by Friedrich Engels. Moscow: Progressive.

Matthews, Gareth. 1980. *Philosophy and the Young Child*. Cambridge, Mass.: Harvard University Press.

————. 1992. *Dialogues with Children*. Cambridge, Mass.: Harvard University Press.

Mattingly, Cheryl. 1998. *Healing Dramas and Clinical Plots: The Narrative Structure of Experience*. Cambridge: Cambridge University Press.

————. 2012. "Moral Selves and Moral Scenes: Narrative Experiments in Everyday Life." *Ethos: Journal of Psychological Anthropology*, doi:10.1080/00141844.2012.691523.

Mauss, Marcel. 1979. "A Category of the Human Mind: The Notion of Person, the Notion of 'Self.'" In *Sociology and Psychology*, translated by Ben Brewster, 57–94. London: Routledge.

Mavalankar, Dileep, Kranti Vora, and Bharati Sharma. 2010. "The Midwifery Role of the Auxiliary Nurse Midwife." In *Health Providers in India: On the Frontlines of Change*, edited by Kabit Sheikh and Asha George, 38–56. Delhi: Routledge.

McGuiness, Brian, ed. 2002. *Approaches to Wittgenstein: Collected Papers*. New York: Routledge.

Mead, George Herbert. 1934. *Mind, Self, and Society*. Chicago: University of Chicago Press.

Mehta, Deepak. 2000. "Circumcision, Body, Masculinity: The Ritual Wound and Collective Violence." In *Violence and Subjectivity*, edited by Veena Das, Arthur Kleinman, Margaret Lock, Mamphela Ramphele, and Pamela Reynolds, 79–102. Berkeley: University of California Press.

Mehta, Deepak, and Roma Chatterji. 2001. "Boundaries, Names, Alterities." In *Remaking a World: Violence, Social Suffering, and Recovery*, edited by Veena Das, Arthur Kleinman, Margaret Lock, Mamphela Ramphele, and Pamela Reynold, 201–25. Berkeley: University of California Press.

Metcalf, J. Z., C. K. Everett, K. R. Steingart, A. Cattamanchi, L. Huang, P. C. Hopewell, et al. 2011. "Interferon-gamma Release Assays for Active Pulmonary Tuberculosis Diagnosis in Adults in Low- and Middle-Income Countries: Systematic Review and Meta-analysis." *Journal of Infectious Diseases* 204 (Supp. 4): S1120–29.

Miguel, Edward, and Michael Kremer. 2004. "Worms: Identifying Impacts on Education and Health." *Econometrica* 72 (1): 159–217.

Misra, Kavita. 2000. "Productivity of Crisis: Disease, Scientific Knowledge and State in India." *Economic and Political Weekly* 35 (43/44): 3885–92.

Mittermaier, Amira. 2011. *Dreams That Matter: Egyptian Landscapes of the Imagination*. Berkeley: University of California Press.

Mohanan, Manoj, Veena Das, Diana Tabak, Brian Chan, Alaka Holla and Jishnu Das. 2011. *Standardized Patieints and the Measurement of Healthcare Quality. Fieldguide, Manual and Sample Instruments. Medical Advice, Quality and Availability in Rural India*. spp.staging.utoronto.ca/sites/default/.../spmanualfieldguide_012012.pdf.

Mol, Annemarie. 1998. "Lived Reality and the Multiplicity of Norms: A Critical Tribute to Georges Canguilhem." *Economy and Society* 27 (2–3): 274–84.

———. 2002. *The Body Multiple: Ontology in Medical Practice*. Durham, N.C.: Duke University Press.

Mol, Annemarie, and John Law. 2004. "Embodied Action, Enacted Bodies: The Example of Hypoglycemia." *Body & Society* 10 (2–3): 43–62.

Morduch, Jonathan, Stuart Rutherford, Daryl Collins, and Orlanda Ruthven. 2009. *Portfolios of the Poor: How the World's Poor Live on $2 a Day*. Princeton, N.J.: Princeton University Press.

Morens, David M., Gregory K. Folkers, and Anthony S. Fauci. 2004. "The Challenge of Emerging and Re-emerging Infectious Diseases." *Nature* 430 (6996): 242–49.

Morris, David B. 1998. *Illness and Culture*. Berkeley: University of California Press.

Mosse, David. 2005. *Cultivating Development: An Ethnography of Aid Policy and Practice*. London: Pluto Press.

Mulhall, Stephen. 2009. *The Wounded Animal: J. M. Coetzee and the Difficulty of Reality*. Princeton, N.J.: Princeton University Press.

Murray, Christopher J. L., and Julio Frenk. 2008. "Global Health Tracking." *Lancet* 371 (9619): 1191–99.

Nelson, Phillip. 1970. "Information and Consumer Behavior." *Journal of Political Economy* 78 (2): 311–29.

Nyamnjoh, Francis B., and Harri Englund, eds. 2004. *Rights and the Politics of Recognition in Africa*. London: Zed Books.

Obeyesekere, Gananath. 1985. "Buddhism, Depression, and the Work of Culture." In *Culture and Depression*, edited by Arthur Kleinman and Byron Good, 134–52. Berkeley: University of California Press.

Pakaslahti, Antti. 1998. "Family-Centered Treatment of Mental Health Problems at the Balaji Temple at Rajasthan." In *Changing Patterns of Family and Kinship in South Asia*, edited by Asko Parpola and Sirpa Tenhunen, 120–66. Helsinki: Finnish Oriental Society.

Pal, Rama. 2012. "Analysing OOP Catastrophic Health Expenditure in India: Concepts, Determinants and Policy Implications." http://hdl.net/2275/105.

Pandolfo, Stefania. 2007. "Testimony in Counterpoint: Psychiatric Fragments in the Aftermath of Culture." *Qui Parle* 17 (1): 64–118.

———. 2008. "The Knot of the Soul: Postcolonial Conundrums, Madness and the Imagination." In *Postcolonial Disorders*, edited by Mary-Jo DelVecchio Good, Sandra Hyde, Sarah Pinto, and Byron Good, 329–58. Berkeley: University of California Press.

———. n.d. "Voix et témoignage en marge d'une rencontre psychiatrique." Manuscript. 48 pages.

———. Forthcoming. *Knot of the Soul: Madness, Psychiatry, Islam*. Chicago: University of Chicago Press.

Patel, Vikram, and Arthur Kleinman. 2003. "Poverty and Common Mental Disorders in Developing Countries." *Bulletin of the World Health Organization* 81 (8): 609–15.

Peabody, John W., M. Omar Rahman, Paul J. Gertler, Joyce Mann, Donna O. Farley, Jeff Luck Jr., and Charles Wolf. 1999. *Policy and Health: Implications for Development in Asia*. Cambridge: Cambridge University Press.

Pedersen, Morten A. 2012. "A Day in the Cadillac: The Work of Hope in Urban Mongolia." Special issue on *Future and Fortune: Contingency, Morality and the Anticipation of Everyday Life*, edited by Giovanni Da Col and Carlone Humphrey, *Social Analysis: The International Journal of Cultural and Social Practice* 56 (2): 136–51.

Petryna, Adriana, and Arthur Kleinman. 2006. "The Pharmaceutical Nexus." In *Global Pharmaceuticals: Ethics, Markets, Practices*, edited by Adriana Petryna, Andrew Lakoff, and Arthur Kleinman, 1–32. Durham, N.C.: Duke University Press.

Pinto, Sarah. 2011. "Rational Love, Relational Medicine: Psychiatry and the Accumulation of Precarious Kinship." *Culture, Medicine, and Psychiatry* 35 (3): 76–395.

———. 2012. "The Limits of Diagnosis: Sex, Law, and Psychiatry in a Case of Contested Marriage." *Ethos* 40 (2): 119–41.

———. 2014. *Daughters of Parvati: Women and Madness in Contemporary India*. Philadelphia: University of Pennsylvania Press.

Povinelli, Elizabeth A. 2011. *Economies of Abandonment: Social Belonging and Endurance in Late Liberalism*. Durham, N.C.: Duke University Press.

Price, Reynolds. 2000. *A Whole New Life*. New York: Scribner.

Prout, Alan, and Allison James. 1997. "A New Paradigm for the Sociology of Childhood? Provenance, Promises, and Problems." In *Constructing and Reconstructing Childhood: Contemporary Issues in the Sociological Study of Childhood*, edited by Allison James and Alan Prout, 7–33. London: Falmer Press.

Pufall, Peter B., and Richard P. Unsworth, eds. 2004. *Rethinking Childhood*. New Brunswick, N.J.: Rutgers University Press.

Raheja, Gloria Goodwin. 1988. "India: Caste, Kingship, and Dominance Reconsidered." *Annual Review of Anthropology* 17:497–522.

Rajeswari, R., V. Chandrasekaran, M. Suhadev, S. Sivasubramaniam, G. Sudha, and G. Renu. 2002. "Factors Associated with Patients and Health System Delays in the Diagnosis of Tuberculosis in South India." *International Journal of Tuberculosis and Lung Disease* 6 (9): 789–95.

Ravallion, Martin. 2012. "Fighting Poverty One Experiment at a Time: A Review of Abhijit Banerjee and Esther Duflo's *Poor Economics: A Radical Rethinking of the Way to Fight Global Poverty*." *Journal of Economic Literature* 50 (1): 103–14.

Reddy, K. Srinath, et al. 2011. "Towards Achievement of Universal Health Care in India by 2020: A Call to Action." *Lancet* 377 (9767): 760–68.

Reidpath, D. D., P. A. Allotey, A. Kouame, and R. A. Cummins. 2003. "Measuring Health in a Vacuum: Examining the Disability Weight of the DALY." *Health Policy and Planning* 18 (4): 351–56.

Reynolds, Pamela. 1996. *Traditional Healers and Childhood in Zimbabwe*. Athens: Ohio University Press.

———. 2012. *War in Worcester: Youth and the Apartheid State*. New York: Fordham University Press.

Riles, Annelise. 2001. *The Network Inside Out*. Ann Arbor: University of Michigan Press.

Robbins, Joel. 2011. "Beyond the Suffering Slot: Toward an Anthropology of the Good." Unpublished manuscript.

Saint-Paul, Giles. 2011. *The Tyranny of Utility: Behavioral Social Science and the Rise of Paternalism*. Princeton, N.J: Princeton University Press.

Sass, Louis A. 1992. *Madness and Modernism: Insanity in the Light of Modern Art, Literature, and Thought*. Cambridge, Mass.: Harvard University Press.

Scheper-Hughes, Nancy. 1992. *Death without Weeping: The Violence of Everyday Life in Brazil*. Berkeley: University of California Press.

———. 2009. "Rotten Trade: Millennial Capitalism, Human Values and Global Justice in Organs Trafficking." In *Human Rights: An Anthropological Reader*, edited by Mark Goodale, 167–97. Malden, Mass.: Wiley-Blackwell.

Scheper-Hughes, Nancy, and Carolyn Sargent, eds. 1998. *Small Wars: The Cultural Politics of Childhood*. Berkeley: University of California Press.

Sedgwick, Eve Kosofsky. 2003. *Touching Feeling: Affect, Pedagogy, Performativity*. Durham, N.C.: Duke University Press.

Seligman, Charles G. 1950. Foreword to *Witchcraft, Oracles and Magic among the Azande*, by E. E. Evans-Pritchard. Oxford: Clarendon Press.

Sen, Amartya K. 1977. "Rational Fools: A Critique of the Behavioral Foundations of Economic Theory." *Philosophy and Public Affairs* 6 (4): 317–44.

Severi, C. 2002. "Memory, Reflexivity and Belief: Reflections on the Ritual Use of Language." *Social Anthropology* 10 (1): 23–40.

———. 2007. *Le principe de la chimère: Une anthropologie de la mémoire*. Paris: Editions Rue d'Ulm & Musée du Quai Branly.

Silverman, Phyllis R. 2000. *Never Too Young to Know: Death in Children's Lives*. New York: Oxford University Press.

Singh, Bhrigupati. 2012. "The Headless Horseman of Central India: Sovereignty at Varying Thresholds of Life." *Cultural Anthropology* 27 (2): 383–407.

———. 2014. *Poverty and the Quest for Life: Spiritual and Material Striving in Contemporary Rural India*. Chicago: University of Chicago Press.

Singh, V., A. Jaiswal, J. D. H. Porter, J. A. Ogden, R. Sarin, P. P. Sharma, V. K. Arora, and R. C. Jam. 2002. "TB Control, Poverty, and Vulnerability in Delhi, India." *International Journal of Tuberculosis and Lung Disease* 7 (8): 693–700.

Singla, R., R. Sarin, U. K. Khalid, K. Malhuria, N. Singla, A. Jaiswal, M. M. Puri, P. Visalakshi, and D. Behara. 2009. "Seven-year DOTS-Plus Pilot Experience in India: Results, Constraints, and Issues." *International Journal of Tubeculosis and Lung Disease* 17 (8): 976–81.

Smith, Frederick M. 2006. *The Self Possessed: Deity and Spirit Possession in South Asian Literature and Civilization*. New York: Columbia University Press.

Soudia, Yehia, 1991. *Dreams and Their Meanings in the Old Arab Traditions*. New York: Vantage Press.

Spilsbury, James C., and Jill E. Korbin. 2004. "Negotiating the Dance: Social Capital from the Perspective of Neighborhood Children and Adults" In *Rethinking Childhood*, edited by Peter B. Pufall and Richard P. Unsworh. 191–206. Rutgers, N.J.: Rutgers University Press.

Sreeramareddy, C. T., Z. Z. Qin, S. Satyanarayana, R. Subbaraman, and M. Pai. 2014. "Delays in Diagnosis and Treatment in Pulmonary Tuberculosis in India: A Systematic Review." *International Journal of Tuberculosis and Lung Disease* 18 (3): 255–66.

Stastny, Peter. 1998. "From Exploitation to Self-Reflection: Representing Persons with Psychiatric Disabilities in Documentary Films." *Literature and Medicine* 17 (1): 68–90.

Steingart, K. R., L. L. Flores, N. Dendukuri, I. Schiller, and S. S. Laal. 2011. "Commercial Serological Tests for the Diagnosis of Active Pulmonary and Extrapulmonary Tuberculosis." *PLoS Medicine* 8 (8) e1001062.

Stephens, Sharon. 1995. *Children and the Politics of Cultures*. Princeton, N.J.: Princeton University Press.

Strathern, Marilyn. 2004. *Partial Connections*. Updated ed. Oxford: Rowman and Littlefield.

Sudhinaraset, M., M. Ingram, H. K. Lofthouse, and D. Montagu. 2013. "What Is the Role of Informal Healthcare Providers in Developing Countries? A Systematic Review." *PLoS ONE* 8 (2): e54978. doi:10.1371/journal.pone.0054978.

Suganthi, P., V. K. Chadha, J. Ahmed, G. Umadevi, P. Kumar, and R. Srivastava. 2008. "Health Seeking and Knowledge about Tuberculosis among Persons with Pulmonary Symptoms and Tuberculosis Cases in Bangalore Slums." *International Journal of Tuberculosis and Lung Disease* 12 (11): 1268–73.

Taneja, Anand V. 2010. "This Is How One Pictures the Jinn of History." Unpublished manuscript, 25 pages.

———. 2013. "Jinnealogy: Everyday Life and Islamic Theology in Post-Partition Delhi." *HAU: Journal of Ethnographic Theory* 3 (3) 139–65.

Tarlo, Emma. 2003. *Unsettling Memories: Narratives of the Emergency in Delhi*. Berkeley: University of California Press.

Thornton, Robert J. 1992. "The Rhetoric of Ethnographic Holism." In *Rereading Cultural Anthropology*, edited by George Marcus, 15–33. Durham, N.C.: Duke University Press.

Trawick, Margaret. 1990a. *Notes on Love in a Tamil Family.* Berkeley: University of California Press.

———. 1990b. "Untouchability and the Fear of Death in a Tamil Song." In *Language and the Politics of Emotion*, edited by C. A. Lutz and L. Abu-Lugodh, 186–206. Cambridge: Cambridge University Press.

Tuitt, Patricia. 2006. "Individual Violence and the Law." *Studies in Law, Politics and Society* 39:3–15.

Turner, Victor W. 1967. *The Forest of Symbols: Aspects of Ndembu Ritual.* Ithaca, N.Y.: Cornell University Press.

Uplekar, M., S. Juvelkar, S. Morankar, S. Rangan, and P. Nunn. 1998. "Tuberculosis Patients and Practitioners in Private Clinics in India." *International Journal of Tuberculosis and Lung Disease* 2 (4): 324–29.

Van Damme, Bruno Meesen, Ir Por, and Katharina Kober. 2012. "Catastrophic Health Expenditure." *Lancet* 362 (9388): 996.

Wagner, Roy. 1991. "The Fractal Person." In *Big Men and Great Men: Personifications of Power in Melanesia*, edited by Maurice Godelier and Marilyn Strathern, 159–73. Cambridge: Cambridge University Press.

Wegenstein, Bernadette. Forthcoming. "The Good and the Bad Breast: Cosmetic Surgery and Breast Cancer." In *An Anthropology of Living and Dying in the Contemporary World*, edited by Veena Das and Clara Han. Berkeley: University of California Press.

Weil, Simone. 1951. "The Love of God and Affliction." In *Waiting for God*, 67–82. New York: Harper Perennial Modern Classics.

Wells, Lloyd A. 2003. "Discontinuity in Personal Narratives: Some Perspectives of Patients." *Philosophy, Psychiatry, and Psychology* 10 (4): 297–303.

Wilce, James M. 1998. *Eloquence in Trouble: The Poetics and Politics of Complaint in Rural Bangladesh.* New York: Oxford University Press.

Wittgenstein, Ludwig. 1953. *Philosophical Investigations.* Translated by G. E. M. Anscombe. New York: Macmillan.

Woodward, David, and Richard D. Smith. 2003. "Global Public Goods for Health: Concepts and Issues." In *Global Public Goods for Health: A Health Economic and Public Health Perspective*, edited by R. D. Smith, R. Beaglehole, D. Woodward, and N. Drager, chap. 1. Oxford: Oxford University Press.

Woody, J. Melvin. 2003. "When Narrative Fails." *Philosophy, Psychiatry, and Psychology* 10 (4): 329–45.

Woolf, Virginia. [1930] 2002. *On Being Ill.* Ashfield, Mass.: Paris Press.

World Bank. 1993. *World Development Report: Investing in Health.* New York: Oxford University Press.

World Health Organization. 2001. *The World Health Report 2001—Mental Health: New Understanding, New Hope.* Geneva: World Health Organization.

———. 2008. *The Global Burden of Disease.* Geneva: World Health Organization.

Nathu Ram, 178–79
neighborhoods: jhuggis, 62n2; neoliberal
    values and, 18; observance by
    neighbors, 49n13
neoliberalism: family and, 18; neigh-
    borhood and, 18
new paradigm of childhood, 79–80
NOIDA Sector V: jhuggi cluster, 61;
    schools, 63, 79
nonhuman forms, connectedness, 128–29
normal, ethnographs and, 111
normativity, ethnographs and, 111
nuri ilm, 23, 141

obligations to kin: borrowing from
    employers, 122–23; duty to parents,
    124; guilt, 127–28
occult practices, 133–34
omens, 69
opinions, related by children, 76
ordinary ethics, 17–18, 117–18
ordinary language, 115n2
organ donation, 120; Ramvila (Billu's
    brother), 122–3. *See also* bio-exchanges
other, the: existence of, proving, 115; finite
    responsibility to, 115; violence and,
    114–15

Padmavat, 156n24
Padmini, 144–49, 151, 152–54, 155–56
pain, picture, 87
Pandolfo, Stefania, 90, 111
Partition, Hafiz Main and, 149–54
Paswan, Sanjay, 133
pathology, creativity of, 104
personal narrative, mental illness and,
    84–85
peshi, 146n16
pharmaceutical companies, 175n7; practi-
    tioners' dependence on, 191–92
pharmacist *versus* practitioner, 43
Philosophical Investigations (Wittgenstein), 69
physical pain, affliction and, 3
politics: family, 70–72; gendered speech,
    108; prepolitical state of children,
    69–74

Poonam Clinic, 166–69
poor theory, 4
possession, demonic, 93–94, 97
poverty: expenditure for health care,
    42n10; illness and, 41–42; treatment
    and, 41–42
Povinelli, Elizabeth, 12–13; case study
    from, 13–14
practitioners: access to, 159–60; advertising,
    165–69; alternative medicine regu-
    lation, 162–63; appearances, 169–76;
    AYUSH, 163; BAMS, 163; Bangali
    Doctors, 169–70; BUMS, 163; certifi-
    cates *versus* efficacy, 170n4; competence
    study, 190–91; consciousness of patient,
    192–93; curse of healing gift, 178;
    degree distribution, 164; describing
    their craft, 160; distant learning
    degrees, 169; distribution, 161; *gunas*,
    168n2; *haath ka hunar*, 176; Indigenous
    Medical Inquiry Committee, 162;
    Institute of Alternative Medicine, 170;
    Integrated Medicine degree, 40n9;
    know-do gap, 191; low-income neigh-
    borhoods, 20–21; medical knowledge
    as craft, 169–71; Medical Registration
    Act of Bombay, 162; medicine,
    matching to disease, 173–75; pharma-
    ceutical companies and, 191–92; *versus*
    pharmacist, 43; protecting patients
    from selves, 198; RMP, 162; social
    norms, 192–93; symbolic efficacy of
    healing, 176–78; tantrics, 167; term use,
    29n1; training, 169–70, 171–73
Prakash, 10–11, 88
prepolitical beings, children as, 69–74
psychiatric asylums, 82–83
psychiatric disorders, 10–11, 82; anthropo-
    logical studies, 89; common mental
    disorders, 89; demographics and, 89;
    diagnosis, 87–88; exorcism and, 93–94;
    loss of self, 86–87; membership in
    human form, 97; modernism and,
    83–84; personal narrative and, 84–85;
    religious symbols and, 111–12; Swapan,
    88–89; treatment conditions, 101n17

forms of living
Stefanos Geroulanos and Todd Meyers, *series editors*

Georges Canguilhem, *Knowledge of Life*. Translated by Stefanos Geroulanos and Daniela Ginsburg. Introduction by Paola Marrati and Todd Meyers.

Henri Atlan, *Selected Writings: On Self-Organization, Philosophy, Bioethics, and Judaism*. Edited and with an Introduction by Stefanos Geroulanos and Todd Meyers.

Catherine Malabou, *The New Wounded: From Neurosis to Brain Damage*. Translated by Steven Miller.

François Delaporte, *Chagas Disease: History of a Continent's Scourge*. Translated by Arthur Goldhammer. Foreword by Todd Meyers.

Jonathan Strauss, *Human Remains: Medicine, Death, and Desire in Nineteenth-Century Paris*.

Georges Canguilhem, *Writings on Medicine*. Translated and with an Introduction by Stefanos Geroulanos and Todd Meyers.

François Delaporte, *Figures of Medicine: Blood, Face Transplants, Parasites*. Translated by Nils F. Schott. Foreword by Christopher Lawrence.

Juan Manuel Garrido, *On Time, Being, and Hunger: Challenging the Traditional Way of Thinking Life*.

Pamela Reynolds, *War in Worcester: Youth and the Apartheid State*.

Vanessa Lemm and Miguel Vatter, eds., *The Government of Life: Foucault, Biopolitics, and Neoliberalism*.

Henning Schmidgen, *The Helmholtz Curves: Tracing Lost Time*. Translated by Nils F. Schott.

Henning Schmidgen, *Bruno Latour in Pieces: An Intellectual Biography*. Translated by Gloria Custance.

Veena Das, *Affliction: Health, Disease, Poverty*.

Kathleen Frederickson, *The Ploy of Instinct: Victorian Sciences of Nature and Sexuality in Liberal Governance*.

Roma Chatterji, ed., *Wording the World: Veena Das and Scenes of Inheritance*.

Jean-Luc Nancy and Aurélien Barrau, *What's These Worlds Coming To?* Translated by Travis Holloway and Flor Méchain. Foreword by David Pettigrew.

CPSIA information can be obtained
at www.ICGtesting.com
Printed in the USA
LVHW111422080119
603154LV00001B/138/P

9 780823 261819